# C++ XML

## Contents At a Glance

# C++ XML

Fabio Arciniegas

**New Riders**

**www.newriders.com**

201 West 103rd Street, Indianapolis, Indiana 46290

An Imprint of Pearson Education

Boston • Indianapolis • London • Munich • New York • San Francisco

# C++ XML

Fabio Arciniegas

## Trademarks

## Warning and Disclaimer

**Publisher**
David Dwyer

**Associate Publisher**
Al Valvano

**Executive Editor**
Stephanie Wall

**Managing Editor**
Gina Kanouse

**Development Editor**
Allison Beaumont Johnson

**Product Marketing Manager**
Stephanie Layton

**Publicity Manager**
Susan Petro

**Senior Project Editor**
Lori Lyons

**Copy Editor**
Gayle Johnson

**Senior Indexer**
Cheryl Lenser

**Manufacturing Coordinator**
Jim Conway

**Book Designer**
Louisa Klucznik

**Cover Designer**
Brainstorm Design, Inc.

**Cover Production**
Aren Howell

**Proofreader**
Katherine Shull

**Composition**
Amy Parker
Rebecca Harmon

**Media Developer**
Jay Payne

❖

*To my mother, my inspiration and strength.*

*"This means something," Tyler says.*
*—Chuck Palahniuk*
❖

# Table of Contents

# About the Author

**Fabio Arciniegas** is the Chief Technical Officer of postgraphy (http://www.postgraphy.com), where he applies his C++ and XML expertise to the development of visual knowledge and image processing applications. He is an active participant in the XML community, both as a developer and as a writer. His contributions include the development of the C++ implementation of the TREX language, XLink software, and numerous articles (especially in www.xml.com) and tutorial programs dealing with XML technologies. He participates frequently as a speaker at XML-related conferences and tutorials, including XML Developers Conference, O'Reilly Open Source Conference, and XML and Distributed Applications (where he is the chair), among others.

# About the Technical Reviewers

These reviewers contributed their considerable hands-on expertise to the entire development process for *C++ XML*. As this book was being written, these dedicated professionals reviewed all the material for technical content, organization, and flow. Their feedback was critical to ensuring that *C++ XML* fits our readers' need for the highest-quality technical information.

**Beth Breidenbach** is a Product Architect for Getronics, a Netherlands-based provider of software and infrastructure solutions throughout the world. Her group develops enterprise-wide software applications targeted to top-tier financial institutions. A self-professed "data geek," she has an abiding interest in all aspects of data design, storage, transmission, and translation. These topics were a natural lead-in to exploring the possibilities inherent in the new family of XML-related technologies. Her most recent project was the application of XML and database technologies to rule processing engines. She is currently exploring data design aspects of natural language interfaces.

**Jason A. Buss** began working with computers at an early age. After working as a CNC programmer, he moved on to technical publications in 1996. He is currently working on the development and enhancement of a single-source SGML/XML publishing system for a major aircraft manufacturer. He spends his free time with his wife and children. His hobbies include building PCs, working with open-source XML software, reading, and playing the guitar. New state regulations regarding mandatory apprenticeship have made this hobby very impractical (at least in Kansas).

# Acknowledgments

Special thanks to Stephanie Wall, Laura Loveall, Allison Johnson, Beth Breidenbach, Jason Buss, and the whole New Riders team for being proof of the great value of a good process.

Finally, many thanks to my family and all those who ultimately pay the price of my obsession with making the best work possible.

# Tell Us What You Think

As the reader of this book, you are the most important critic and commentator. We value your opinion and want to know what we're doing right, what we could do better, what areas you'd like to see us publish in, and any other words of wisdom you're willing to pass our way.

As an Executive Editor for the Web Development team at New Riders Publishing, I welcome your comments. You can fax, email, or write me directly to let me know what you did or didn't like about this book—as well as what we can do to make our books stronger.

*Please note that I cannot help you with technical problems related to the topic of this book, and that due to the high volume of mail I receive, I might not be able to reply to every message.*

When you write, please be sure to include this book's title and author, as well as your name and phone or fax number. I will carefully review your comments and share them with the author and editors who worked on the book.

Fax:       317-581-4663
Email:     stephanie.wall@newriders.com
Mail:      Stephanie Wall
           Executive Editor
           New Riders Publishing
           201 West 103rd Street
           Indianapolis, IN 46290 USA

# Introduction

This book is not a tender introduction to XML for all audiences. On the contrary, this book is for programmers interested in creating high-performance and high-quality applications using exclusively XML and C++.

In a market saturated with entry-level information, this book provides valuable, high-level, to-the-point techniques and tools for the successful construction of real-world C++ XML programs ranging from XML editors and databases to 3D applications and distributed systems.

## What Does This Book Cover?

From a skill-oriented point of view, this book covers the following:

- All aspects of efficient server-side, standalone, and client-side C++ development for XML
- Advanced techniques for the development of Windows and Linux XML applications
- The crucial details of the successful application of all major XML C++ toolkits and frameworks
- Cross-platform integration and extension techniques
- The latest on distributed application development using XML and C++

From the technology side, this book covers *the C++ manipulation* of all the following technologies:

- XML 1.0+ namespaces
- SAX 2.0
- DOM 2.0
- Non-SAX/DOM parsers
- XPath
- XPointer
- XMLSchema and other modeling languages
- Encodings in C++
- XML and databases

- XSLT

- Extension languages for C++ applications using XML

- Extended models for XML processing using C++-exclusive features (such as templates)

- Server topics such as XML+XSLT+Apache integration using C++

# Who Is This Book For?

This book is for programmers looking to build applications with XML and C++.

If you need a book that explains the complexities and power of manipulating all major XML technologies with C++, you have arrived at the right choice.

Whether you want to construct software such as an OpenGL SAX application with XML as its 3D file format, a Windows MFC application using SOAP or XML-RPC messages, a Linux GTK application using DOM, Windows applications using XML views of ADO and ODBC databases, extension language interpreters that use C++ XSLT, or any other C++ XML use, this book gives you the theory, code, and inside information necessary to understand and create it.

# Who Is This Book Not For?

This is a C++-specific book. If you need a different exposition of the XML topics discussed here, you should refer to general books such as *Inside XML* (New Riders, 2001) or *XML Developer's Guide* (McGraw-Hill, 2000).

# Level of the Book and Design Principles

The level of this book is intermediate to advanced. It has been written with the following principles in mind:

- **Thoroughness.** This book addresses all the relevant technologies, techniques, and tips required to create nontrivial C++ XML applications (see Chapter 2 for the complete organization).

- **Absolute code support for the theory.** Every API, construct, and methodology is supported by working code. *Every line of code shown in this book is part of a fully working C++ application that is included with complete source code on the CD.*

- **Reusability.** The programs, modules, and patterns throughout this book have been written so that they can be as reusable as possible in your own projects.

# What Are the Requisites for This Book?

From the reader's point of view, the only requirement is familiarity with C++. Some minimal idea of the format of XML is also helpful (even though Chapter 1 fully explains all the constructs of XML 1.0+ namespaces).

The software and hardware requirements are a personal computer and a C/C++ compiler. The examples were developed mainly under Visual Studio C++ 6.0 for Windows, and most of the executables are Win32 applications. However, with this book's Linux applications, ELFs are provided. Whenever possible, makefiles for Linux using gcc 2.91 or later and Cygnus gcc 2.95 or later for Windows have been included.

# I

# XML Basics

# XML: Constructs and Concepts

THIS BOOK IS NOT AN INTRODUCTION TO XML for all readers (countless books and free Web resources cover that). Instead, this book concentrates on the advanced treatment of XML technologies using the C++ language, so it assumes that you have a basic familiarity with both.

For the sake of completeness, however, this chapter summarizes the constructs and concepts of XML, from well-formedness to namespaces. If you are already comfortable with XML, feel free to skip this chapter and use it merely as a reference.

This chapter is divided into three sections. The first section reviews the basic constructs and concepts of XML, the second goes through Document Type Definitions (DTDs), and the third explains namespaces.

Finally, it is important to note that this chapter addresses XML 1.0 plus namespaces as a language, not the XML family of technologies (and their relation to C++). That is the subject of the next chapter.

# Basic Constructs

The starting place for our discussion are the basic constituents of an XML document: elements and attributes. The following sections explain their structure and usage.

## Elements, Attributes, and Nesting

All XML documents are formed by elements. Elements are delimited by start and end tags and may contain other elements and text. A start tag is composed of a tag name and a set of attributes. An end tag contains only the name of the element, preceded by /. Some examples are shown in Listing 1.1.

Listing 1.1    **Elements**

```
<show>
    <name><simpleName>Tymon Phonty</simpleName></name>
    <episode>
        <description>A Man who speaks in anagrams.
            <note>they are really only spoonerisms</note>
        </description>
    </episode>
</show>
```

For the sake of convenience, if a tag has no content, it can be abbreviated as follows:

```
<russian></russian>
```

can be abbreviated to

```
<russian/>
```

An attribute is a name/value pair separated by an equal sign (=). Attribute values must be enclosed in single or double quotation marks (the choice is irrelevant as long as the usage is consistent). The spacing between the element name and the attributes, as well as the spacing between attribute names and values, is irrelevant, thus allowing indentation such as the following:

```
<link href="http://www.foucaultspendulum.com/dictionary/style.css"
      rel="stylesheet"
      type="text/css"/>
```

The single most important aspect of well-formedness in XML is correct nesting. In short, an element is correctly nested if its start and end tag are within the same parent element:

```
<someElement>
    <correct/>  <!-- a correct, empty tag -->
    <someOtherElement> <correct> </correct> </someOtherElement>
    <someOtherElement> <incorrect>   </someOtherElement> </incorrect>
<!-- the above error makes the whole document malformed -->
</someElement>
```

Last, as you undoubtedly have guessed already, comments start with `<!--` and end with `-->`. The string `--` is invalid inside a comment.

> ### XML Names
>
> This chapter uses the term *XML name* quite often, so I should describe it formally. An XML name is a string of characters beginning with a letter (not necessarily an English one), underscore (_), or colon (:), and followed by any number of name characters, such as letters, digits, hyphens, underscores, colons, or full stops.
>
> All the names starting with the string XML (or any case variation of it, such as xMl) are considered reserved.
>
> All XML names are case-sensitive.

## XML Declaration

An XML document may (and, as a matter of good practice, should) begin with an XML declaration:

```
<?xml version="1.0" encoding="utf-8" standalone="true"?>
```

The XML declaration specifies three things: the version of XML used (there is only one version—1.0—but it is mandatory to include this information for extensibility purposes), the encoding of the document, and whether it is standalone. The last two points deserve special attention and will be revisited when I introduce the necessary concepts. (The concept of standalone refers to external DTD declarations and is explained in the sidebar titled "Standalone" later in this chapter. The concept of encoding is an extremely important and tricky topic and is discussed in Chapter 8.)

Most of the time, when dealing with English-based XML documents, you will see the simple version of the declaration:

```
<?xml version="1.0"?>
```

## *CDATA* Sections

In order to escape large quantities of character data that might contain reserved characters (such as < ), you can use a CDATA section. A CDATA section begins with the string `<![CDATA[` and ends with the string `]]>`. All the characters inside these two strings are considered character data and are not interpreted as markup.

```
<paragraph>
If you are doing a tutorial on XHTML, you may want to show some code,
but you don't want its tags to be part of your document, instead,
you want them to be just text:
<![CDATA[
<para><b>Showing the usage of b.</b></para>
]]> <!-- Multiple CDATA sections may not be nested -->
</paragraph>
```

The other escaping mechanism are character references, strings such as &#x424; and &#1040;, which allow the inclusion of reserved and special characters in a document. Character references will be discussed more when I introduce the concept of entities.

## Processing Instructions

Processing instructions (commonly called PIs) are a rarely used feature of XML that allow a document to pass direct and specific data to the application (not the parser). They have a simple syntax:

```
<?target instruction?>
```

The PI's target is an XML name identifying the application that is supposed to receive the instruction. The instruction is a free-form string that gets passed to the application. XML does not put any constraint on the format of PIs, except that it considers the targets that start with the string xml(or any capitalization variation of it) reserved.

The following is a typical PI used to bind XML stylesheets to documents on certain browsers:

```
<?xml-stylesheet type="text/css" href="aeneid.css" media="screen"?>
```

The following is a much more ad hoc (but equally valid) PI:

```
<?emacs (set-foreground-color "blue")?>
```

Processing instructions may appear at any point of an element's content.

## Natural Language

In order to explicitly identify the natural language used in the contents of a given attribute, you must use the special attribute xml:lang.

The value of xml:lang must fall into one of the following categories:

- A two-letter code defined by ISO-639. This is the most commonly used and intuitive form (en for English, es for Spanish, de for German, and so on). The complete list can be accessed at

  http://www.egt.ie/standards/iso639/iso639-1-en.html

- An IANA (Internet Assigned Numbers Authority) identifier, such as I-navajo. All IANA identifiers must start with I-. You can find a list of IANA language identifiers at

  http://www.isi.edu/in-notes/iana/assignments/languages/

- A user-defined name prefixed by x-. Needless to say, this is a rather uncommon choice.

If the value of xml:lang starts with a two-letter ISO639 code, it may be expanded with subcodes for particular locales. The following are some examples:

```
<films>
    <filmtitle xml:lang="fr">L'enfer</filmtitle>
    <filmtitle xml:lang="en-US">Arizona Dream</filmtitle>
</films>
```

## Well-Formedness

Now that we have covered the basic concepts, we are ready to formulate a working definition of well-formedness. (The later sidebar titled "Well-Formedness Versus Validity" discusses the difference between well-formedness and validity.)

A document is well-formed if it follows the syntax described here, has a root element, and has all of its subelements correctly nested.

# DTDs

DTDs (document type definitions) are the most basic and widely used form of type specification for XML documents. They are used to specify the type of elements that may appear in a document, their order and attributes, and their content.

DTDs are made up of markup declarations: element type, attribute list, notation, and entity declarations. The following sections examine each of these four types of constructs and show how they are tied to the document.

## Element Type Declarations

An element type declaration constrains the types of values that may appear inside a particular element.

An element type declaration has the following form:

```
<!ELEMENT name contentspec>
```

name is an XML name, and contentspec has one of the following forms (see examples in Listing 1.2):

- **EMPTY**. This indicates that the element has no children whatsoever.
- **ANY**. The element may contain any combination of character data (commonly called #PCDATA) and any other elements in the DTD. (This content model is very general and usually indicates underspecification.)
- **"Children"**. In this case, the content model is a parentheses-enclosed sequence (separated by commas) or choice (separated by | ). The elements of a sequence or choice may be either element names or groups of choices or sequences themselves.

Each group of sequences or choices may be affected by one of the three multiplicity modifiers: ? for zero or one, + for one or more, or * for zero or more.

- **Mixed.** In this case, the content model is represented as a parentheses-enclosed choice between #PCDATA (the reserved word for character data inside an element type declaration) and all the elements that may appear interspersed with the character data. The whole sequence must be finished by the modifier *. Note that this means that you cannot constrain element order inside a mixed-content element. All you can say is that some elements might appear, and they will do so amid character data.

Listing 1.2  **Element Type Declarations**

```
<!--
    Name: Shows
    Description: A DTD for the description of TV shows
    Version : $Id: shows.dtd,v 1.3 2001/01/21 16:10:00 Default Exp $
-->

<!-- It is always recommended to document your DTDs as shown above -->


<!-- **** Element Type Declarations **** -->

<!-- a simple 'Children' model, using a sequence with no modifiers -->
<!ELEMENT show (name,episode)>

<!-- A more complex 'Children' model -->
<!-- It shows a choice of either an element, or a sequence of elements -->
<!ELEMENT name (simpleName | (officialName,aka))>

<!-- 'Mixed' models -->
<!-- note how "zero or more" is specified with the familiar '*' -->
<!ELEMENT simpleName    (#PCDATA|note)* >
<!ELEMENT aka           (#PCDATA|note)* >

<!-- The only special case of 'Mixed' models: only #PCDATA -->
<!ELEMENT officialName (#PCDATA)>
<!ELEMENT note         (#PCDATA)>

<!-- more examples -->
<!ELEMENT episode       (number?,description)>
<!ELEMENT description   (#PCDATA|note)* >
<!ELEMENT number         (#PCDATA)>
```

## Binding a Document to a DTD

Before going any further, it is important to see how to associate a document to a DTD for validation purposes.

Right after the XML declaration (`<?xml version="1.0"?>`), the document may have a document type declaration that uses one of the following two forms:

```
<!-- Form 1: Public Identifier + System Identifier -->
<!DOCTYPE name PUBLIC "publicId"  "systemId">

<!-- Form 2: System Identifier only -->
<!DOCTYPE name SYSTEM "systemId">
```

In either case, `systemId` is a URI used to directly retrieve the DTD. It can be as simple as the name of the file that holds the DTD, or a URL such as "http://www.foo.net/bar.dtd". `publicId` is a string used to identify well-known DTDs (such as HTML 4.0 or DocBook). A parser might use the public ID to try to fetch the DTD, using a catalog, for example.

Listing 1.3 shows a valid instance of the DTD in Listing 1.2.

Listing 1.3    **Valid Instance of shows.dtd**

```
<?xml version="1.0"?>
<!DOCTYPE show SYSTEM "shows.dtd">
<show>
  <name>
    <!-- note that element names are case-sensitive -->
    <simpleName>tymon thonpy</simpleName>
  </name>
  <episode>
    <number>32</number>
    <description>A man who speaks only in anagrams <note>Actually,
                they are only spoonerisms</note>.
   </description>
  </episode>
</show>,
```

## Attribute List Declarations

The next type of markup constraint is the attribute list declaration. An attribute list declaration states the name, type, and default value (if any) of every attribute for a given element.

Attribute lists have the following general structure:

```
<!ATTLIST elementName  attrName attrType attrDefaultDeclaration
                       attrName attrType attrDefaultDeclaration ...>
```

There are three types of attributes: string type, tokenized type, and enumeration type. The following sections discuss the specific form that each ATTLIST declaration takes.

### String Types

The simplest type of attribute is the string type. In a declaration of this type, the attrType is the string CDATA, signaling that the value of this attribute is a free-form string containing any characters except <.

> **Element and Attribute Declaration Uniqueness**
>
> Because you can write several <!ELEMENT ...> or <!ATTLIST ...> clauses, it is perfectly legitimate to wonder how the parser should behave in such cases.
>
> Element declarations must be unique. It is an error to declare an element more than once.
>
> Different attribute list declarations referring to the same element are condensed into one. If multiple declarations for the same attribute are found, only the first one is taken into account. The rest are ignored.

String types may exhibit (just as any other type) an attribute default declaration, which specifies whether the attribute is required, as well as a default value (if one exists).

### Default Declaration

In order to specify required and default values, the type string (or any other attribute type) may be followed by one of the following specifiers:

- **#REQUIRED.** Indicates that every instance of the element must have a value for this attribute. No default value is provided for this type of attribute.
- **#IMPLIED.** Indicates that the attribute is not required and that no default value is provided.
- **Default.** Indicates that the default value for the attribute is *Default*. If the element specified in the declaration does not provide a specific value for this attribute, *Default* is assumed.
- **#FIXED Default.** Indicates that the attribute might or might not be present, but if it is, it must have the value *Default*. This is generally useful to model "flag" attributes such as official, as shown in Listing 1.4.

Listing 1.4 shows an example of string types, extending the DTD of Listing 1.1.

Listing 1.4   **String Type Attributes**

```
<!-- required string attributes -->
<!ATTLIST episode
          recorded   CDATA   #REQUIRED
          aired      CDATA   #REQUIRED>

<!-- a fixed string attribute -->
```

```
<!ATTLIST description
        official   CDATA    #FIXED "YES">

<!-- another attlist declaration for the same element (legitimate) -->
<!-- an author is not required -->
<!ATTLIST description
        author    CDATA    #IMPLIED>
```

## DTD Limitations

After careful examination of Listing 1.4, you might feel a vague sensation of underspecification. , For example, there is nothing saying that a description can be official only if it has an author.

This illustrates just one of the many shortcomings of DTDs as a modeling language. Others include complex types (such as dates), cardinality operators (there is no way to say "between four and nine occurrences of this element"), and compound element IDs.

DTDs achieve a high level of usability at the cost of some expressiveness. They are the first and most important of all type definition languages for XML, and no XML developer can ignore them. However, learning another type definition language, such as Trex, Schematron, or XML Schema, can prove useful for cases in which the expressive power of DTDs and application-level contracts are not enough.

XML Schema and its programmatic use in C++ are discussed in Chapter 15. For the moment, let's stay focused on what DTDs can offer.


## Tokenized Types

Tokenized types are special types defined by the XML specification. Their values are one or more tokens. They are dependent on the rules explained next.

A tokenized type has one of the following values in the `attrType` specification:

- **ID.** Indicates that the value of this attribute is a *unique* name (no other attribute of type ID may have the same value) that identifies the element throughout the document.

- **IDREF.** Indicates that the value of the attribute is the name of an ID somewhere else in the document. This is useful to model a simple type of link inside a document.

- **IDREFS.** Indicates that the value of the attribute is a collection of space-separated IDREFS.

- **ENTITY.** Indicates that the value of the attribute is the name of a properly defined unparsed entity. For more information, see the appropriate entities section later in this chapter.

- **ENTITIES.** Indicates that the value of the attribute is a list of space-separated entity names.

- **NMTOKEN.** Indicates that the value of the attribute is a collection of name characters (see the earlier sidebar "XML Names"). These are different from names because they can begin with any XML character, not just with a letter, underscore, or colon.

- **NMTOKENS.** Indicates that the value of the attribute is a collection of NMTOKENS.

As you have probably guessed, the most useful tokenized types are ID and IDREFS. Listing 1.5, an addendum to the Listing 1.1 DTD, shows the declaration of tokenized types.

Listing 1.5    **Tokenized Types (Only Changed Types Are Shown)**

```
<!-- note the change in the note element -->
<!ELEMENT note        (#PCDATA|see)*>


<!-- required string attributes -->
<!ATTLIST episode
          recorded   CDATA      #REQUIRED
          aired      CDATA      #REQUIRED
          key        ID         #REQUIRED>

<!ELEMENT see        EMPTY>
<!-- a required idref -->
<!ATTLIST see
          also       IDREF      #REQUIRED>

<!ELEMENT related    EMPTY>
<!-- a required idref -->
<!ATTLIST related
          terms      NMTOKENS   #REQUIRED>
```

As shown in the listing, the default declaration structure (as defined in the section of that name) is the same for this and every other type of attribute.

The DTD does not show, so far, the usage of entities and entity-type attributes. Those will be added when I formally present those concepts.

### Enumerated Types

Enumerated types fall into one of two categories:

- **Enumerations.** Marked as a parentheses-enclosed, pipe-separated choice of NMTOKENS, this type explicitly defines the set of values that the attribute may have.

- **Notation types.** A choice list preceded by the keyword NOTATION specifies that the value of the attribute must be the name of a notation declared on the DTD. An element bearing a notation attribute has a content of the type specified by it.

Before I go into the details of notations, let's see an example of simple enumerations:

```
<!ATTLIST episode
          rated      (PG|PG13|R|NC17) #IMPLIED>
```

## Notations

A notation is a string denoting the format of an unparsed entity (a part of the document that is not XML, and perhaps not even text, and therefore is not processed by the parser). Notations are declared using the following syntax:

```
<!NOTATION name PUBLIC "publicID" {SYSTEM "systemID"}>
```

or

```
<!NOTATION name SYSTEM "systemID">
```

It is important to note that the URIs for the definition of IDs do not point to examples of the notation, but to formal string definitions of their type. For example, the following are the correct notation declarations for some common types of images:

```
<!NOTATION tif PUBLIC
    "-//Aldus Corporation//NOTATION Tagged Image File Format//EN">
<!NOTATION pcx PUBLIC
    "-//ZSoft//NOTATION PCX: IBM  PC Raster Graphics Format//EN">
<!NOTATION gif PUBLIC
    "-//Compuserve Information Services//NOTATION Graphics Interchange
        Format//EN">
```

Even though notations are not nearly as common as other constructs, it is good to become acquainted with them as yet another tool for DTD modeling.

## Interim: The *show* DTD

Up to this point, we have analyzed almost every major structure in XML (we have only entities left to explore). Let's make a quick stop and review our DTD, enhanced with different types of attributes and notation declarations. Listing 1.6 shows the enhanced version of the show DTD, and Listing 1.7 shows a valid instance document that is conformant with it.

Listing 1.6  **Enhanced *show* DTD**

```
<!ELEMENT show (name,episode+)>

<!ELEMENT name (simpleName | (officialName,aka))>

<!ELEMENT simpleName    (#PCDATA|note)* >
<!ELEMENT aka           (#PCDATA|note)* >

<!ELEMENT officialName (#PCDATA)>
<!ELEMENT number       (#PCDATA)>
```

*continues*

Listing 1.6 **Continued**

```
<!ELEMENT episode        (number?,graphic?,description)>
<!ELEMENT description    (#PCDATA|note|related)* >
<!ELEMENT note           (#PCDATA|see)*>


<!ATTLIST episode
          recorded    CDATA            #REQUIRED
          aired       CDATA            #REQUIRED
          rated       (PG|PG13|R|NC17) #IMPLIED
          key         ID               #REQUIRED>

<!ELEMENT see     EMPTY>
<!ATTLIST see
          also      IDREF    #REQUIRED>

<!ELEMENT related     EMPTY>

<!ATTLIST related
          terms     NMTOKENS    #REQUIRED>


<!ATTLIST description
          official   CDATA    #FIXED "yes">

<!ATTLIST description
          author     CDATA    #IMPLIED>

<!NOTATION ps SYSTEM "application/postscript"> <!-- a mime type -->
<!NOTATION gif PUBLIC
"-//Compuserve Information Services//NOTATION Graphics Interchange Format//EN">
<!-- a public id -->

<!ELEMENT graphic (#PCDATA)>
<!ATTLIST graphic
          type      NOTATION (ps|gif) "ps">
```

Listing 1.7 **Valid Instance of the *show* Type**

```
<?xml version="1.0"?>
<!DOCTYPE show SYSTEM "shows_1_2.dtd">
<show>
  <name>
    <!-- note that element names are case-sensitive -->
    <simpleName>tymon thonpy</simpleName>
  </name>
  <episode recorded = "12/11/1971"
        aired    = "11/9/1972"
        rated    = "PG"
```

```
        key      = "mp-anagram">
    <number>30</number>
    <description author="Eric">A man who speaks only in anagrams
                <note>Actually, they are only spoonerisms
                        <see also="mp-proust"/>
                </note>.
    </description>
  </episode>
  <episode recorded="4/24/1972"
        aired="11/16/1972"
        key="mp-proust">
<!-- The following element illustrates two things: default
     attribute values (for attribute type) and how to embed
     postscript in an XML document using notations. Naturally,
     the technique can be extended to other types.
-->
    <graphic>
/Times-Roman findfont
32 scalefont
setfont

100 200 translate
25 rotate
2 1 scale
newpath
0 0 moveto
(Hail Guilliam!) true charpath
0.5 setlinewidth
0.4 setgray
stroke

showpage
    </graphic>
    <description official="yes"
                author="John">The All-England summarize Proust
                competition  <related terms="Marcel Proust"/>
    </description>
  </episode>
</show>
```

## Conditional Sections

In order to easily include or ignore certain parts of a DTD, you can use conditional sections.

A conditional section has the following form:

```
<![includeDirective[
... all desired markup declarations ...
]]>
```

*includeDirective* is either `INCLUDE` or `IGNORE`. The markup declarations inside the section are considered a part of the DTD or are plainly ignored, accordingly.

## Entities

The last major features of DTDs (and XML as a language) are entity declaration and references. Before studying their syntax, let's review the concept of entities.

All XML documents are physically made up of entities: individual pieces of content, identified by a name.

Entities are classified into four groups: internal general, external parsed general, unparsed, and parameter. The following sections analyze the declaration and usage of each group.

### The Only Anonymous Entity

The starting point for the parser is known as the document entity (normally the main file that holds the XML declaration, the document type declaration, and the root element). The document entity is the only entity that is not identified by a name.

### Internal General (Parsed)

Internal general entities are the simplest parsed entities. They contain replacement text that becomes part of the document. You define them inside entity declarations by specifying their name and explicitly providing their replacement text.

The following declaration shows an example:

```
<!ENTITY isbn   "0-14-004259-8">
```

An internal entity (as it is normally called) can only be referenced inside the document, not the DTD. To reference it, you simply include its name inside the characters & and ; as follows:

```
&isbn; <!-- the effect of this is simply to include the replacement
text -->
```

### External General (Parsed)

External general entities (external general for short) are a powerful mechanism of modularization. They specify, using a public or system identifier, the name of an external resource that holds the entity's replacement text:

```
<!ENTITY chapter1 SYSTEM "C++XMLBook-Chapter1-Author.xml">
```

External general entities are included in the document using the same notation as their internal counterpart:

```
&chapter1; <!-- this can only appear in the document, not in the DTD -->
```

## Unparsed

Unparsed entities are the least-common entities. They are pieces of content that might not be text, and if they are, they might not be XML. You declare them by specifying their name, their location (using a public or system identifier), and their notation (their type).

The following example shows the declaration syntax (note the keyword NDATA and the notation name):

```
<!NOTATION tiff PUBLIC
    "-//Aldus Corporation//NOTATION Tagged Image File Format//EN" >
<!ENTITY aras-tiff SYSTEM "/usr/local/images/sa.tiff" NDATA tiff>
```

Unparsed entities are referenced by name in the value of entity-type attributes.

## Parameter

Parameter entities are a powerful reuse mechanism for DTDs. They basically work like general entities, but they can be used only inside the DTD. They are commonly used to encapsulate reusable parts of the DTD and to improve its readability and maintainability, as shown here:

```
<!-- note the % character, which indicates the nature of this entity -->
<!ENTITY % number        "CDATA">
<!ENTITY % months        "jan|feb|mar|apr|may|jun|jul|
                          aug|sep|oct|nov|dec">
```

Parameter entities can be used only inside the document. They are referenced by placing their name between % and ;:

```
<!ELEMENT date           (#PCDATA)>
<!ATTLIST date
        day      %number;    #IMPLIED
        month    (%months;)  #IMPLIED
        year     %number;    #REQUIRED>
```

### Standalone

Near the beginning of this chapter, I mentioned the possibility of adding a standalone string to the XML declaration:

```
<?xml version="1.0" standalone="yes"?>
```

Now that you know about entities, I am ready to give a precise definition of its semantics.

In a standalone document declaration, the value "yes" indicates that there are no markup declarations external to the document entity (in the DTD external subset) that affect the information passed from the XML processor to the application.

For example, if the external subset contains an attribute with a default value, the document cannot be marked as standalone, because the attribute declaration would affect the information passed by forcing the existence of a value, even when it was not specified in the document.

## Character References

A character reference is an explicit inclusion of a Unicode character. (See Chapter 8 for a discussion of Unicode and encodings.) This is especially helpful for including characters that are not available on the keyboard, and to escape special characters such as <.

A character reference starts with either &#x or &# and ends with ;. The numeric code in between is either the hexadecimal or decimal representation of the character code, respectively. The following code shows an example:

```
&#x424; &#x2E; &#x410; &#46; &#1040;
<!-- This would display: Ф.А.А. -->
```

## Internal and External DTD Subsets

I'll finalize our discussion of DTDs by presenting a final feature: internal versus external DTD subsets.

A document may specify some local markup declarations without having to change the original DTD. This is performed by enclosing them in square brackets at the end of the doctype declaration:

```
<?xml version="1.0"?>
<!DOCTYPE show SYSTEM "shows_1_3.dtd"
[
 <!ENTITY lastModified "$Id: show_1_3.dtd,v 1.3 02/02/02 6:10 Exp $">
 <!ENTITY otherEpisodes SYSTEM "otherEpisodes.xml">
]>
<show>
<!-- rest of the document -->
  &otherEpisodes;
</show>
```

These local declarations are known as the internal DTD subset. The whole DTD is the union of both subsets.

This section concludes our review of XML. The remainder of this chapter explains the next most important specification in the XML family: namespaces.

> **Well-Formedness Versus Validity**
>
> A document is well-formed as long as it follows the basic syntactic rules defined in the first part of this chapter—in particular, correct nesting.
>
> A document is valid if it contains a document declaration and complies with the rules specified by its DTD.
>
> Parsers are often classified as being validating or not, depending on whether they check validity or merely well-formedness, respectively.

### More Examples

For more examples of complex markup declarations and reusable libraries of DTDs and parameter entities, see the files on the CD.

# Namespaces

This final part of the chapter discusses a specification so important that it has come to be regarded as basic to XML as core structures and DTDs. I am talking, naturally, about namespaces (W3C recommendation: `http://www.w3.org/TR/1999/REC-xml-names-19990114/`).

## Rationale

As a C++ programmer, you are no doubt familiar with the concepts of variable scoping and name clashes. In XML, the same situations arise with the names of elements and attributes, especially when mixing different vocabularies (such as when you embed your financial XML language in the multimedia XML language SMIL, and you don't know whether the element `rate` refers to an interest rate or a screen refresh rate).

XML namespaces are designed to be the simplest mechanism to tackle the problem of name clashes within XML. Their principle is very simple: enrich an element or attribute with a unique identifier, thus escaping the problem of possible name collisions with others.

## Declaration

The declaration for using a namespace is a reserved attribute of this form:

```
<x xmlns:prefix = "name" >
...
</x>
```

This indicates that the namespace identified with *prefix* will be available on element x and all throughout the elements inside it.

If the prefix is not included, the namespace is supposed to apply as the default namespace for the element and its content.

If the prefix is specified, it can be used before any attribute or element name, thus identifying it as part of the namespace.

Listing 1.8 illustrates these ideas.

Listing 1.8 **Namespaces**

```
<?xml version="1.0"?>
<booknotes xmlns:xyz = "http://www.w3.org/1999/xyzar"
           xmlns       = "http://www.thefaactory.com/booknotes">
<!-- booknotes are part of the default namespace,
     so are all the subelements, unless they specify a different
```

*continues*

Listing 1.8   **Continued**

```
      prefix or define a new default namespace -->

    <p>
  <!-- the universal name of p is:
   {http://www.thefaactory.com/booknotes}p -->
        <b xmlns = "http://www.w3c.org/xhtml">
           <c/>
           <!-- both b and c belong to the new default namespace -->
        </b>
        <c/> <!-- this c is out of the scope of the new default, so it
                belongs to the original default namespace -->
        <xyz:anElement xyz:anAttribute="value">
           <!-- the universal name of xyz:anElement is
              {http://www.w3.org/1999/xyzar}:anElement -->
        </xyz:anElement>
    </p>
  </booknotes>
```

## Qualified and Universal Names

A qualified name has this form:

```
prefix:localpart
```

The prefix acts as a placeholder for the URI of the namespace associated with it. When a namespace-aware parser processes a QName (as they are familiarly called), it expands the name to its full form, the universal name, which is simply the URI plus the local part (see Listing 1.8—in particular, the p element).

See Chapter 7 for an application dealing with programmatic analysis of namespaces. (In Chapter 7, we construct an XML editor using a namespace-aware C++ parser.)

## Declaring Namespaces on the DTD

Note that the rules for namespaces refer to the existence of the xmlns attribute in the document itself. However, using the default declaration techniques discussed in the second part of this chapter (DTDs), you can include namespace declarations on the DTD, frequently improving the document's readability.

The following #FIXED attributes illustrate this point:

```
<!ELEMENT planet (system,moons+)>
<!ATTLIST planet
        xmlns:xlink CDATA #FIXED   "http://www.w3.org/1999/xlink"
        xmlns:booknotes      CDATA #FIXED
                        "http://www.thefaactory.com/booknotes">
```

After this declaration, you may freely use the `xlink` and `booknotes` prefixes, because the parser will include the `xmlns:xlink` and `xmlns:booknotes` attributes upon reading.

## Scope and Visibility

A namespace declaration is in scope for the element where it is defined and all its contents, as long as it is not overwritten by a declaration with the same prefix (see Listing 1.8).

One important last point of namespace visibility is that default namespace declarations do not apply to attributes. Take care of defining explicit prefixes for namespaces if you intend to use them with attribute names.

```
<!-- There is no harm in declaring an extra prefix pointing to the same URI,
     so you can use it with attributes -->
<!ATTLIST planet
          booknotes:name       CDATA   #REQUIRED
          xmlns:xlink CDATA #FIXED   "http://www.w3.org/1999/xlink"
          xmlns        CDATA #FIXED
                       "http://www.thefaactory.com/booknotes">
          xmlns:booknotes       CDATA #FIXED
                                 "http://www.thefaactory.com/booknotes">
<!--
   <planet booknotes:name="pluto">...
 <!-- both planet and name are in the same namespace -->
   </planet>
-->
```

## Semantics

One key characteristic of namespaces is their lack of high-level semantics. When developers first encounter namespaces, they normally think a namespace's URI points to a DTD, or a schema, or some sort of catalog with a description of the namespace. However, that is not the case. *A namespace is merely a unique identifier,* a string that you append to element and attribute names so that you don't confuse them. No further assumptions must be made.

Namespaces don't enhance the notion of validation, either. The XML mechanism for DTDs is exactly the same with or without namespaces; they are not a magical solution for doing anything else but disambiguate.

Namespaces are a simple and easy-to-use abstraction on top of XML. The following chapters use them intensively to create cleanly separated applications and enhance your documents with constructs from other XML vocabularies, such as Xlink and XHTML.

# Summary

This chapter reviewed the whole XML language—from the basic notions of elements to namespaces covering entities, declaration, types, and notations. Special attention was given to DTDs and all the types of markup declarations that may appear in them (such as element, attribute list, entity, and notation declarations).

Several examples of DTD modeling and XML documents were given, as well as plenty of examples and reusable components for your own DTDs.

This chapter is intended as a general reference for the syntax and semantics of XML. Subsequent chapters deal with specific applications and extensions of what was covered here, such as Xpointers, Xlink, and the ways to manipulate them programmatically using C++.

# 2

# XML/C++ Overview

THE OPPORTUNITIES FOR COLLABORATION BETWEEN XML and C++ are numerous and spawn several technologies, specifications, application types, and programming paradigms.

Examples of the C++/XML liaison include things as diverse as XML extension languages for C++ applications, C++ extensions to XML-related browser behavior, C++ modules to access databases as XML documents (and vice versa), XML specification implementations (XPath, XLink, XPointer), and implementation patterns over well-known APIs using C++-specific features (such as using templates to visit DOM trees).

Needless to say, it is easy to get lost in such a myriad of options and seemingly dissimilar things. The goal of this chapter is to give you a complete and clear mental framework of the XML/C++ technologies: what they are, how they are grouped, where to apply them, and where to find them in this book.

This chapter is divided into two parts. The first part discusses the XML family of technologies. The second part discusses the basic APIs for general-purpose XML programming. It gives an overview of the main kinds of C++ XML applications and how they build on the previous parts.

# The XML Family of Technologies

XML, in the most common and useful sense, is far more than just the XML 1.0 specification. It is a set of technologies, concepts, and APIs designed around the idea of a universal representation of hierarchical data.

The WWW Consortium (W3C) and other organizations such as OASIS (Organization for the Advancement of Structured Information Standards) have worked for years to build specifications on top of XML 1.0. These specifications cover things as diverse as linking, advanced data modeling, and encryption. The union of the most important of these specifications is commonly called the "XML family of technologies." The following sections explain the role and position of each member.

## Core XML

The absolute core of XML is defined in the XML 1.0 specification. This is where the important concepts of elements, attributes, entities, and so on get defined. From a conceptual point of view, all the contents of this specification amount to two key points upon which everything else is constructed: well-formedness and validity.

### Well-Formed Documents

Well-formed XML documents must adhere to only the most basic syntax defined in the specification. In other words, they are only required to be a correctly nested set of elements, each probably having some attributes and content.

No formal restrictions are made on the type of elements that may appear in the document, or what content they may have. This might be good in some situations where the level of formality is not required, and checking the correctness of the document from a purely (and minimal) syntactical point of view is enough. Listing 2.1 shows a well-formed document.

Listing 2.1   **A Minimalistic Well-Formed Document**

```
<?xml version="1.0"?>
<!-- The line above is known as the XML declaration. It states this is an
    XML file -->
<job>
<!-- There is a root node on every WF document (job, in this case) -->
  <title>Software Developer</title>
  <duties>
   <duty>Design</duty><duty>Test</duty>
   <duty>Program</duty><duty>Improve</duty>
   <duty priority="highest">Enjoy it</duty>
  </duties>
  <salary>Not specified</salary>
</job>
```

In a more general case, you need to constrain the contents of the document and explicitly state rules such as "The job description is optional, but the duties are not." This is the higher level of abstraction added by validity.

## Valid Documents

XML 1.0 defines a basic constraint mechanism called DTD (Document Type Definition). DTDs specify a particular type of document, such as the names of elements that may appear in a document, their attributes, and their content.

Listing 2.2 shows the DTD formalizing the structure of the job type of documents.

### Listing 2.2    *job* **DTD**

```
<!ELEMENT job (title,description?,duties,salary)>
<!ELEMENT title       (#PCDATA)> <!-- title has character data only -->
<!ELEMENT description (#PCDATA)>
<!ELEMENT duties      (duty+)>    <!-- at least one duty -->
<!ELEMENT salary      (#PCDATA)>
<!ELEMENT duty        (#PCDATA)>
<!ATTLIST duty  priority (low¦high¦highest)   #IMPLIED>
```

DTDs are tied to their instances by a DOCTYPE declaration, as shown here:

```
<?xml version="1.0"?>
<!DOCTYPE job SYSTEM "job.dtd">
<job>
  <!-- ...all the rest of the content, as in Listing 1.1 -->
</job>
```

When a document exhibits a DOCTYPE declaration, and it complies with all the rules in the associated DTD, the document is said to be valid. Naturally, all valid documents are also well-formed, but not vice versa.

## Namespaces

Namespaces are a simple mechanism to avoid name collision. A namespace is declared by appending an xmlns:*prefix* attribute to an element, whose value is a unique URL. The element and its contents are from then on considered part of the namespaces and can be unambiguously identified. (Listing 2.3, shown in a moment, shows an example.)

Even though in the strictest sense XML 1.0 defines all the basics, namespaces are also considered part of the core XML because of their importance for the real-world environment, where multiple vocabularies and extensions must coexist in one document.

Namespaces can be used with either plain well-formed documents or with valid ones. Namespaces are used in every other specification of the XML family, so it's important to know them. For details of this and the other components of the core XML, refer to Chapter 1.

Several types of key technologies build on the core. Most of them are vocabularies for particular domains (such as a chemical markup language, XHTML, and even the job description just given). Some others are more fundamental in the sense that they expand the semantics of the core XML in order to help create more powerful vocabularies and applications. These technologies are the rest of the XML family of specifications (shown in Figure 2.1) and may be divided into three groups: advanced data modeling, transformation, and pointing and linking.

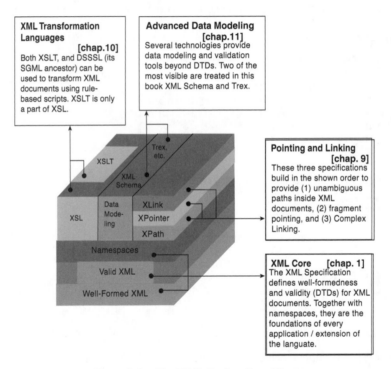

**XML Transformation Languages**    **[chap.10]**
Both XSLT, and DSSSL (its SGML ancestor) can be used to transform XML documents using rule-based scripts. XSLT is only a part of XSL.

**Advanced Data Modeling**    **[chap.11]**
Several technologies provide data modeling and validation tools beyond DTDs. Two of the most visible are treated in this book XML Schema and Trex.

**Pointing and Linking**    **[chap. 9]**
These three specifications build in the shown order to provide (1) unambiguous paths inside XML documents, (2) fragment pointing, and (3) Complex Linking.

**XML Core    [chap. 1]**
The XML Specification defines well-formedness and validity (DTDs) for XML documents. Together with namespaces, they are the foundations of every application / extension of the languate.

Trex, etc.
XSLT
XML Schema
XSL
Data Mode-ling
XLink
XPointer
XPath
Namespaces
Valid XML
Well-Formed XML

**Figure 2.1**    The XML family of specifications.

## Advanced Modeling and Validation

DTDs are an excellent tool for a wide variety of applications where the degree of formalism needed is moderate and definitions such as "the content is character data" are enough. Other applications, however, require much more precise definitions, such as "The content is character data representing a floating point smaller than 9.69." For such applications, the W3C has created XML Schema.

XML Schema is a language for defining complex structures and data types for XML documents. Using XML Schema, you can define, derive, extend, and compose very precise constructs, thus providing higher-level semantics on the document and higher automatic validation from the parser level.

Listing 2.3 shows an example of XML Schema. It's a classic purchase order example that has become a "hello world" of sorts for the XML Schema specification. (Don't worry if not all the details are clear at the moment—this listing is intended to give you only a taste of the syntax. The details, especially the C++ manipulation, are explored in Chapter 9.)

**Listing 2.3    The Purchase Schema (as Defined in the XML Schema Spec Part 0)**

```
<xsd:schema xmlns:xsd="http://www.w3.org/2000/08/XMLSchema">

<!-- This document originally defined on the XML Schema
     specification part 0 -->

 <xsd:annotation>
  <xsd:documentation>
   Purchase order schema for Example.com.
   Copyright 2000 Example.com. All rights reserved.
  </xsd:documentation>
 </xsd:annotation>

 <xsd:element name="purchaseOrder" type="PurchaseOrderType"/>

 <xsd:element name="comment" type="xsd:string"/>

 <xsd:complexType name="PurchaseOrderType">
  <xsd:sequence>
   <xsd:element name="shipTo" type="USAddress"/>
   <xsd:element name="billTo" type="USAddress"/>
   <xsd:element ref="comment" minOccurs="0"/>
   <xsd:element name="items"  type="Items"/>
  </xsd:sequence>
  <xsd:attribute name="orderDate" type="xsd:date"/>
 </xsd:complexType>

 <xsd:complexType name="USAddress">
  <xsd:sequence>
   <xsd:element name="name"   type="xsd:string"/>
   <xsd:element name="street" type="xsd:string"/>
   <xsd:element name="city"   type="xsd:string"/>
   <xsd:element name="state"  type="xsd:string"/>
   <xsd:element name="zip"    type="xsd:decimal"/>
  </xsd:sequence>
  <xsd:attribute name="country" type="xsd:NMTOKEN"
     use="fixed" value="US"/>
 </xsd:complexType>
```

*continues*

Listing 2.3    **Continued**

```
<xsd:complexType name="Items">
 <xsd:sequence>
  <xsd:element name="item" minOccurs="0" maxOccurs="unbounded">
   <xsd:complexType>
    <xsd:sequence>
     <xsd:element name="productName" type="xsd:string"/>
     <xsd:element name="quantity">
      <xsd:simpleType>
       <xsd:restriction base="xsd:positiveInteger">
        <xsd:maxExclusive value="100"/>
       </xsd:restriction>
      </xsd:simpleType>
     </xsd:element>
     <xsd:element name="USPrice"     type="xsd:decimal"/>
     <xsd:element ref="comment"    minOccurs="0"/>
     <xsd:element name="shipDate" type="xsd:date" minOccurs="0"/>
    </xsd:sequence>
    <xsd:attribute name="partNum" type="SKU"/>
   </xsd:complexType>
  </xsd:element>
 </xsd:sequence>
</xsd:complexType>

<!-- Stock Keeping Unit, a code for identifying products -->
<xsd:simpleType name="SKU">
 <xsd:restriction base="xsd:string">
  <xsd:pattern value="\d{3}-[A-Z]{2}"/>
 </xsd:restriction>
</xsd:simpleType>
</xsd:schema>
```

XML Schema is not the only, nor necessarily the most popular, available language for advanced modeling and validation cases. It has a reputation for bloatedness and "over-specification." (My own opinion is reserved until Chapter 9, where a fair, comparative assessment can be made.) The fact remains that XML Schema is bound to evolve along with, and with the help of, other competitor languages.

Despite not being officially supported by the W3C, other high-level definition languages, such as TREX, Schematron, and Hook, have enjoyed a certain amount of success. Chapter 9 compares TREX and XML Schema, especially from the point of view of C++ performance and availability.

## Pointing and Linking Technologies

Whether we are talking about Web applications or high-performance C++ APIs for XML databases, unambiguous pointing and linking mechanisms are an essential tool.

## XLink

The official form of linking in XML comes in the form of XLink, a specification defining complex and simple links in terms of a handful of special attributes (possibly only via namespaces).

XLink provides the XML equivalent of <A HREF ...> in HTML: a mechanism to bind resources. In the XML world, however, links are semantics-oriented and may be associated with any element.

Listing 2.4 gives you an idea of the look and feel of XLink by showing a fragment of an XML document for the description of a legal act accusing people of certain crimes.

Listing 2.4    **An Abridged XLink-Aware Document for the Knights Templar Trial**

```
<?xml version="1.0"?>
<act xmlns:xlink="http://www.w3.org/1999/XLink">
  <date>March 14, 1310</date>
  <description>Knights Templar Trial</description>

  <article number="1" xlink:type="extended" >
    <!-- an extended link contains resources and locators, as well as
         the arcs that bind them together -->
    <defendant xlink:type="locator"
               xlink:href="templars.xml#xpointer(id['jmolay'])"
               xlink:label="molay">Jaques de Molay</defendant>
    <defendant xlink:type="locator"
               xlink:href="templars.xml#xpointer(id['jsivry'])"
               xlink:label="sivry">Jean de Sivry</defendant>
    <!-- ... and many other defendants -->
    <crime xlink:type="resource"
           xlink:label="absolution">That the Grand Master absolved the
                                     brothers of their sins</crime>
    <crime xlink:type="resource"
           xlink:label="night">That the brothers held their meetings in secret
                                and at night.</crime>
    <!-- ... and many other crimes (127 in total) -->

    <!-- and now the accusations. These are xlink arcs,
         connecting resources -->
    <accussation xlink:type="arc"
                 xlink:from="absolution"
                 xlink:to="molay"/>

    <accussation xlink:type="arc"
                 xlink:from="night"
                 xlink:to="molay"/>

    <accussation xlink:type="arc"
                 xlink:from="night"
                 xlink:to="sivry"/>
```

*continues*

Listing 2.4    **Continued**

```
    <!-- ... and many other accusations -->
  </article>
</act>
```

**An Irrelevant Fun Fact**

The act shown in Listing 2.4 reflects some of the 127 charges brought by order of Phillip IV of France against the order of the Knights Templar.

## XPointer

If you examine the value of the `xlink:href` attribute in Listing 2.4, you will see a URL that is somewhat reminiscent of old HTML fragment identifiers (such as `index.html#someId`). This is, in fact, an XPointer: an unambiguous, URL-friendly way of pointing to any element or attribute inside an XML document.

XPointer syntax is based on paths and functions. Paths are similar to those used in filesystems, indicating the nesting relationship between elements, while functions enrich the language with useful comparison and processing expressions (such as to get the substring of an element name or compare an id).

XPointer is simply an extension of the XML Path Language, XPath.

## XPath

XPath is the foundation of all pointing features in XLink, XPointer, and XSLT (discussed in the next section). It defines the concepts of location steps (the different parts of a path), axes (collections of related nodes), and a core function library for the manipulation of strings and numbers, all for the purpose of unambiguously addressing parts of an XML document.

XPath expressions are not expressed in XML in order to allow them to be integrated as URLs and attribute values. Instead, they are simple strings such as the ones shown here:

| | |
|---|---|
| `/xhtml/para/@name` | Selects the `name` attribute of the `/xhtml/para` node. |
| `@*` | Selects all the attributes of the current node (called the context). |
| `para[1]` | Selects the first `para` child of the context node. |
| `para[last()]` | Selects the last `para` child of the context node. |

XPath, the XPointer extensions, and XLink are explained in Chapter 10, with a special emphasis on available C++ tools for their manipulation and the implementation strategies for their successful use.

# XML Transformation

One popular operation with XML is to transform it using declarative languages such as XSLT (XML Stylesheet Transformations). This is common for two reasons:

- It is a powerful and maintainable way of performing certain operations, such as transforming to rendering formats (such as HTML or PDF)
- A rule-based language is easy to learn and provides a reasonable manipulation tool for individuals with different skill levels

The single most common transformation language is W3C's XSLT (currently in version 1.1). XSLT provides a way to write rule-based stylesheets, such as the one shown in Listing 2.6. A rule is composed of two parts: a matching expression (an XPath expression, naturally) and a body. The body may contain non-XSLT tags that get copied directly into the output. Listings 2.5 through 2.7 show a source document, a stylesheet, and the result of processing it, respectively.

Listing 2.5   **A Simple Source Document**

```
<?xml version="1.0"?>
<films>
   <filmtitle xml:lang="fr">L'enfer</filmtitle>
   <filmtitle xml:lang="en-US">Arizona Dream</filmtitle>
</films>
```

Listing 2.6   **XSLT Stylesheet**

```
<xsl:stylesheet version="1.0"
            xmlns:xsl="http://www.w3.org/1999/XSL/Transform">

<xsl:template match="/films"> <!-- the rule expression -->
<!-- the rule body -->
<html>
   <head>
      <title>Movies!</title>
   </head>
   <body>
     <h2>The movies are:</h2>
      <ul>
      <xsl:for-each select="filmtitle">
      <xsl:call-template name="film"/>
      </xsl:for-each>
       </ul>
   </body>
</html>
</xsl:template>
```

*continues*

Listing 2.6   **Continued**

```
<!-- this template is called for each film -->
<xsl:template name="film">
   <li><xsl:value-of select="text()"/>
     ( <xsl:value-of select="@xml:lang"/> )
   </li>
</xsl:template>

</xsl:stylesheet>
```

Listing 2.7   **XSLT Transformation Result**

```
<html>
 <head>
  <title>Movies!</title>
 </head>
 <body>
  <h2>The movies are:</h2>
    <ul>
      <li>L'enfer ( fr ) </li>
      <li>Arizona Dream ( en-US ) </li>
    </ul>
 </body>
</html>
```

Even though the language itself is explained in Chapter 11, the true core and value of that portion of the book lies in explaining how to integrate this technology into your C++ applications so that you can provide advanced extensions and rendering capabilities to C++ programs dealing with XML.

Chapter 11 also explains the basics of DSSSL, an SGML predecessor of XSLT, and shows you how to integrate DSSSL modules (Jade, in particular) into your application in order to create PDF and TeX output.

# APIs

A complementary view of XML technologies comes from the study of the APIs available to process it. APIs for XML are mainly divided into three levels:

- All-purpose basic APIs
- APIs implementing noncore XML specifications
- Vocabulary-specific APIs

## All-Purpose Basic APIs

Figure 2.2 shows the layout of the all-purpose APIs for programmatic manipulation of XML in C++. The following sections explore each of the components shown.

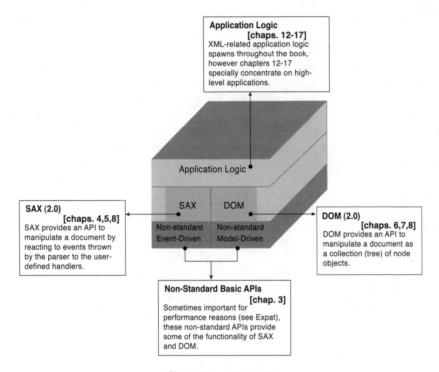

**Figure 2.2**    XML APIs.

### Event-Oriented Interfaces

Event-oriented interfaces are based on a push model, in which the application registers with a parser and gives it a document to process. The parser sends messages to the application, telling it about the items it sees as it processes the document. (All the details, and a much more precise description of the process, are given in Chapters 3 through 5.)

### Non-SAX Interfaces

Event-oriented interfaces can take many different shapes, including the industry-standard Simple API for XML, SAX (discussed in Chapters 4 and 5). Nonstandard interfaces are also worth studying, specially when extreme performance issues are being considered or a pure C solution is preferred. To cover these cases, Chapter 3 presents expat, the fastest XML-compliant parser.

### SAX Interfaces

SAX is an API originally developed for Java and later ported to C++. It is commonly regarded as the de facto standard for event-oriented XML processing. Chapters 4 and 5 present the structure and rationale of C++ SAX, and Chapter 8 considers some advanced C++ issues related to it (such as char types and their relation to Unicode).

### Object-Model-Oriented Interfaces

On the other side of the basic-processing arena are object-model-oriented interfaces. This denomination covers all the parsing environments in which the document is first totally read and represented as objects, and then the application can manipulate it by querying and modifying their state. The most popular and important of all such interfaces is W3C's Document Object Model (DOM).

DOM (as well as other technologies mentioned in this book) is well documented at an introductory level in other resources (including my book *XML Developer's Guide*). The important twist of Chapters 6 through 8 is their focus on its C++ implementation.

### Non-DOM Models

Some C/C++ libraries for XML manipulation—notably, libxml for Linux—expose a non-DOM model of the document. Even though Chapter 3 provides a sample of libxml in this mode, non-DOM model interfaces are uncommon and generally are somewhat provincial. The model-oriented programming parts of this book concentrate on the C++ DOM.

### DOM

Chapters 6 and 7 present the structure and usage of C++ DOM. Despite its memory footprint, DOM is just as important as SAX for XML manipulation. Choosing which one to use is a decision that involves performance and architectural considerations and therefore should not be taken lightly. Chapter 8 presents advanced DOM and SAX issues and shows you how to connect them using C++.

## Non-Core Interfaces

An important group of APIs are those that allow you to programmatically manipulate advanced XML abstractions such as XPointers and schemas. This book dedicates a whole part to their structure, usage, and glitches, from the point of view of C++.

In each chapter that discusses a noncore specification (such as pointing and linking, schema, and transformation, throughout Chapters 9 through 11), a succinct presentation of the language is provided, and then the bulk of the chapter presents the programmatic C++ manipulation.

### Vocabulary-Specific API

Advanced XML vocabularies sometimes present a C++ API specifically designed for their manipulation or interpretation. This is the case with certain elements of SOAP and other XML-based distributed protocols, as well as that of APIs for XML-database translations.

Two important examples of this type of API are presented in Chapters 14 and 15.

# Applications

The ultimate point of this book is to provide you with the concepts to create high-performance quality C++ applications. The actual examples and logic for application creation are extended throughout this book, not only in a couple of chapters. However, it is important to see some of the types of applications you will be creating and their relative position throughout the book (see Figure 2.3).

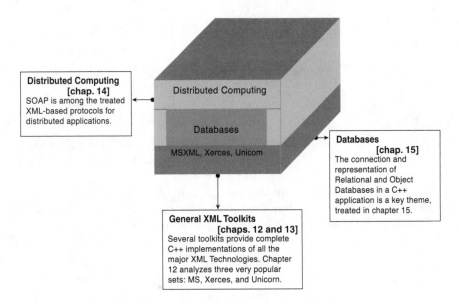

**Figure 2.3**    Applications.

### Pure XML Manipulation

Pure XML manipulation deals with C++ SAX and DOM programs, the implementation logic on top of specific vocabularies (whether homemade or not), and the programmatic choices for their representation and composition.

These types of applications are explored in Chapters 4 through 8.

Complex and interesting C++ applications of these technologies (such as data and metadata configuration, extension languages, and vocabulary-specific browser plug-in development) are explored in Chapters 12 through 15.

### Relational Persistence

C++ applications dealing with advanced XML persistence (such as relational and object databases) are an important topic that recurs in almost every commercial application. The C++ implementation of database/XML modules is the focus of Chapter 15.

### Distributed XML Applications

Distributed C++ applications using XML-based protocols are a growing and interesting field. Their general rationale, structure, performance, and security are explored in Chapter 14.

### Case Studies

This book finishes with the construction of two complete, real-life XML C++ applications, using the APIs and technologies studied throughout the book.

## Summary

This chapter presented an overview of the XML technologies and APIs and how they interact and lay upon each other. It also provided pointers to the chapters where each specification and/or API is discussed.

It is important to note that although I discuss general XML technologies, the focus and value of this book are not so much in the presentation I give of the specifications themselves as in the knowledge of how to manipulate them programmatically using C++.

# II

# Processing XML with C++

# 3

# Event-Driven Processing

THIS CHAPTER DISCUSSES THE FIRST AND MOST COMMON way of working with XML documents in a program: event-driven processing.

During event-driven processing, the parser notifies the program of events that occur while the parser reads the document. Examples of such events include finding a new start tag and encountering more character data.

This chapter discusses the two main parts of event-driven processing:

- The concepts and usage of event-driven parsers and handlers
- The strategies and patterns used to manipulate the data after it is received

The parser used in most of this chapter is James Clark's expat. Because of its ubiquity in C/C++ XML projects (expat is the parser behind projects such as Mozilla and the Perl XML modules), it will be discussed in more detail than other mentioned toolkits, such as Gnome's libxml.

## The Event-Driven Model

In order to get a complete view of event-driven processing, you must understand it from two complementary points of view: the physical process that an application goes through when using an event-driven XML parser, and the development process by which such an application is created.

The actual control flow of the event-driven application (the physical process of parsing and reporting) is simple:

1. The application creates a new parser instance.

2. The application registers the handler functions with the parser.

3. The application asks the parser to start processing a particular document.

4. The parser goes through the document sequentially, raising calls to the application handlers for each construct it finds (tags, cdata sections, comments).

5. The application receives the data (as parameters of its handlers) and uses it at will.

Figure 3.1 illustrates the process as a Unified Modeling Language (UML) sequence diagram.

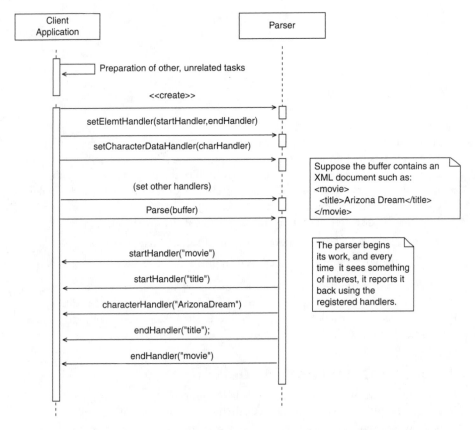

**Figure 3.1**    A sequence diagram for typical event-driven applications.

On the other hand, there is the application construction view of the process:

1. Define the nature of your handler functions. (In the case of C++ wrappers to expat and the C++ toolkits in Chapter 4, these functions are bundled into handler classes.)

2. Accommodate your handler functions' implementation to a format that is congruent with the parser's interface (black-box design fitness).

3. Accommodate your handler functions' implementation so that it takes into account the nuances and details that are not explicit in the parser's interface (white-box design fitness).

4. Validate the quality of your design according to traditional and domain-specific criteria.

Understanding both of these views is fundamental in creating high-quality event-driven XML programs. This chapter considers both views in the light of performance-oriented C/C++ parsers and their C++ wrappers, especially expat. The next chapter tackles the same issues in the light of more object-oriented approaches, especially SAX2 parsers.

# expat

expat is the fastest nonvalidating XML parser in the world (it is included on the companion CD). It is the cornerstone of key industrial XML applications and is an obligatory item for anyone interested in C/C++ XML development.

The following sections focus on the syntax and code-level issues of expat usage. Some design tips are also given.

## A Hands-On Introduction

In order to start the discussion of expat, let's begin with an actual application. This first example constructs a syntax tree from an arithmetic XML file and then evaluates it.

The XML files that you will use as inputs for your program are XML representations of simple arithmetic expressions. They look like the following:

```
<?xml version="1.0"?>
<!DOCTYPE calculation SYSTEM "calculation.dtd">
<calculation>
  <!-- an XML document representing the expression
                ((4 * 3) + 3) * (4/2)
  -->

  <mul>
    <add>
      <value>3</value>
      <mul>
      <value>4</value>
```

```
        <value>3</value>
        </mul>
      </add>
      <div>
        <value>4</value>
        <value>2</value>
      </div>
    </mul>
  </calculation>
```

This document, as stated in its prologue, is conformant with the following DTD:

```
<!ENTITY % operation "add | sub | mul | div">

<!ELEMENT calculation (%operation;)>
<!ELEMENT value       (#PCDATA)>

<!ELEMENT add   ((%operation; |value),(%operation; |value))>
<!ELEMENT sub   ((%operation; |value),(%operation; |value))>
<!ELEMENT mul   ((%operation; |value),(%operation; |value))>
<!ELEMENT div   ((%operation; |value),(%operation; |value))>
```

**About the DTD**

It is important to mention that this DTD is included only for didactical purposes. Because expat is a non-validating parser, the conformance of the document to the DTD will not be taken into account.

### The Syntax Tree Classes

The whole point of the syntax tree exercise is to create a suitable object representation of the data in the document in order to evaluate an arithmetic expression. The place to start is the definition of the classes that represent the arithmetic syntax tree.

Figure 3.2 shows the syntax tree class structure (a classical application of the composite pattern).

The ideas behind the syntax tree class structure are simple:

- Every object in the tree is a term and can be evaluated to a floating-point value (using getValue).

- Some objects are simple values, and others are math operators.

- Math operators have two associated terms. Different types of operators do different things to their operands (division, multiplication, and so on).

The use of this class hierarchy is straightforward. Figure 3.3 shows the equivalence between an arithmetic expression, a conceptual syntax tree, and the code needed to implement it, using our representation.

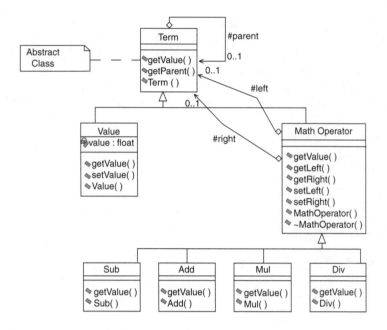

**Figure 3.2**   The syntax tree class structure.

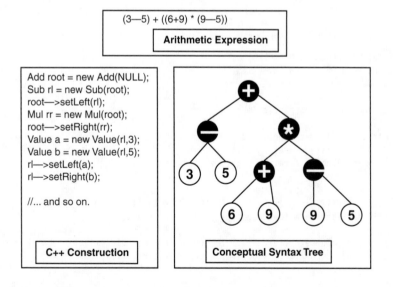

**Figure 3.3**   One expression, three models.

Listings 3.1 through 3.4 show the implementation of the `Term`, `MathOperator`, `Value`, and `Add` classes. (The implementation of `Sub` and the other operations is almost identical and will be obvious when you go through this code.)

Note that as with the rest of the code embedded in this book, the classes presented here omit DOC++ comments and other organizational features to save space. For the complete code, including Visual Studio projects and makefiles, refer to the CD.

Listing 3.1    **Term Implementation**

```
#ifndef TERM_H
#define TERM_H


class Term {
 public:
   virtual float getValue() = 0;

   Term *getParent() { return parent; }

    Term(Term *new_parent) { parent = new_parent; }

 protected:
   Term *parent;
};

#endif TERM_H
```

Listing 3.2    **MathOperator Implementation**

```
#ifndef MATHOPERATOR_H
#define MATHOPERATOR_H
#include "Term.h"

class MathOperator : public Term {
 public:
   virtual float getValue() = 0;
   Term *getLeft()  { return left; }
   Term *getRight() { return right; }


   void setLeft(Term *new_left)   { left = new_left; }
   void setRight(Term *new_right) { right = new_right; }

   inline MathOperator(Term *t) : Term(t) { left = NULL; right = NULL; }
   inline ~MathOperator() { delete(left); delete(right); }

  protected:
   Term *left;
   Term *right;
};
#endif MATHOPERATOR_H
```

Listing 3.3 **Value Implementation**

```
#include "Term.h"

class Value : public Term {
 public:
  float getValue() { return value; }
  void setValue(float new_value) { value = new_value; }

  Value(Term *t,float new_value = 0) : Term(t) { value = new_value; }

  private:
   float value;

};
```

Listing 3.4 **Add Implementation**

```
#include "MathOperator.h"

class Add : public MathOperator {
 public:
   float getValue() { return left->getValue() + right->getValue(); }
   inline Add(Term *t): MathOperator(t) { }
};
```

## Handlers

Handlers are called whenever the parser finds something that must be reported to the application. For example, when the parser encounters a start tag such as the following:

```
<actor name="John" Surname="Malkovich">
```

it issues a call to the start handler, passing the name of the tag and an array with the attributes. An extra parameter of type void *, containing arbitrary user data, is also passed to all handlers. It is used to help the application keep a state between different handler calls.

The application must have a handler for each construct (start tags, character data, end tags, and so on) it is interested in. The following text discusses all the available types of handlers. For the moment, let's concentrate on the practical implementation of the startElement and endElement handlers that will take care of constructing our syntax tree from an XML document.

For the startElement handler implementation, the startElement handler receives, as mentioned already, the name of the tag and the attributes (sent in only one null-terminated array of strings const char **atts, where atts[0] contains the name of the first attribute and atts[1] its value, and so on). It also receives a parameter with arbitrary data. We will use this parameter to pass the tree's current term.

The rationale behind the `startElement` handler is simple: Determine what type of term the tag represents, create an instance of it, and add it as a child of the current node:

```
void
startElement(void *data, const char *el, const char **attr) {
  Term *child = NULL;
  if(strcmp(el,"calculation") == 0)
        return;
  // We are certain that whenever start is called,
  // the parent is a MathOperator
  MathOperator *parent = (MathOperator *)((nodeAndParser *)data)->currentTerm;
  if(strcmp(el,"add") == 0)
    child = new Add(parent);
  if(strcmp(el,"sub") == 0)
    child = new Sub(parent);
  if(strcmp(el,"mul") == 0)
    child = new Mul(parent);
  if(strcmp(el,"div") == 0)
    child = new Div(parent);
  if(strcmp(el,"value") == 0)
  {
      double value = atof(attr[1]); //attr[0] == "number" attr[1] == the value
      child = new Value(parent,(float)value);
  }

  if(parent->getLeft() == NULL)
    parent->setLeft(child);
  else
    parent->setRight(child);
  ((nodeAndParser *)data)->currentTerm = child; // Data simply contains
                       // the tree and a reference to the parser.
                       // See definition below.
}
```

As you can see in the last lines of the `startElement` handler, in order to correctly construct the tree, you must update the user data so that it points to the newly created node. Otherwise, you would always be adding subnodes to the same term!

When an element ends, the opposite procedure takes place: The user data must be updated to point to the parent of the current node. This is taken care of in the `endElement` handler:

```
void endElement(void *data, const char *name)
{
  Term *current = ((nodeAndParser *)data)->currentTerm;
  ((nodeAndParser *)data)->currentTerm = current->getParent();
}
```

## *main*

The `main` procedure of the program is very simple but represents the steps mentioned earlier (create a parser, register the handlers, and start parsing):

```c
#include "stdafx.h"
#include "xmlparse.h"
#include "string.h"
#include "math.h"
#include "LittleMathLanguage.h"
#include "syntaxTree.h"


typedef struct
{
  XML_Parser parser; // We will use in other examples
                     // for extra error info.
  Term    *currentTerm;
} nodeAndParser;

int main(int argc, char* argv[])
{
  char buf[BUFSIZ];
  XML_Parser parser = XML_ParserCreate(NULL);
  int done;

  Add *root = new Add(NULL);
  root->setLeft(new Value(root,0)); // Just a way to set up
                                    // a harmless root

  nodeAndParser *np = new nodeAndParser();
  np->parser = parser;
  np->currentTerm = root;

  XML_SetUserData(parser, np);
  XML_SetElementHandler(parser, startElement, endElement);
  do {
    size_t len = fread(buf, 1, sizeof(buf), stdin);
    done = len < sizeof(buf);
    if (!XML_Parse(parser, buf, len, done)) {
      fprintf(stderr,
           "%s at line %d\n",
           XML_ErrorString(XML_GetErrorCode(parser)),
           XML_GetCurrentLineNumber(parser));
      return 1;
    }
  } while (!done);
  printf("The result of evaluating the tree is %.2f\n",root->getValue());
  delete(root);
  XML_ParserFree(parser);
  return 0;
}
```

### The Result

The following is a transcription of an invocation using the XML file shown at the beginning of this example:

```
C:\XMLC++\syntaxTree\bin>type test.xml | syntaxTree
The result of evaluating the tree is 30.00
```

## expat Structure

Now that you know the rationale and implementation structure behind expat applications, it's time to take a look at the complete API.

expat has a total of 33 functions (all of them documented in the original source code, included on the CD), of which only a few are really relevant for the vast majority of applications. The following sections enumerate and classify all the functions and comment on the use of the most relevant ones. The examples in the case studies show most of the functions of expat in a large application.

expat's functions can be divided into the five groups shown in Figure 3.4.

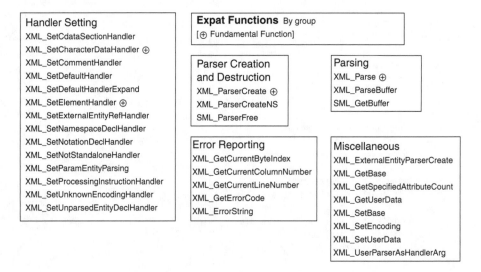

**Figure 3.4**    The basic expat structure.

**Fundamental Functions**

As mentioned before, of the myriad of functions in Figure 3.4, a small subset provides 80 percent of expat's power. The following six functions are the most important in the whole expat distribution:

- `XML_ParserCreate(const XML_Char*encoding)`. Constructs a new parser. If called with a non-null encoding name, it specifies the character encoding of the document to parse. Only UTF-8, UTF-16, US-ASCII, and ISO8859-1 are natively supported.

- `XML_SetElementHandler(XML_Parser p, XML_StartElementHandler start, XML_EndElementHandler end)`. Sets the element handler methods for a particular parser. The handler methods must follow the structure prescribed:

```
typedef void
(*XML_StartElementHandler)(void *userData,
                           const XML_Char *name,
                           const XML_Char **atts)


typedef void
(*XML_EndElementHandler)(void *userData,
                         const XML_Char *name)
```

- `int XML_Parse(XML_Parser p, const char *s, int len, int isFinal)`. Unlike other parsers, expat provides the ability to control on a very low level the actual reading of the document. The `XML_Parse` function lets you read the part of the document contained in the first `len` characters of the `s` buffer. The `isFinal` parameter tells the parser whether this is the final part of the document. The classic structure of a program using this function is shown in the earlier `syntaxTree` example.

- `XML_SetCharacterDataHandler(XML_Parser p, XML_CharacterDataHandler charhndl)`. Another key function of the kit is the character data handler. It works just like `setElement` handler (or any of the other handlers in the kit, for that matter): It receives a pointer to a handler function and registers it with the parser. The function must comply with the following structure:

```
typedef void
(*XML_CharacterDataHandler)(void *userData,
                            const XML_Char *s,
                            int len);
```

Note the existence of a third argument, `len`. The string sent to the application is not a *clean,* 0-terminated string. Instead, the application must deal only with the valid characters by knowing that only the first `len` of them are significant.

- Another very important point is the following: As with the other handlers, the characters received here are `XML_Char`—that is, UTF-8 characters (unless you defined it otherwise when recompiling expat). This will always be the case, regardless of the original document encoding.

- `XML_SetUserData(XML_Parser p, void *userData)`. As you saw in the `syntaxTree` example, the key to communicating a state between handler calls is the `userData` that gets passed around them. Note that the type of the user data is the very general `void *`. This has two consequences: You can pass a pointer to anything as user data, even the parser itself, and you must properly cast back the `userData` on every handler.

- `void XML_ParserFree(XML_Parser p)`. The final key function is, naturally, the cleanup function, `XML_ParserFree`. One very important point about it is that it does not free the user data registered with the parser. That is left as an application responsibility.

## Object-Oriented Wrappers for expat

So far you have seen expat as an extremely fast and convenient C parser. Now it is time to see how can it also be wrapped in very elegant C++ classes that might fit better in an object-oriented C++ project.

The basic principles behind expat wrappers such as expatpp (a C++ wrapper by Andy Dent, used by me to create applications and as a base for my own wrapper classes) are discussed and put to use in the following sections.

### Creating a Wrapper Interface

The first step is to create a class that exposes the handler interfaces:

```
class expatpp {
public:
     expatpp(bool createParser=true);
     virtual ~expatpp();

     operator XML_Parser() const;

     bool emptyCharData(const XML_Char *s, int len);  // utility often
                                       // used in overridden charData

// overrideable callbacks
     virtual void startElement(const XML_Char* name, const XML_Char** atts);
     virtual void endElement(const XML_Char*);
     virtual void charData(const XML_Char*, int len);
     virtual void processingInstruction(const XML_Char* target,
                                 const XML_Char* data);
```

```
        virtual void defaultHandler(const XML_Char*, int len);
        virtual int notStandaloneHandler();
        virtual void unparsedEntityDecl(const XML_Char* entityName,
                                 const XML_Char* base,
                                 const XML_Char* systemId,
                                 const XML_Char* publicId,
                                 const XML_Char* notationName);
        virtual void notationDecl(const XML_Char* notationName,
                              const XML_Char* base,
                              const XML_Char* systemId,
                              const XML_Char* publicId);
        virtual void startNamespace(const XML_Char* prefix,
                                const XML_Char* uri);
        virtual void endNamespace(const XML_Char*);

// XML interfaces
        int XMLPARSEAPI XML_Parse(const char* buffer, int len, int isFinal);
        XML_Error XMLPARSEAPI XML_GetErrorCode();
        int XMLPARSEAPI XML_GetCurrentLineNumber();
protected:
        XML_Parser mParser;


// interface functions for callbacks
public:
        static void startElementCallback(void *userData, const XML_Char* name,
                                    const XML_Char** atts);
        static void endElementCallback(void *userData, const XML_Char* name);
        static void startNamespaceCallback(void *userData,
                                      const XML_Char* prefix,
                                      const XML_Char* uri);
        static void endNamespaceCallback(void *userData,
                                    const XML_Char* prefix);
        static void charDataCallback(void *userData, const XML_Char* s,
                                int len);
        static void processingInstructionCallback(void *userData,
                                           const XML_Char* target,
                                           const XML_Char* data);
        static void defaultHandlerCallback(void* userData, const XML_Char* s,
                                      int len);
        static int notStandaloneHandlerCallback(void* userData);
        static void unParsedEntityDeclCallback(void* userData,
                                          const XML_Char* entityName,
                                          const XML_Char* base,
                                          const XML_Char* systemId,
                                          const XML_Char* publicId,
                                          const XML_Char* notationName);
        static void notationDeclCallback(void *userData,
                                    const XML_Char* notationName,
                                    const XML_Char* base,
                                    const XML_Char* systemId,
                                    const XML_Char* publicId);
```

```
// utilities
    static int skipWhiteSpace(const char*);

};
```

As you can see from the code, not only virtual functions are provided for public use—some protected static functions are also included. The idea behind those functions becomes evident when you analyze the implementation of this base class:

```
expatpp::expatpp(bool createParser)
{
  if (createParser) {
            mParser = XML_ParserCreate(0);
            ::XML_SetUserData(mParser, this);
            ::XML_SetElementHandler(mParser, startElementCallback,
                                    endElementCallback);
            ::XML_SetCharacterDataHandler(mParser, charDataCallback);
            ::XML_SetProcessingInstructionHandler(mParser,
                                    processingInstructionCallback);
            ::XML_SetDefaultHandler(mParser, defaultHandlerCallback);
            ::XML_SetUnparsedEntityDeclHandler(mParser,
                                    unParsedEntityDeclCallback);
            ::XML_SetNotationDeclHandler(mParser, notationDeclCallback);
            ::XML_SetNotStandaloneHandler(mParser,
                                    notStandaloneHandlerCallback);
            ::XML_SetNamespaceDeclHandler(mParser, startNamespaceCallback,
                                    endNamespaceCallback);
    }
}



void
expatpp::startElementCallback(void *userData, const XML_Char* name,
                                const XML_Char** atts)
{
      ((expatpp*)userData)->startElement(name, atts);
}
```

You are passing the object itself as user data, and you are registering the protected callbacks as the handlers. This way, when the callback gets called, you can take the user data (the wrapper object itself) and call its implementation of the particular handler. Because it is a virtual function, if no handler is defined in the subclass, the default empty implementation is called:

```
void  expatpp::startElement(const XML_Char*, const XML_Char**) {}
```

This nifty wrapper design allows applications that use expat in C++ context to make very object-oriented use of it in two easy steps: subclass the base wrapper and override only those handlers in which they have interest.

The following section shows the application of the above two steps.

## expatpp Example

The following application uses a subclass of C++ wrapper to create a visual representation (TreeView) of the elements in the document. It was written using Borland C++ controls, but it can be easily ported to other environments. As a matter of fact, the next section shows an equivalent for Visual C++ (the environment of choice for the majority of these examples), and the final part of the chapter (other toolkits) shows it for Gnome under Linux.

```cpp
//~Description A simple example of how to use C++ wrappers.
//~             It overrides the startelement handler in order to
//~             construct a visual representation of elements
//~             in a tree view.

#ifndef myParserH
#define myParserH

#include "expatpp.h"
#include <vcl.h>

class myParser : public dexpatpp
{
    private:
        TTreeView *mTreeView; // The tree view in which the
                              // atts will be shown
        TTreeNode *lastNode;
    public:

        inline myParser(TTreeView *treeToUse);
        inline void startElement(const XML_Char* name, const XML_Char** atts);
        inline void endElement(const XML_Char* name);
};

inline
void myParser::startElement(const XML_Char* name, const XML_Char** atts)
{
    lastNode = mTreeView->Items->AddChild(lastNode, name);
}

inline
void myParser::endElement(const XML_Char* name)
{
    lastNode = lastNode->Parent;
}

inline myParser::myParser(TTreeView *treeToUse)
{
    mTreeView = treeToUse;
    lastNode = NULL;
}

#endif
```

The resulting TreeView, after parsing a simple XML document, looks like Figure 3.5. For the complete listing and final executable, refer to the CD.

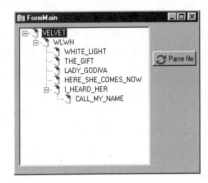

**Figure 3.5**   The TreeView result.

## Integrating expat in Windows Projects (Optional)

This section shows the steps to integrate expat to a visual C++ project.

If you already know about the use of third-party library files under Visual C++, chances are that by looking at the expat distribution, you already know what to do, so feel free to skip this section if that is the case.

The steps to include expat in your Visual C++ project are as follows:

1. Open/create your project.

2. Go to fileView and add the xmlparse.lib library as part of the project.

3. Include the "xmlparse.h" header in your application.

4. Make sure that "xmlparse.h" is visible within your project.

5. Before running, make sure that the expat DLLs are visible. (It's a good idea to copy them to your project's output directory.)

The CD includes a sample project (that also displays a tree, but this time using the MFC) with the preceding characteristics. Please refer to it, or to the syntaxTree project, for practical examples of the steps mentioned.

# Other C/C++ Toolkits

Useful as it is, expat is not the only C/C++ XML parser available. Depending on your needs (such as validation or compliance with a particular project such as Gnome), you might want to try one of the following alternatives:

- **RXP.** A free validating XML parser written in C. Pointers to it are available on the CD.
- **libxml.** This fast implementation by Daniel Veillard is also one of the most complete C/C++ parsers available. Originally written in C, this validating parser has wrappers for C++ available. It is the core of the XML support in the Linux Gnome Project.
- **IBM's xml4c2 and Apache's Xerces.** This toolkit provides powerful event-driven and model based XML parsers written in C++. It includes garbage collection and compliance with most current XML-related standards. It is discussed in detail in the next chapters.
- **MSXML3.** This Microsoft toolkit provides a complete and very fast implementation of most current XML standards, including a C++ event-driven parser (for SAX). Several examples using this tool are introduced in the following chapters.

In order to give you an idea of the flavor of these other packages, the following code presents the same tree view application for Linux and libxml. This code is presented only to show the different design of libxml. No GTK (the UI toolkit used) experience is expected or required.

You will note that instead of registering handlers, this example receives a tree that represents the document and traverses it. This mode of processing will be explored in Chapters 6 and 7. It's presented here only as a teaser, showing how much two APIs can differ.

```
// THIS EXAMPLE IS OPTIONAL AND IN ESSENCE IS SEPARATE FROM THE REST
// OF THE CHAPTER. PLEASE SKIP IT IF IT IS A SOURCE OF CONFUSION.

#include <gnome.h>
#include "parser.h"

static void print_tree(xmlDocPtr doc,xmlNodePtr cur,GtkWidget *root) {
  GtkWidget *subtree;
  GtkWidget *label;

  if(!strcmp(cur->name,"text")){
    label = gtk_tree_item_new_with_label(xmlNodeListGetString(doc, cur, 1));
  }
  else
    label = gtk_tree_item_new_with_label(cur->name);
```

```
    gtk_widget_show(label);
    gtk_tree_append(GTK_TREE(root),label);

    if(cur->childs) {
      subtree = gtk_tree_new();
      gtk_tree_item_set_subtree(GTK_TREE_ITEM(label),subtree);
      print_tree(doc,cur->childs,subtree);
    }
    if(cur->next)
      print_tree(doc,cur->next,root);
}


static void
 button_clicked(GtkWidget *button,gpointer data) {
  GtkWidget *tree;
  GtkWidget *rootLabel;
  GtkWidget *subtree;

  xmlDocPtr doc;
  xmlNodePtr cur;

  /*
   * build an XML tree from the file;
   */
  doc = xmlParseFile("test.xml");
  if (doc == NULL) return;

  cur = doc->root;
  if (cur == NULL) {
      g_print("empty document\n");
      xmlFreeDoc(doc);
      return;
  }

  tree = gtk_tree_new();
  rootLabel = gtk_tree_item_new_with_label(cur->name);
  gtk_widget_show(rootLabel);
  gtk_tree_append(GTK_TREE(tree),rootLabel);

  cur = cur->childs;
  subtree = gtk_tree_new();
  gtk_tree_item_set_subtree(GTK_TREE_ITEM(rootLabel),subtree);

  print_tree(doc,cur,subtree);
```

```
    xmlFreeDoc(doc);

    gtk_box_pack_start(GTK_BOX(data),GTK_WIDGET(tree),TRUE,FALSE,0);
    gtk_widget_show_all(data);

}

static gint delete_event(GtkWidget *widget, GdkEvent *event ,gpointer data) {
    // two things to do: finish the loop and return FALSE, so the
    // gtk continues the closing of the window
    gtk_main_quit();
    return FALSE;
}

int
main(int argc,char *argv[]) {

    GtkWidget *app;
    GtkWidget *button;
    GtkWidget *hbox;

    gnome_init("XML view tree","1,0",argc,argv);
    app = gnome_app_new("XML view","XML Tree View");
    gtk_signal_connect(GTK_OBJECT(app),"delete_event",
                    GTK_SIGNAL_FUNC(delete_event),
                    NULL);
    hbox = gtk_hbox_new(TRUE,5);
    gnome_app_set_contents(GNOME_APP(app),hbox);
    button = gtk_button_new_with_label("Read test.xml");
    gtk_box_pack_start(GTK_BOX(hbox),GTK_WIDGET(button),TRUE,FALSE,0);
    gtk_signal_connect(GTK_OBJECT(button),"clicked",
                    GTK_SIGNAL_FUNC(button_clicked),
                    hbox);

    gtk_widget_show_all(app);
    gtk_main();
    return 0;
}
```

# Summary

This chapter presented the rationale and praxis of event-driven processing, especially using expat, a widely used C parser. Discussions and examples of C++ wrapping of C parsers were also provided.

The next chapter continues the discussion of event-oriented XML programming by presenting SAX and advanced techniques behind complex handler design.

# 4

# SAX C++

**C**HAPTER 3 DISCUSSED THE BASICS OF A KEY PARADIGM to process XML:
event-oriented programming. This chapter discusses the most important attempt to
standardize an interface for such a paradigm: Simple API for XML (SAX).

Chapter 3 showed how different event-oriented libraries can use unique ways to
send messages to a handler. Consider, for example, how much the two following functions differ, even though they have the same goal (namely, to inform the application of
the encounter of a startElement tag and its attributes):

```
// See how a custom-made class for attributes is used here
void classX::startElement (const char *fullname,
                               AttributeList & atts)
// See how an array of strings is used here for the attributes
// (expat and libxml style)
void classY::startElement  (void *ctx,
                               const xmlChar *fullname,
                               const xmlChar **atts);
```

Perhaps the most evident differences are the void * parameter in the second function
and the different forms to pass the attribute list. Other, more subtle differences will
arrive from the actual definition of xmlChar. (In libxml, from which the second function was taken, xmlChar is defined as unsigned char, which is different from the mere
char * in the first function.)

All these differences (on all the methods of an event-driven library) amount to a simple fact: lack of interoperability. If two parsers differ in how they inform the application of events, they simply cannot be used interchangeably (at least, not without changing the calling code or writing wrapper classes for each new implementation!).

SAX is an independent (non-W3C) effort to standardize event-driven interfaces, thus bringing interoperability among different parsers. SAX (now on version 2.0) was originally designed for Java by David Megginson and the Open Source community in xml-dev. Within Java, SAX has become the industry standard and has truly achieved its objectives as the lingua franca of event-driven parsing.

As time progressed, the necessity of a C++ version of SAX became evident, and several efforts have taken place to create a unified version. These efforts, however, are not at an end yet. The C++ specification of SAX is an ongoing process, and even though the main C++ parsers agree on the vast majority of points, there are still differences. (The CD contains pointers to the sites with the latest versions of SAX C++.)

This chapter analyzes the C++ SAX interfaces as defined by Xerces (Apache), pointing out when necessary the differences with other toolkits and possible changes in the future. Despite the small changes the C++ SAX API might undergo, becoming familiar with the interfaces and putting them into practice now is essential for any serious C++ XML programmer.

# A Hands-On Introduction

Above all, this book deals with practical development, so let's begin with a simple application that demonstrates the basic notions behind SAX parsing.

## The Document Type

For our first example, let's take the problem of creating a small XML vocabulary for drawing geometric figures. Listing 4.1 is the DTD for the first version of our drawing vocabulary. (This small application will be augmented in future chapters in order to show advanced design issues and strategies.)

Listing 4.1   **simpleGraphics.dtd**

```
<!-- General Parameter entities -->
<!ENTITY % int "CDATA">

<!-- ELEMENT and ATTLIST declarations -->

<!ENTITY % instruction "circle | rectangle | text">

<!ELEMENT graphic (%instruction;)*>

<!ELEMENT circle EMPTY>
<!ATTLIST circle
```

```
            x      %int;    #REQUIRED
            y      %int;    #REQUIRED
            rad    %int;    #REQUIRED>

<!ELEMENT rectangle EMPTY>
<!ATTLIST rectangle
            xi     %int;    #REQUIRED
            yi     %int;    #REQUIRED
            xf     %int;    #REQUIRED
            yf     %int;    #REQUIRED>

<!-- A short line of text to be drawn on  the screen -->
<!ELEMENT text (#PCDATA)>
<!ATTLIST text
            x      %int;    #REQUIRED
            y      %int;    #REQUIRED>
```

This document type is straightforward. It simply states the following: "A document of this type is a graphic composed of drawing instructions. There are three types of instructions: circles, rectangles, and text. Each instruction has certain parameters (such as x,y and radius for the circle)."

Listing 4.2 is a valid instance of the preceding DTD.

Listing 4.2    **SimpleGraphics Instance**

```
<?xml version="1.0" ?>
<!DOCTYPE graphic SYSTEM "simpleGraphics.dtd">
<graphic>
  <rectangle xi="15" yi="200" xf="225" yf="225"/>
  <circle x="30" y="30" rad="12"/>
  <circle x="30" y="60" rad="24"/>
  <circle x="30" y="90" rad="36"/>
  <circle x="30" y="120" rad="48"/>
  <circle x="30" y="150" rad="60"/>
  <circle x="30" y="30" rad="12"/>
  <circle x="60" y="60" rad="24"/>
  <circle x="90" y="90" rad="36"/>
  <circle x="120" y="120" rad="48"/>
  <circle x="150" y="150" rad="60"/>
  <circle x="30" y="30" rad="12"/>
  <circle x="60" y="30" rad="24"/>
  <circle x="90" y="30" rad="36"/>
  <circle x="120" y="30" rad="48"/>
  <circle x="150" y="30" rad="60"/>
  <text x="17" y="204">Sense is a line, mind is a circle</text>
</graphic>
```

Our goal is to create a program that takes an instance document such as this one and presents its graphical interpretation (in other words, a renderer).

## Strategy

SAX is an event-oriented API, so it follows the same structure as any other of its kind. This structure (discussed in Chapter 3) can be summarized in five steps:

1. The application creates a new parser instance.

2. The application registers the handlers with the parser.

3. The application asks the parser to start processing a particular document.

4. The parser goes sequentially through the document, raising calls to the application handlers for each construct it finds.

5. The application receives the data (as parameters of its handlers) and uses it at will.

However, SAX is also an object-oriented API, so it exhibits important differences from other toolkits, such as the one seen in the preceding chapter. Here are the two most important differences:

- Handler functions are bundled into cohesive classes such as DocumentHandler (for character data, start tags, and end tags) and ErrorHandler (for parse error handling).

- Because handlers are implemented as objects, which can hold attributes, there is no longer a need to pass user data every time a handler call is made (remember the void * first parameter of expat calls). Each object can maintain its state, thus leading to a much cleaner implementation.

The following code creates a Handler class that derives from HandlerBase. HandlerBase is a simple base object in SAX 1.0. (This book discusses both SAX 1.0 and 2.0. It starts with 1.0 because of its simplicity, but examples of both versions are included.) It implements a void behavior for every handler method of every handler interface. (Remember that this first section is designed only to give you a basic feel for what a SAX implementation looks like. Details about the API will come in the second part of this chapter.)

The class is going to implement the startElement and characters methods in order to capture the data for each instruction. Based on the element name (passed as the first argument of the startElement method), the handler will be able to determine which figure to draw. Based on the element attributes (passed as the second argument of startElement), it will be able to determine the particular parameters for each figure.

Listing 4.3 shows the implementation of our SAXGraphicsHandler class.

Listing 4.3   *SAXGraphicsHandler*

```
#include "SAXGraphicsHandler.h"

/**@name SAX Handler Methods
 */
//@{
  /**
```

```
     receives notification for start elements.
     <p>For this particular example, it simply reads the attributes of the new
     element and <b>dispatches the appropriate drawing method</b>.</p>
     @param
     @return
     @exception
     @param name The element type name.
     @param attributes The specified or defaulted attributes.
     @exception SAXException Any SAX exception, possibly
               wrapping another exception.
  */
inline void SAXGraphicsHandler::startElement(
                              const   XMLCh* const   name,
                              AttributeList&  attributes)
{

     if(strcmp(XTOC(name),"circle") == 0)
     {

/*
Note the use of XTOC and CTOX. These macros are used to convert classic char * to
the XMLCh * used by the xml4c library, and vice versa. XMLCh will be discussed
more in the second part of this chapter.
*/

int r =  atoi(XTOC(attributes.getValue(CTOX("rad"))));
               int x =  atoi(XTOC(attributes.getValue(CTOX("x"))));
               int y =  atoi(XTOC(attributes.getValue(CTOX("y"))));

               canvas->Ellipse(x-r/2,y-r/2,x+r/2,y+r/2);
     }

     if(strcmp(XTOC(name),"rectangle") == 0)
     {
               int x1 =  atoi(XTOC(attributes.getValue(CTOX("xi"))));
               int y1 =  atoi(XTOC(attributes.getValue(CTOX("yi"))));
               int x2 =  atoi(XTOC(attributes.getValue(CTOX("xf"))));
               int y2 =  atoi(XTOC(attributes.getValue(CTOX("yf"))));
               canvas->Rectangle(x1,y1,x2,y2);
     }

     if(strcmp(XTOC(name),"text") == 0)
     {
               textX =  atoi(XTOC(attributes.getValue(CTOX("x"))));
               textY =  atoi(XTOC(attributes.getValue(CTOX("y"))));
     }
}
   /**
     Receive notification of character data inside an element.
     <p>In this case, simply output the text to the window. Note that this
     method is always called <b>after</b> the startElement invocation for the
```

*continues*

Listing 4.3   **Continued**

```
        &lt;text&gt; element, so the attributes for the positioning of the text
        are already set. </p>
        @param chars The characters.
        @param length The number of characters to use from the
                      character array.
        @exception SAXException Any SAX exception, possibly
                   wrapping another exception.
        @see DocumentHandler#characters
    */
    inline void SAXGraphicsHandler::characters (
                                const          XMLCh* const    chars,
                                const  unsigned int            length)
{
    if(textX != -1)
            canvas->TextOut(textX,textY,XTOC(chars));
    textX = -1; // Note that this will work only with short strings
                // that get passed in only one call (the padding and
                // wrapping complications of doing otherwise are
                // unnecessary for our example)
}
  //@}


//--------------------------------------------------------------------------
// Constructors / Destructors
//--------------------------------------------------------------------------

  /**@name Constructors / Destructors
   */
  //@{
  /**
     Create a new SAXGraphicsHandler, to draw on the canvas provided.
     @param canvas the pointer to the CDC (windows class that
     encapsulates the printing area)
   */
SAXGraphicsHandler::SAXGraphicsHandler(CDC* newCanvas)
{
  canvas = newCanvas;
  textX = textY = -1;
}
```

## DOC++ and Other Documentation

All the examples developed for this book contain copious documentation in the form of DOC++ comments such as the ones shown in Listing 4.3. In subsequent examples, however, some of these comments are not discussed in the text for space reasons.

All the code shown in this book is completely functional and is commented on the CD. Refer to the doc directory of this and the other applications for generated DOC++ HTML pages, such as the one shown in Figure 4.1.

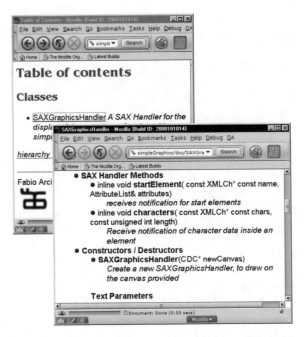

**Figure 4.1**    DOC++ documentation for `SAXGraphicsHandler`.

The preceding code shows the implementation of our graphics handler. Now let's connect this with a main Windows program in order to finally present the graphic to the user (see Listing 4.4).

To save space and keep the focus, I have abridged the code of the Windows program to only the `OnDraw` function where the SAX parser is created and tied to the handler (actually, the rest is identical to what the Application Wizard would generate for a new project). The complete code can be found on the CD.

Listing 4.4    *OnDraw* **(Member of the Windows Main Program)**

```
void CGraphView::OnDraw(CDC* pDC)
{

  SAXParser parser;
  SAXGraphicsHandler handler(pDC);
  parser.setDocumentHandler(&handler);
  parser.parse("simplegraphic.xml");


}
```

> **OnDraw**
>
> In a Windows application, OnDraw is called every time the contents of the window must be painted.

The result, given the contents of simplegraphic.xml, is the window shown in Figure 4.2.

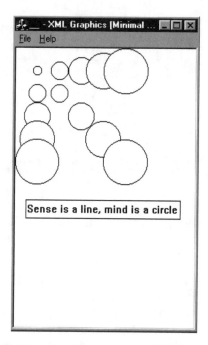

**Figure 4.2**  SAXGraphicsHandler.

# SAX C++ Structure

SAX C++ interfaces, for both versions 1.0 and 2.0, can be classified into the following groups:

- **Handlers.** These define cohesive groups of methods that can be implemented to deal with events during the parsing of an XML resource (such as ContentHandler and ErrorHandler).

- **Sources.** These define the interfaces for sources of SAX events (such as Parser). Instances of Handler classes hook up with instances of SAX sources in order to receive event notifications.

- **Helpers and exceptions.** These provide the Handler classes with the auxiliary definitions needed to complete their tasks (such as AttributeList and Locator).

In the following sections, we'll see the members exclusive to SAX 1.0. The following chapter explores the areas of overlap and advanced techniques. The reasons to spend time discussing both versions are simple and can be summarized as follows: In today's C++ world, both SAX 1.0 and SAX 2.0 are relevant tools. You need to be familiar with both if you expect to interact with other people's code (see Figure 4.3).

Let's start with the SAX 1.0 interfaces.

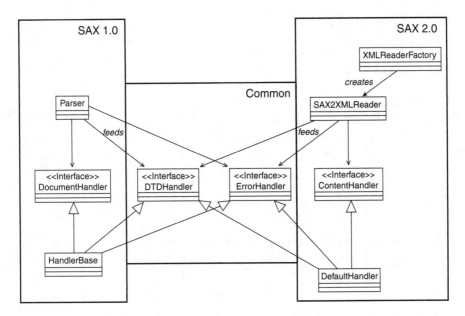

**Figure 4.3**    SAX 1.0 versus 2.0 Map

# SAX 1.0

The following sections describe the components of SAX 1.0 in its C++ incarnation.

## Handlers

SAX 1.0 offers three types of handlers:

- DocumentHandler
- ErrorHandler
- DTDHandler

Each type is an interface—a pure abstract class—that bundles a set of very cohesive (highly related) functions.

> **Abstract Classes as Ideal SAX Contracts**
>
> An *abstract class* is, as you probably know, a class with one or more pure virtual functions (such as void f() = 0;). Abstract classes exclusively made up of virtual functions are both the equivalent of Java's interfaces and the ideal mechanism for the description of a contract such as a SAX handler. In other words, if a handler claims to provide support for document content, it must implement *all* the methods of DocumentHandler.

The process of becoming proficient with SAX starts with a good understanding of the methods of each handler. The following sections explain the most important of them: DocumentHandler. The other two will be left for the next chapter, because they are shared with SAX version 2.0.

## *DocumentHandler*

DocumentHandler is by far the most important and commonly used handler in SAX 1.0. It is designed to receive notification of all general document events, such as the start and end of elements and the appearance of character data. It is composed by the following methods.

### *void startDocument()*

Called only once per document, before any other notification methods in this interface.

### *void startElement(XMLCh* const name, AttributeList& atts)*

Called every time a start element tag or an empty element tag is found. For each call to startElement, there is a corresponding call to endElement.

Note that unlike in other APIs (such as expat), the attribute list is passed as an object of a specific class created for this particular purpose. Details about AttributeList and its version 2.0 successor are given in the "Helpers and Exceptions" section of Chapter 5.

> **XMLCh**
>
> As mentioned in Chapters 1 and 2, all XML parsers must understand documents in at least two encodings (UTF-8 and UTF-16), but this doesn't mean they have to present the data to the application in so many different ways. The parser may choose to present all the applications with only one type of character, even if it understands multiple encodings (more than 150 in the case of IBM's toolkit).
>
> XMLCh is the name given in the Xerces, IBM, and other SAX implementations to a character type used to represent all the characters after they are read inside the program. As you saw in the first example, this is the type used in all the SAX handlers and helpers.
>
> The definition of XMLCh (in Apache's Xerces, IBM's xml4c, and other key implementations) is simple: An XMLCh is a **wide character**: wchar_t (whatever that is on each particular platform).
>
> Even though you can safely implement your programs accepting XMLCh as a fact of life (that is, without knowing these details), if this explanation is not totally clear to you, and you want to know all about characters in C++, please refer to Appendix A.
>
> As a last note for the low-level curious, it must be mentioned that in Win32, the actual definition of XMLCh is unsigned short (2 bytes).

### void endElement(XMLCh* const name)

Called every time an element ends (when an element tag is found or the end of an empty element tag is reached). Note that the name of the element is somewhat redundant here. If the document is well-formed XML, the name of the ending element will always match that of the last invocation to startElement.

### void endDocument( )

Simply receives the notification of the end of the document.

### void characters(const XMLCh* const chars, const unsigned int length)

This handler receives notifications of character data (such as the string "Untouchables" in the element

```
<movie studio="paramount">Untouchables</Movie>)
```

The characters method receives two parameters: a constant array of XMLCh, filled with the character data, and an integer, indicating the length of the valid data in the characters array. When receiving a characters notification, it is very important to read only the first length elements of the array (chars is not zero-terminated).

Admittedly, it would be easier for the beginner if characters would only receive a zero-terminated string, but that would imply costs on the efficiency of the API and its congruency with its Java counterpart.

It is very important to note that the parser is *not* required to return all the character data of an element in only one call to this method (not even if the only content of the element is character data). The parser may return one string in several pieces, each one in a different call to this method.

### void ignorableWhitespace(const XMLCh* const chars, const unsigned int length)

This method is analogous to the previous characters method. Its function is to return all the nonrepresentative white space used in the document (such as tabs and carriage returns between attributes, or tabs used only for indentation of elements).

It is important to note that not all the white space might be returned in a single piece (just as all the character data is not required to be returned in one call to the characters method).

### void processingInstruction(const XMLCh* const target, const XMLCh* const data)

This interface gets notified of the processing instructions (PIs) as they appear on the document. Simple enough. This method responds to declarations such as

```
<? target "data" ?>
```

Note, however, that the XML and text declaration (<? xml version="1.0" ?>) are not considered PIs. Therefore, they are not reported through this method.

*void SetDocumentLocator(const Locator\* const locator)*

A locator is an object that can return the position information of a SAX event (such as "The `startElement` tag occurred on line 3, character 66"). Parsers use this method to pass their locators (note that a pointer to the object is passed), thus ensuring that they'll have position information for the client if it is requested.

   This is not a client-oriented method (so you don't need it to construct your programs), but it must be mentioned for the sake of completion.

*void resetDocument( )*

This final member of the `DocumentHandler` interface is especially simple and somewhat low-level. It takes care of resetting all the document implementation defaults associated with the document. Its usage is far less frequent than any other method in this interface (such as `startElement`).

### Using DocumentHandler: The Trimmer Application

Listing 4.5 shows how to use a subclass of `DocumentHandler` to produce a "trimmer" that can erase elements, or attributes, according to user criteria. Such a program could be used to delete content that a censor might consider inappropriate, because it is shown after the code.

   The first part of the code is, naturally, the `TrimmerSAXHandler` itself. Besides the methods for `DocumentHandler`, it has three arrays of strings to hold the candidates for deletion. (I recommend that you see the program running first and then come back to this listing.)

Listing 4.5   *SAXTrimmerHandler.h*

```
#include    <sax/DocumentHandler.hpp>
#include    <sax/AttributeList.hpp>
#include    <iostream.h>
#include    <util/XMLString.hpp>
#include    "StrX.h"

#ifndef XTOC
#define XTOC(x) XMLString::transcode(x) // Use iff x is a char *
#define CTOX(x) XMLString::transcode(x) // Use iff x is an XMLCh *
#endif


class SAXTrimmerHandler : public DocumentHandler
{
public:

    SAXTrimmerHandler ();
    ~SAXTrimmerHandler();
```

```
    void endDocument();

    void endElement(const XMLCh* const name);

    void characters(const XMLCh* const chars, const unsigned int length);

    void ignorableWhitespace
    (
        const    XMLCh* const    chars
        , const unsigned int     length
    );

    void processingInstruction
    (
        const    XMLCh* const    target
        , const XMLCh* const     data
    );

    void startDocument();

    void startElement(const XMLCh* const name, AttributeList& attributes);

    void resetDocument();
    void setDocumentLocator(const Locator* const a);

  // Handler-specific declarations
  void addTrimmableElement(const char*name);
  void addTrimmableElementByAttribute(const char*name);
  void addTrimmableAttribute(const char*name);

private :
  // In this first, simple implementation we use vectors of char*.
  // In more advanced versions we will use STL containers
  char *elements[50];
  int te;
  char *attributes[50];
  int ta;
  char *elementsByAttribute[50];
  int tea;
  int ignoreData;
};
#endif SAXTrimmerHandler_H
```

The implementation of this interface is very simple. For each presentable element, simply print its contents to standard output. If the element is not presentable, simply ignore the data. This is illustrated in Listing 4.6.

Listing 4.6 *SAXTrimmerHandler.cpp*

```cpp
#include "SAXTrimmerHandler.h"



// ---------------------------------------------------------------------
//   SAXTrimmerHandler: Constructors and Destructor
// ---------------------------------------------------------------------
 SAXTrimmerHandler::SAXTrimmerHandler( )
{
  ignoreData = 0;
  te = 0;
  ta = 0;
  tea = 0;
  for(unsigned int i = 0;i < 50; i++)
  {
    elements[i] = NULL;
    attributes[i] = NULL;
    elementsByAttribute[i] = NULL;
  }

}

SAXTrimmerHandler::~SAXTrimmerHandler()
{
  for(unsigned int i = 0;i < 50; i++)
  {
    if(elements[i] != NULL)
      delete[] elements[i];
    if(attributes[i] != NULL)
      delete[] attributes[i];
    if(elementsByAttribute[i] != NULL)
      delete[] elementsByAttribute[i];
  }
}



// ---------------------------------------------------------------------
//   SAXTrimmerHandler: Overrides of the SAX DocumentHandler interface
// ---------------------------------------------------------------------
void SAXTrimmerHandler::characters(const     XMLCh* const    chars
                             , const   unsigned int    length)
{
  XMLCh *realChars = new XMLCh[length+1];
  XMLString::copyNString(realChars,chars,length);
  realChars[length] = '\0';
  if(!ignoreData)
      cout << XTOC(realChars);
```

```
    delete(realChars);
}


void SAXTrimmerHandler::endDocument()
{
  // In this case, there is no need to do anything here.
}


void SAXTrimmerHandler::endElement(const XMLCh* const name)
{
  if(ignoreData)
  {
    ignoreData--;
    return;
  }
  cout << "<" << "/" << XTOC(name) << ">";
}


void SAXTrimmerHandler::ignorableWhitespace( const    XMLCh* const chars
                                            ,const   unsigned int length)
{
  // In this case, there is nothing to do.
}


void SAXTrimmerHandler::processingInstruction(const   XMLCh* const target
                                            , const XMLCh* const data)
{
  // In this case, there is nothing to do about this. If you want to preserve
  // the processing instructions, mimic the characters method here.
}


void SAXTrimmerHandler::startDocument()
{
  cout << "<?xml version=\"1.0\"?>\n";
}

void SAXTrimmerHandler::resetDocument()
{ // do nothing
}
void SAXTrimmerHandler::setDocumentLocator(const Locator* const a){
      // do nothing
}

void SAXTrimmerHandler::startElement(const    XMLCh* const    name,
                                              AttributeList&  attributes)
{
```

*continues*

Listing 4.6 **Continued**

```cpp
bool marked = false;
unsigned int len = attributes.getLength();


for(unsigned int i = 0; i < 50 && elementsByAttribute[i] != NULL; i++)
{
  for (unsigned int index = 0; index < len; index++)
  {
    if(strcmp(XTOC(attributes.getName(index)),elementsByAttribute[i])==0)
          marked = true;
  }
}

for(i = 0; i < 50 && elements[i] != NULL; i++)
{
    if(strcmp(XTOC(name),elements[i])==0)
          marked = true;
}

if(ignoreData ||
   marked)
{
  ignoreData++; // Keep track of how many open tags are being ignored.
                // When the end-element for the ignored element comes,
                // ignoreData will go back to zero.
  return;
}

// It is ok, we must output this element.
cout << "<" << XTOC(name);


  for (unsigned int index = 0; index < len; index++)
  {
    bool ignore = false;

    // Check the attributes.
    for(i = 0; i < 50 && this->attributes[i] != NULL; i++)
          if(strcmp(XTOC(attributes.getName(index)),this->attributes[i])==0)
                ignore = true;
    if(!ignore)
       { // if it wasn't marked, just output it
       cout        << " " <<XTOC(attributes.getName(index))
                << "=\""
                << XTOC(attributes.getValue(index))
                << "\" ";
       }
  }
  cout << ">\n";
```

```
}

void SAXTrimmerHandler::addTrimmableElement(const char*name)
{
  elements[te] = new char[strlen(name)+1];
  strcpy(elements[te++],name);
}
void SAXTrimmerHandler::addTrimmableElementByAttribute(const char*name)
{
  elementsByAttribute[tea] = new char[strlen(name)+1];
  strcpy(elementsByAttribute[tea++],name);
}

void SAXTrimmerHandler::addTrimmableAttribute(const char*name)
{
  attributes[ta] = new char[strlen(name)+1];
  strcpy(attributes[ta++],name);
```

The preceding code is the bulk of the program. However, it is important to see how an instance of this class is tied to a particular parser. This is the job of the `main` procedure, shown in Listing 4.7.

Listing 4.7  **SAXTrimmer.cpp (Main File)**

```
#include <util/PlatformUtils.hpp>
#include <util/TransService.hpp>
#include <parsers/SAXParser.hpp>
#include "StrX.h"
#include "SAXTrimmerHandler.h"



  /**@name Helpers
     Helper Methods for the main application
   */
  //@{
  //@}
  /**
     Show the program usage
   */
static void usage()
{
    cout <<  "\nUsage: SAXTrimmer [trims] file\n"
             "This program trims the data of the provided xml file, according"
             "with the trim options ([trims]) specified.\n"
             "The format for the trim options is:\n"
             "-e=name erases the elements with the specified name\n"
             "-a=name erases the attributes with the specified name\n"
```

*continues*

Listing 4.7 **Continued**

```
                    "-ea=name erases the elements with the specified attribute\n"
                    " of the element)\n"
        << endl;
}



  /**
     main program
     Instantiates the parser and the SAXTrimHandler, putting them together to
     produce the result.
   */
class SAXTrimHAndler;

int main(int argC, char* argV[])
{
    // Initialize the XML4C2 system
    try
    {
        XMLPlatformUtils::Initialize();
    }

    catch (const XMLException& toCatch)
    {
        cerr << "Error during initialization! :\n"
             << StrX(toCatch.getMessage()) << endl;
        return 1;
    }

    // Check command line and extract arguments.
    if (argC < 2)
    {
        usage();
        XMLPlatformUtils::Terminate();
        return 1;
    }

    // Watch for special case help request
    if ((argC == 2) && !strcmp(argV[1], "-?"))
    {
        usage();
        XMLPlatformUtils::Terminate();
        return 2;
    }

    SAXTrimmerHandler *trimmer = new SAXTrimmerHandler();

    int parmInd;
    for (parmInd = 1; parmInd < argC; parmInd++)
    {
        // Break out on first parm not starting with a dash
        if (argV[parmInd][0] != '-')
```

```
        break;

    if (!strncmp(argV[parmInd], "-e=", 3)
    ¦¦  !strncmp(argV[parmInd], "-E=", 3))
    {
        const char* const element = &argV[parmInd][3];
          trimmer->addTrimmableElement(element);
    }
    else if (!strncmp(argV[parmInd], "-ea=",4)
          ¦¦  !strncmp(argV[parmInd], "-EA=",4))
    {
        const char* const attribute = &argV[parmInd][4];
          trimmer->addTrimmableElementByAttribute(attribute);
    }
     else if (!strncmp(argV[parmInd], "-a=", 3)
          ¦¦  !strncmp(argV[parmInd], "-A=", 3))
    {
        const char* const attribute = &argV[parmInd][3];
          trimmer->addTrimmableAttribute(attribute);
    }
     else
    {
        cerr << "Unknown option '" << argV[parmInd]
             << "', ignoring it\n" << endl;
    }
}

//
//  And now we have to have only one parameter left and it must be
//  the file name.
//
if (parmInd + 1 != argC)
{
    usage();
    return 1;
}
char *xmlFile = argV[parmInd];

//
//  Create a SAX parser object. Then, according to what we were told on
//  the command line, set it to validate or not.
//
SAXParser parser;

//
//  Create the handler object and install it as the document and error
//  handler for the parser. Then parse the file and catch any exceptions
//  that propogate out
//
try
{
```

*continues*

Listing 4.7 **Continued**

```
        parser.setDocumentHandler(trimmer);
        parser.parse(xmlFile);
        delete trimmer;
    }

    catch (const XMLException& toCatch)
    {
        cerr << "\nAn error occured\n  Error: "
             << StrX(toCatch.getMessage())
             << "\n" << endl;
        return -1;
    }

    // And call the termination method
    XMLPlatformUtils::Terminate();

    return 0;
```

The usage of this program is straightforward. Suppose you are (extremely) concerned about the presentation of potentially offensive material on your XML. The preceding program could be used to filter the hazards.

For example, suppose the file sample.xhtml has the following XML document:

```
<?xml version="1.0"?>
<html>
<head>
<title>Betty Boop</title>
</head>
<body>
<h1>Betty Boop</h1>
<p>Betty Boop has been around since the early 1930's. She was designed by
Fleischer studio and animator Grim Natwick. She began her life without much
bright, and ended up a character with timeless appeal. Her first appearance
was as a singer, August 8, 1930, in "Dizzy Dishes ...</p>
<img src="boop.gif" explicit="yes"/>
<description>
   Here betty is seen dancing in the 1932's classic ...
   <!-- etc. -->
</description>
</body>
</html>
```

The description and explicit images can be trimmed by using an invocation such as the following:

```
SAXTrimmer -e=description -ea=explicit sample.xhtml > afterCensorship.xhtml
```

The two files in this invocation, sample.xhtml and afterCensorship.xhtml, are shown in Figures 4.4 and 4.5, respectively. They are also available on the CD.

Figure 4.4    The XHTML file before censorship.

Figure 4.5    The XHTML file after censorship.

# Summary

This chapter explored the fundamentals of SAX and presented the interfaces exclusive to SAX version 1.0. All the basic techniques were introduced, along with detailed explanations of each major interface. Two nontrivial examples of visual and command-line applications with SAX were introduced. The next chapter presents SAX 2.0, the common interfaces between versions 1.0 and 2.0, and advanced examples of their use.

# SAX C++ 2.0 and Advanced Techniques

**5**

CHAPTER 4 DISCUSSED THE FUNDAMENTALS OF SAX and the interfaces exclusive to its first version: SAX 1.0. This chapter complements that with two discussions:

- Common interfaces between SAX and SAX2 (SAX C++ 2.0)
- Interfaces exclusive to SAX2

In Chapter 8, after seeing the advanced uses of both SAX and DOM, we will analyze quality measures and discuss C++ tips for the design and implementation of both SAX and DOM.

Let's begin by exploring the first item: interfaces that appear in both SAX and SAX2.

## Common Interfaces

There are two common handler interfaces (pure abstract classes) between SAX and SAX2: DTDHandler and ErrorHandler. The first one takes care of basic DTD-related events (read on, because there are some surprises along the way), and the second one takes care of receiving parser reports on malformed or invalid data in the document.

## *DTDHandler*

Despite its name, `DTDHandler` does not receive events for all the declarations present in a document type definition. Instead, it reports only two types of events: notation declarations and unparsed entity declarations.

`DTDHandler` is composed of the following two methods.

### *void notationDecl (const XMLCh const name, const XMLCh const publicId, const XMLCh const systemId)*

This method receives notifications for notation declarations. For a declaration such as the following:

```
<!NOTATION ISO3166 PUBLIC
"ISO/IEC 3166:1993//NOTATION Codes for the Representation of
Languages//EN" "ie3166">
```

the parser must make a call to `notationDecl` using the following values:

- name:`"ISO3166"`
- publicId: `"ISO/IEC 3166:1993//NOTATION Codes for the Representation of Languages//EN"`
- systemId: `"ie3166"`

One important aspect to highlight is that there is no assurance about the order in which the calls to `notationDecl` are made. (In other words, just because a notation declaration is physically first in the DTD doesn't mean it will be reported first.) The only guaranteed thing is that all notations will be reported before calling `startElement` for the first time.

### *void unparsedEntityDecl(const XMLCh const name, const XMLCh const publicId, const XMLCh const systemId, const XMLCh const notationName)*

This method receives notification of unparsed entity declarations such as the following:

```
<!ENTITY myVRMLmap
         PUBLIC "-//Iceland/VRML Map"  "vrml/Iceland.vrml"
         NDATA vrml >
```

It receives the content of the declaration in the form of four strings—one for each component. For example, given the following definitions:

```
<!NOTATION gif PUBLIC
    "-//Compuserve Information Services//NOTATION Graphics Interchange
        Format//EN">
<!ENTITY marylin
        SYSTEM "fabio/marylin.gif"
        NDATA gif >
```

the parser calls `unparsedEntityDecl` with the following parameters:

- name. `"marylin"`
- publicId. `null`
- systemId. `"fabio/marylin.gif"`
- notationName. `"gif"`

### An Important Absentee

In Java implementations of SAX2, it is very common to find an extension interface called `DeclHandler` that listens to notifications about other DTD components such as `Element` and `Attribute` and lists declarations. This interface is missing from most C++ SAX2 implementations (which is OK in theory, because it is not a mandatory part of SAX2), so alternative methods to access the DTD must be implemented.

In IBM's xml4c, you can find a non-SAX way of accessing the DTD data in the example `enumVal`.

## ErrorHandler

The second common handler interface is `ErrorHandler`. Predictably enough, this interface provides methods for the report of both fatal and nonfatal errors that might occur during the parsing of the document.

The `ErrorHandler` interface provides three methods—one for each kind of problem that might arise from XML parsing: nonfatal errors, fatal errors, and warnings.

### void warning(const SAXParseException& exception)

This method must be called by the parser every time it finds a potential problem that cannot be classified as an error in XML 1.0. The parser must continue to provide normal events after it issues the call to this interface, and it is quite likely that it can finish parsing the document despite the problem.

The one parameter to `warning` is `SAXParseException`, a simple type of exception that groups together (in the form of a base class) the different parsing and reading exceptions that may occur during the SAX parsing process.

### virtual void error(const SAXParseException& exception)

This method is called by the parser every time a nonfatal error occurs. After calling this method, the parser must be able to continue providing normal events.

One common call to this method is the encounter of validity errors. They might not prevent the parser from continuing its reading, but they are serious problems that must be reported.

**XML 1.0 Error Definitions**

error—A violation of the rules of the specification; results are undefined. Conforming software may detect and report an error and may recover from it.

fatal error—An error in which a conforming XML processor must detect and report to the application. After encountering a fatal error, the processor may continue processing the data to search for further errors and may report such errors to the application. In order to support correction of errors, the processor may make unprocessed data from the document (with intermingled character data and markup) available to the application. As soon as a fatal error is detected, however, the processor must not continue normal processing (it must not continue to pass character data and information about the document's logical structure to the application in the normal way).

### *void fatalError(const SAXParseException& exception)*

The `fatalError` method receives the same parameter as its counterparts but has a much more serious consequence. After a call to this method, the application must assume that the document is unusable; the only reason to allow the parser to continue is to try to detect further errors.

A call to this interface occurs in cases such as wrong nesting of elements or any other violation of well-formedness constraints.

### Using *ErrorHandler*

Listing 5.1 presents an implementation of the `ErrorHandler` interface. It can be reused in a number of projects that replicate the basic need of an `ErrorHandler`: simple logging.

Listing 5.1   *ErrorHandlerImpl.cpp*

```
void ErrorHandlerImpl::error(const SAXParseException& e)
{
    cerr << "\nError at file " << XToC(e.getSystemId())
        << ", line " << e.getLineNumber()
        << ", char " << e.getColumnNumber()
        << "\n  Message: " << XToC(e.getMessage()) << "\n";
}

void ErrorHandlerImpl::fatalError(const SAXParseException& e)
{
    cerr << "\nFatal Error at file " << XToC(e.getSystemId())
        << ", line " << e.getLineNumber()
        << ", char " << e.getColumnNumber()
        << "\n  Message: " << XToC(e.getMessage()) << "\n";
}

void ErrorHandlerImpl::warning(const SAXParseException& e)
{
```

```
    cerr << "\nWarning at file " << XToC(e.getSystemId())
         << ", line " << e.getLineNumber()
         << ", char " << e.getColumnNumber()
         << "\n  Message: " << XToC(e.getMessage()) << "\n";
}
```

When used with a faulty .xml file, this handler prints something like the following:

```
Error at file C:\temp\sax2\sample.xml, line 8, char 28
  Message: No character data is allowed by content model
```

# The Base Handlers

As you may recall from Figure 4.3, both SAX 1.0 and 2.0 provide a default implementation of all the handler interfaces. These classes (`HandlerBase` in the case of 1.0, and `DefaultHandler` in 2.0) provide empty implementations for all the methods in all the interfaces. Thus, they are a great starting point for simple programs that need only a few SAX methods.

Using `DefaultHandler` as a base class is a significant time-saver, especially if you are using very few methods on one interface.

# Interfaces and Classes Exclusive to SAX 2.0

This section discusses the interfaces and helper classes exclusive to SAX2. It follows the typology suggested in Chapter 4 for SAX in general (handlers, sources, and helpers/exceptions).

## Main Differences from SAX 1.0

SAX 1.0 is a powerful and simple interface that seems to correctly address the needs of event-driven processing. Having experienced this, the immediate questions are why is there a version 2.0 of SAX, and what does it add to the original?

The answer is straightforward: SAX 2.0 was born from the need to add namespace support to the API. In the process of creating such support, the mechanisms for features and properties were introduced as a standard way of extending and empowering SAX drivers.

These two aspects (namespace support and features/properties) are the two main differences from SAX 1.0. They will be introduced as we study the component interfaces.

**Deprecated from SAX 1.0 (from the Original SAX Documentation)**

The following interfaces and classes have been deprecated and will be removed from a future version of SAX. They should be used only for interaction with SAX1 drivers or applications:

```
Parser
DocumentHandler
AttributeList
HandlerBase
ParserFactory
AttributeListImpl
```

## A Map of SAX2

Figure 5.1 shows the UML class diagram for the main classes and interfaces in SAX2. The remainder of this section presents each of the new ones, as well as some examples of their use.

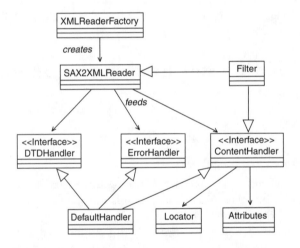

**Figure 5.1**  SAX2 class diagram.

### *ContentHandler*

The equivalent of `DocumentHandler` in SAX2 is `ContentHandler`. `ContentHandler` provides all the old methods for document events, plus some new versions of functions that can help you deal better with namespaces. The following sections summarize the interface.

*void startDocument( )*

This remains unchanged from version 1.0.

*void startElement(const XMLCh const uri, const XMLCh const localname, const XMLCh const qname, const Attributes& attrs)*

The changes in `startElement` tackle the first difference mentioned in the previous section: namespaces. Namespaces in SAX can be easily manipulated thanks to the four parameters that get passed:

- `uri`. Contains a string identifying the namespace URI.
- `localname`. Contains the element name without the namespace prefix.
- `qname`. Contains the qualified version of the element name (with a prefix).
- `atts`. Contains the collection of attributes encapsulated in an instance of the SAX-defined class Attributes.

For example, given the following document,

```
<movies xmlns:kubrick="http://www.kubrick_movies.com">
  <kubrick:movie>Eyes Wide Shut</kubrick:movie>
</movies>
```

when the parser gets to the start element `movie`, it must issue a call to `startElement` with the following parameters:

- `uri`. `"http://www.kubrick.movies.com"`
- `localname`. `"movie"`
- `qname`. `"kubrick:movie"`
- `atts`. Empty attributes

*void endDocument()*

This remains unchanged from version 1.0.

*void endElement (const XMLCh const uri, const XMLCh const localname, const XMLCh const qname)*

The changes in `endElement` (and the semantics of those changes) are analogous to those of `startElement`.

*void ignorableWhitespace(const XMLCh const chars, const unsigned int length)*

Remains unchanged from version 1.0.

*void characters(const XMLCh const chars, const unsigned int length)*

Remains unchanged from version 1.0.

*virtual void startPrefixMapping(const XMLCh const prefix, const XMLCh const uri)*

This method is called whenever a new prefix mapping is encountered. A prefix mapping always takes the form of the special attribute xmlns:[optional name] (as mentioned in Chapter 2).

For example, given the following element:

```
<artist xmlns:mondigliani="http://www.mondigliani.org"> ... </artist>
```

a call to this method is issued, using mondigliani as the value of the first argument and "http://www.mondigliani.org" as the value of the second.

*void setDocumentLocator(const Locator const locator)*

Remains unchanged from version 1.0.

*void processingInstruction(const XMLCh const target, const XMLCh const data)*

Remains unchanged from version 1.0.

*void endPrefixMapping(const XMLCh const prefix)*

Notifies you about the end of the scope of a particular namespace prefix mapping.

### Using ContentHandler

The following code was extracted from the classical application SAXPrint (Xerces version). I include it here because it uses the vast majority of the methods in the interfaces. Other less didactical but much more challenging applications of ContentHandler are included on the CD and in Chapter 8.

The code simply throws to standard output a character representation of the events it receives. (In other words, it simply prints the document.)

```
void SAX2PrintHandlers::characters(const      XMLCh const      chars
                                   , const    unsigned int     length)
{
   //The application uses fFormatter to pre-format the output of XMLChs.
   // fFormatter is a simple class that makes sure the output characters are
   // well suited for each particular platform.
   //If you are curious about the implementation of this object, please refer
   // to the documentation on the CD for a complete explanation
   fFormatter.formatBuf(chars, length, XMLFormatter::CharEscapes);
}
void SAX2PrintHandlers::endDocument()
{
}
void SAX2PrintHandlers::endElement(const XMLCh const uri,
                                   const XMLCh const localname,
                                   const XMLCh const qname)
{
   fFormatter << XMLFormatter::NoEscapes << gEndElement ;
      if ( fExpandNS )
         {
```

```
                  if (XMLString::compareIString(uri,XMLUni::fgEmptyString) != 0)
                          fFormatter  << uri << chColon;
                  fFormatter << localname << chCloseAngle;
          }
          else
                  fFormatter << qname << chCloseAngle;
}
void SAX2PrintHandlers::ignorableWhitespace( const   XMLCh const chars,
                                                const  unsigned int length)
{
    fFormatter.formatBuf(chars, length, XMLFormatter::NoEscapes);
}


void SAX2PrintHandlers::processingInstruction(const  XMLCh const target,
                                                const XMLCh const data)
{
    fFormatter << XMLFormatter::NoEscapes << gStartPI  << target;
    if (data)
        fFormatter << chSpace << data;
    fFormatter << XMLFormatter::NoEscapes << gEndPI;
}



void SAX2PrintHandlers::startDocument()
{
}

void SAX2PrintHandlers::startElement(const XMLCh const uri,
                                     const XMLCh const localname,
                                     const XMLCh const qname,
                                     const Attributes& attributes)
{
    fFormatter  << XMLFormatter::NoEscapes << chOpenAngle ;
      if ( fExpandNS )
      {
            if (XMLString::compareIString(uri,XMLUni::fgEmptyString) != 0)
                      fFormatter  << uri << chColon;
            fFormatter << localname ;
      }
      else
            fFormatter << qname ;

    unsigned int len = attributes.getLength();
    for (unsigned int index = 0; index < len; index++)
    {
        fFormatter   << XMLFormatter::NoEscapes << chSpace ;
            if ( fExpandNS )
            {
                  if (XMLString::compareIString(
                      attributes.getURI(index),XMLUni::fgEmptyString) != 0)
                        fFormatter  << attributes.getURI(index) << chColon;
```

*continues*

```
                        fFormatter  << attributes.getLocalName(index) ;
            }
            else
                    fFormatter  << attributes.getQName(index) ;

            fFormatter  << chEqual << chDoubleQuote
                << XMLFormatter::AttrEscapes
                << attributes.getValue(index)
                << XMLFormatter::NoEscapes
                << chDoubleQuote;
        }
        fFormatter << chCloseAngle;
    }
```

## Sources: *SAX2XMLReader*

It is now time to analyze the other key component of the SAX2 API, the source of
parsing events: SAX2XMLReader.

SAX2XMLReader is the C++ counterpart of XMLReader in the Java distribution
(the somewhat bloated name is subject to change after standardization). It provides
the interface that a SAX2 parser must implement in order to allow a client to order
the following:

- Register handlers
- Get and set features and properties such as namespace support
- Parse a document

SAX2XMLReader replaces the old parser interface and implements the second key
improvement of SAX2: features and properties. Before we get into the details of the
interface, let's see what those are so that you can appreciate the improvement from
SAX 1.0.

### Features and Properties

A SAX2 parser (that is, a SAX2XMLReader) may expose certain capabilities such as validation and namespace support. Those capabilities are called features and are identified
by fully qualified URIs (in practice, they usually refer to well-known URLs).

A SAX2 parser may be queried about its compliance to a feature using the
particular URI:

```
IsValidating = myParser.getFeature("http://xml.org/sax/features/validation")
```

Because of its Boolean nature, features can only be turned on or off. For example, the
following code disables validation on the parser:

```
try {
  r.setFeature("http://xml.org/sax/features/validation", false);
}
```

Different `XMLReaders` might recognize different features, but two features are always required to be recognized by SAX2-compliant parsers:

- `http://xml.org/sax/features/namespaces`
- `http://xml.org/sax/features/namespace-prefixes`

Unlike features, properties are not Boolean. They are arbitrary objects used to extend a SAX2 parser in an organized and standard way. The most useful example of properties is the registration of extended handlers. For example, the following code registers a `DeclHandler` with the parser g. (Unfortunately, as mentioned earlier, the Xerces SAX implementation currently does not provide a `DeclHandler` extension.)

```
DeclHandler  myDH = new DeclHandlerImpl();
g.setProperty("http://xml.org/sax/handlers/DeclHandler",myDH);
```

Properties prevent multiple and incompatible vendor-specific versions of SAX, even if their implementations vary significantly.

## *SAX2XMLReader* Methods

Now that you know what features and properties are, you are ready to see the contents of the `SAX2XMLReader` interface.

### Handler Registration Methods

The `SAX2XMLReader` provides, naturally, methods to get and set the different types of handlers. These methods are self-explanatory and are listed here only for the sake of completion:

- `ContentHandler getContentHandler()`
- `DTDHandler getDTDHandler()`
- `ErrorHandler getErrorHandler()`

Analogous methods are included for setting handlers.

### *bool getFeature(const XMLCh const name)*

This method is used to query the status (true or false) of a feature. Each feature is identified by a fully-qualified URI (the only parameter of this method).

If a parser does not recognize a particular URI, theoretically it will throw a `SAXNotRecognizedException`. Because it is possible for a reader to recognize a feature name but be unable to determine its value, this method can also throw a `SAXNotSupportedException`.

Some toolkits currently do not support these mandatory exceptions.

### *void setFeature(const XMLCh const name, const bool value)*

This method is used to request a feature's change of status. The same rules for recognition and support of exceptions that were described for `getFeature` apply here, but they are complemented by three facts that are not commonly included in API documentation:

- All XMLReaders are required to support setting http://xml.org/sax/features/namespaces to true.

- All XMLReaders are required to support setting http://xml.org/sax/features/namespace-prefixes to false.

- There is no guarantee that a supported feature can change its value at a given point (some features are immutable, some can be changed only before parsing begins, and so on). Therefore, depending on when it is invoked, this method might throw an exception even if the feature is indeed supported.

### *void setProperty(const XMLCh const name, void value)*

This method sets the value of the property identified with the URI name. Naturally, the same rules for exception throwing used for setFeature apply to this method.

### *void parse(const XMLCh const systemId)*

This method starts parsing the document identified by the only parameter. There are other versions of parse, including other types of parameters, such as InputSource, but this is the most commonly used.

### Using *SAX2XMLReader*

The next program, a new version of our trimmer, provides the user with a -v switch that can be used to set which type of validation the parser performs. See how the feature methods are used in this example to get a fine degree of control over the parser behavior. (It is important to note that the snippets of code shown here and in other parts of this book are not full programs. They need the definitions of several other files. The complete, unabridged code for every program is on the CD.)

```
static void usage()
{
    cout <<  "\nUsage: SAXTrimmer [-v=scheme] [trims] file\n"
             "This program trims the data of the provided xml file, according"
             "with the trim options ([trims]) specified.\n"
             "The format for the trim options is:\n"
             "-e=name erases the elements with the specified name\n"
             "-a=name erases the attributes with the specified name\n"
             "-ea=name erases the elements with the specified attribute\n"
             "-v=scheme  Validation scheme [always ¦ never ¦ auto]\n"
             " of the element)\n"
        <<  endl;
}
```

```
    /*
        main program
        Instantiates the parser and the SAXTrimHandler, putting them together to
        produce the result.
    /
class SAXTrimHAndler;

int main(int argC, char argV[])
{
    // Initialize the XML4C2 system
    try
    {
        XMLPlatformUtils::Initialize();
    }

    catch (const XMLException& toCatch)
    {
        cerr << "Error during initialization! :\n"
            << StrX(toCatch.getMessage()) << endl;
        return 1;
    }

    // Check command line and extract arguments.
    if (argC < 2)
    {
        usage();
        XMLPlatformUtils::Terminate();
        return 1;
    }

    // Watch for special case help request
    if ((argC == 2) && !strcmp(argV[1], "-?"))
    {
        usage();
        XMLPlatformUtils::Terminate();
        return 2;
    }

    SAXTrimmerHandler trimmer;
    SAX2XMLReader::ValSchemes valScheme     = SAX2XMLReader::Val_Auto;

    int parmInd;
    for (parmInd = 1; parmInd < argC; parmInd++)
    {
        // Break out on first parm not starting with a dash
        if (argV[parmInd][0] != '-')
            break;

        if (!strncmp(argV[parmInd], "-e=", 3)
        || !strncmp(argV[parmInd], "-E=", 3))
        {
            const char * const element = &argV[parmInd][3];
```

```
            trimmer.addTrimmableElement(element);
        }
        else if (!strcmp(argV[parmInd], "-ea")
                || !strcmp(argV[parmInd], "-EA"))
        {
            const char * const attribute = &argV[parmInd][3];

            trimmer.addTrimmableElementByAttribute(attribute);
        }
        if (!strncmp(argV[parmInd], "-v=", 3)
        || !strncmp(argV[parmInd], "-V=", 3))
        {
            const char * const parm = &argV[parmInd][3];

            if (!strcmp(parm, "never"))
                valScheme = SAX2XMLReader::Val_Never;
            else if (!strcmp(parm, "auto"))
                valScheme = SAX2XMLReader::Val_Auto;
            else if (!strcmp(parm, "always"))
                valScheme = SAX2XMLReader::Val_Always;
            else
            {
                cerr << "Unknown -v= value: " << parm << endl;
                return 2;
            }
        }
        else if (!strncmp(argV[parmInd], "-a=", 3)
                || !strncmp(argV[parmInd], "-A=", 3))
        {
            const char * const attribute = &argV[parmInd][3];
            trimmer.addTrimmableAttribute(attribute);
        }
        else
        {
            cerr << "Unknown option '" << argV[parmInd]
                << "', ignoring it\n" << endl;
        }
    }

    //
    // And now we have to have only one parameter left and it must be
    // the file name.
    //
    if (parmInd + 1 != argC)
    {
        usage();
        return 1;
    }
    char * xmlFile = argV[parmInd];
```

```
//
//  Create a SAX parser object. Then, according to what we were told on
//  the command line, set it to validate or not.
//
SAX2XMLReader * parser = XMLReaderFactory::createXMLReader();
if (valScheme == SAX2XMLReader::Val_Auto)
{
    parser->setFeature(CTOX("http://xml.org/sax/features/validation"), true);
    parser->setFeature(CTOX("http://apache.org/xml/features/
              validation/dynamic"),
                        true);
  }
if (valScheme == SAX2XMLReader::Val_Never)
  {
    parser->setFeature(CTOX("http://xml.org/sax/features/validation"),
                        false);
  }
  if (valScheme == SAX2XMLReader::Val_Always)
  {
    parser->setFeature(CTOX("http://xml.org/sax/features/validation"),
                        true);
    parser->setFeature(CTOX("http://apache.org/xml/features/
              validation/dynamic"),
                        false);
  }


//
//  Create the handler object and install it as the document and error
//  handler for the parser. Then parse the file and catch any exceptions
//  that propogate out
//
try
{
    parser->setDocumentHandler(&trimmer);       parser->parse(xmlFile);
}

catch (const XMLException& toCatch)
{
    cerr << "\nAn error occurred\n  Error: "
         << StrX(toCatch.getMessage())
         << "\n" << endl;
    return -1;
}

// And call the termination method
XMLPlatformUtils::Terminate();

return 0;
}
```

### Reader Factories

The creation of SAX2XMLReaders rarely takes place as an invocation to a constructor. Instead, a mechanism based on the factory pattern (introduced by the "Gang of Four" in the seminal book *Design Patterns*) is implemented.

Instead of knowing exactly what class it will receive, the client knows whom to ask for it. This special factory class takes care of instantiating a parser that fits the client's needs and complies with interface expectations.

In code, this process takes the following form:

```
SAX2XMLReader parser = XMLReaderFactory::createXMLReader();
```

The natural consequences are portability and interoperability. By decoupling the client expectations from the toolkit's implementation, you have one less point of dependency to worry about.

## Helpers and Exceptions

The final category of SAX interfaces and classes has already been introduced by the code presented in this and the previous chapter. However, two interfaces are worth mentioning here: Attributes and Locator.

Attributes provides the SAX2 equivalent of AttributeList. The one advantage it provides is the addition of methods to get the URI and localname of an attribute qualified by namespaces, and the ability to query an attribute by name.

The following code illustrates the use of both additions:

```
public void startElement (String uri,
                          String localpart,
                          String QName, Attributes atts) {
   for (int i = 0; i < atts.getLength(); i++) {
     String Qname = atts.getQName(i);
             String URI   = atts.getURI(i);
             String local = atts.GetLocalName(i);
     String type = atts.getType(i);
     String value = atts.getValue(i);
   }
 }
 </pre>
```

Attributes by name:

```
public void startElement (String uri, String localpart, String QName,
                          Attributes atts) {
   String identifier = atts.getValue("id");
   String label = atts.getValue("label");
 }
```

The `Locator` interface, as mentioned in the previous chapter, provides the physical location information for events (`getPublicID`, `getColumnNumber`, `getLineNumber`). Note that the results returned by a `Locator` are valid only during normal parsing and the scope of each handler. Attempting to access the `Locator` data at any other time will yield unspecified results.

## Summary

This chapter introduced common interfaces between SAX 1.0 and SAX 2.0, as well as examples of their use. Several examples, such as a trimmer tool, showing the specifics of SAX 2.0 C++ implementations in the Windows environment were introduced.

The fundamental advantages of the SAX approach are speed, its low impact on memory, and the freedom of not having a preconceived model to work with. Some of these features are key in applications such as the censorship tool developed in Chapter 4, where massive documents may be processed with a marginal amount of memory. However, not all problems fall into that category, so you must get acquainted with other mechanisms and their trade-offs.

The next two chapters discuss a totally different way of manipulating XML documents—the Document Object Model. Then we will compare the two approaches and tie them together using advanced design techniques in Chapter 8.

# 6

# DOM Level 2.0

THIS CHAPTER INTRODUCES THE DOCUMENT OBJECT MODEL 2.0 (DOM) and the most important implementations of its C++ binding. It also discusses the programming techniques behind their correct use.

In order to keep the discussion grounded in practical development, this chapter introduces representative examples along with their DOM explanation. The most important example is the construction of an XML analyzer application.

## DOM Basics

The previous chapters discussed the event-driven approach to XML processing, its mechanisms, and techniques. This chapter covers the other main paradigm for XML parsing and manipulation: the Document Object Model (DOM).

In event-driven processing, the result of parsing an XML file was a series of events caught by handlers. In the Object Model approach, the result of parsing an XML file is a collection of objects forming a tree that represents the whole document (see Figure 6.1).

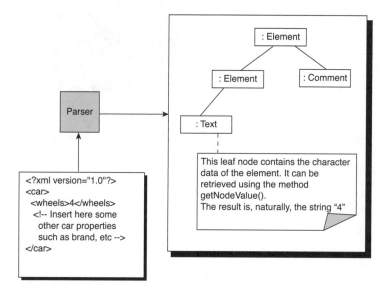

**Figure 6.1** DOM result.

In the event-driven case, the role of the XML manipulation code is that of a catcher, a reactive approach to small pieces of XML information (events) thrown by the parser. In the Object Model case, the role of your code changes to that of a visitor, an explorer of a final and complete result. Such exploration can be performed in any order you prefer (including random access).

### An Important Distinction

Please note that the DOM presents an object model of *the document,* not an object model of the *data on the document.* The difference becomes evident when you think about the proper representation of the data encapsulated in the document in Figure 6.1: It would be preferable to have a `car` class with a simple `int wheels` attribute.

The two-way transformation between document and data models is one of the most recurrent problems in DOM XML processing. It's also one of the topics of this chapter.

The following sections analyze four subjects:

- **DOM history and nature.** The rationale and definition of the interfaces that constitute the DOM.

- **A hands-on example.** A syntax-oriented example dealing with the key interfaces.

- **Guide to core interfaces.** A detailed guide to the most important interfaces.

- **A complete example.** A final, nontrivial example in which we finish an XML editor and discuss implementation trade-offs.

# DOM History

DOM, as with so many other Web-related technologies, was born amid the chaos of multiple vendors offering proprietary solutions to an evident global problem.

During the first years of the Web, it became clear that an object model for HTML pages was desperately needed for operations such as client-side validation and the transformation of page data. Needless to say, there are an infinite number of ways to model an HTML page as a collection of objects. (For example, attributes can be modeled as data members of the element class, or they can be modeled as objects on their own.)

The first object models were initially created within the space (and looking after the requirements) of HTML browsers. They were dissimilar between each other, forcing script programmers to duplicate code in order to provide portability. The solution to such fragmentation came with DOM 1.0. (The previous, vendor-specific attempts are collectively called DOM 0.) DOM 1.0 is a series of interfaces developed by the W3C, a development contract to which every implementor adheres in order to maximize interoperability.

Further extensions to DOM (including version 2.0, which is the topic of this chapter) have provided interfaces for much more than HTML, covering not only an (almost complete) object model for XML, but also interfaces for Cascading Style Sheets (CSS), iterators, and so on.

# DOM Nature

In order to be successful and avoid confusion, DOM must be specified in a way that is implementation language-independent. Such a solution would ideally come from the specification of the interfaces using Interface Definition Language (IDL).

IDL is CORBA's mechanism for specifying the methods exposed by a particular type of object before implementing them in any particular language. The result of compiling IDL is the translation of the IDL interface into its correct representation for a particular language. For example, consider the following IDL interface:

```
interface Calculator

{
    float sum(float a, float b);
    // etc.
};
```

When translated into C++ (using a tool such as Borland's idl2cpp), the result looks like the following:

```
Class Calculator
{
    virtual double sum(double a, double b);
}
```

The interface can later be implemented by a subclass..

**The IDL Usage Scope**

It is very important to know that IDL was used for the DOM specification only as a reference and because it was the most common and well-known of all the interface description languages. No particular CORBA/COM knowledge is required, and no explicit connection with CORBA/COM is made in the spec (or this chapter).

Just as there is a C++ binding of the IDL, there are Java, Python, and Emacs versions, so the decision to specify a cross-language model in IDL seems almost ideal. However, there is a serious drawback: The DOM specification's IDL is loose and is merely a documentation tool. In other words, no real working interface is expected to come out of its compilation.

This problem can lead to fragmentation and differences between implementations (there is a normative Java implementation, but there is no such thing for every possible language). It is important to mention this so that you will not be taken by surprise when you encounter the differences between toolkits.

The examples in this and the following chapter use both Microsoft's and IBM's C++ implementations of the DOM.

## Structure

DOM defines the interfaces for the object representation of an XML document and its manipulation. In order to do so, it must provide basic abstractions such as element, attribute, character data, and so on, as well as helper classes such as collections of nodes (NodeList), therefore allowing for manipulation such as the following:

```
void doSomethingWithTheAttributes(DOM_Element MyElement)
{
  DOM_NodeList attributes = MyElement.getAttributes();
  int attrCount = attributes.getLength();
  for (int i = 0; i < attrCount; i++)
  {
    DOM_Node  attribute = attributes.item(i);
    //Do something with the attribute (perhaps print it)
  }
}
```

There are a couple of important points to highlight from this example:

- **Evident paradigm shift.** The paradigm shift (from SAX) that I have been talking about becomes evident in this simple example. Instead of waiting for the parser to push the attributes in a call, you pull them out of the element. Traversal and manipulation of tree nodes are the two processes you will repeat for all your DOM applications.

- **Program to the interface, not the implementation.** The design of DOM revolves around the notion of the *node,* a base interface that every element of the tree conforms to. Programs make use of the fact that all components in a tree are nodes (they share the common base class Node) in order to easily iterate through them, regardless of whether they are elements, character data, or even attributes. More examples of this visiting mechanism will be presented in this chapter when I introduce the reading/writing sections of our small XML editor.

The following sections and figures (Figures 6.2 through 6.6) show the structure of all the DOM's core interfaces. After that, an example will be studied.

### Core DOM

DOM Level 2.0 is a specification full of history. It must be backward-compatible with previous versions (which dealt only with HTML problems) while modeling new challenges. This has lead to a somewhat bloated standard composed of eight modules:

- Core interfaces
- HTML
- Views
- Stylesheets
- Cascading Stylesheets
- Events
- Traversal
- Range

We will concentrate on the core module, for it is where the interfaces for XML manipulation are found. Refer to the CD for the documentation for the other modules, if needed.

Core DOM (keep in mind that I am referring to version 2.0) is divided in four basic groups, presented here in order of importance and frequency of use.

### Essential Interfaces

The essential interfaces are those used to represent the basic abstractions in an XML document: elements, attributes, document fragments, and the idea of the document itself. All interfaces in this group are descendants of the basic node.

Figure 6.2 shows the UML class diagram for the essential core interfaces and their Xerces C++ implementations.

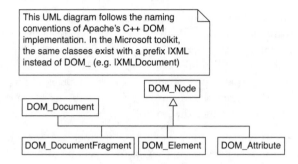

**Figure 6.2** DOM essentials.

### Interfaces Versus Implementations

When referring to "DOM interfaces," I mean (unless stated otherwise) the original DOM Level 2.0 specifications. On the other hand, the implementations shown in the class diagrams refer to the standard Xerces C++ implementation, used in the Apache project and the IBM toolkit. The programming examples for this chapter are also based on Xerces C++.

As you can see in Figure 6.2, the core interfaces provide the most basic and natural objects to represent an XML document. The examples in the next section will give you a good idea of their use. Later, I will formalize these basic notions with concise API descriptions.

## Collections

Nodes are often grouped into collections, especially as the result of queries such as the following:

```
DOM_NodeList attributes = MyElement.getAttributes();
```

This would return all the nodes representing an element's attributes. For such cases, instead of returning null-terminated arrays of `Attribute` objects or Standard Template Library (STL) collections two collection interfaces are provided: `NodeList` and `NamedNodeMap`.

Figure 6.3 shows the UML class diagram for the `Collection` group and its Xerces implementation.

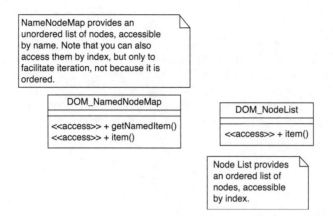

**Figure 6.3**  DOM collections.

## Text

Strings of characters are modeled as DOMString objects. However, in order to have a homogeneous tree, there must be a natural representation for groups of characters as nodes. That is why the DOM includes three (increasingly specialized) types of nodes for character data representation: CharacterData, Text, and CDataSection. An extra text-oriented class named Comment also derives from CharacterData.

Figure 6.4 shows the UML class diagram for the CharacterData group. Note that for most practical cases, the DOM_CharacterData classes serve only as node wrappers for their DOMString content.

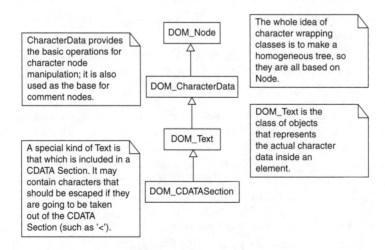

**Figure 6.4**  DOM character data.

### Entities

The last group of core interfaces is the `Entity` interfaces. The members of this group provide the functionality to obtain and manipulate entities and their references. It is important to note that DOM Level 2.0 has no support for DTD manipulation or querying.

This part of the core module is by far the least used. It is included here mostly for the sake of completion. Figure 6.5 shows the UML class diagram for the `Entity` interfaces.

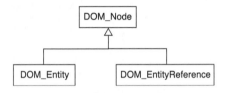

**Figure 6.5**   DOM entities.

# A Hands-On Example: An XML Editor

In order to thoroughly explore the core interfaces, I will avoid basic examples (which can be found as part of the standard distributions on the CD). Instead, we will construct an XML editor. (Naturally, this editor will be a simple one, without many of the features of commercial tools such as XMLSpy, but it will be complex enough to be a good learning challenge.)

Here are the three goals we will achieve in the process of constructing our editor:

- Construct the visual representation using MFC (Microsoft Foundation Classes) visual components
- Allow the user to select a node in order to obtain a list of the namespaces visible in that particular node
- Save the tree to disk

The first of these problems is emblematic of the routine involved in creating a DOM application: Create the parser, read a document, and walk the tree, applying different pieces of logic depending on the type of node.

Let's see this strategy in the coding terms of `ConstructTreeVisitor`, a simple class that has the responsibility of creating the visual representation of the DOM tree (see Listing 6.1).

Listing 6.1   **DOM Visualization Implementation**

```
void ConstructTreeVisitor::constructTree(DOM_Node &   domTree,
                                         CTreeCtrl *   mfcTree,
                                         HTREEITEM * parent = NULL)
```

```
{
  HTREEITEM current;
  char * text = NULL;
  switch(domTree.getNodeType())
  {
  case DOM_Node::ELEMENT_NODE:
        current = mfcTree->InsertItem(
            ((DOM_Element &)domTree).getTagName().transcode(),
            0,3,parent == NULL ? TVI_ROOT: *parent);
            break;
  case DOM_Node::TEXT_NODE:
        text = ((DOM_Text &)domTree).getNodeValue().transcode();
        text = trim(text);
        if(strlen(text))
           current = mfcTree->InsertItem(text,
                1,3,parent == NULL ? TVI_ROOT: *parent);
        delete[] text;
        break;
  case DOM_Node::ATTRIBUTE_NODE:
         current = mfcTree->InsertItem(
              ((DOM_Attr &)domTree).getName().transcode(),
              2,3,parent == NULL ? TVI_ROOT: *parent);
         current = mfcTree->InsertItem(
              ((DOM_Attr &)domTree).getValue().transcode(),
                1,3,current);
            break;
  default:
        return;
  }
  DOM_NodeList aList = domTree.getChildNodes();
  for(unsigned int i = 0; i < aList.getLength() ; i++)
    constructTree(aList.item(i),mfcTree,&current);
}
```

Even though this example makes pretty clear the mechanisms by which simple walks
through the tree get made, it doesn't shed any light on the problems of actually parsing
the file and finding the first element to pass to this function. The remaining piece of
ConstructTreeVisitor, shown in Listing 6.2, illustrates this point.

Listing 6.2   **DOM Basic Parsing**

```
void ConstructTreeVisitor::constructTree(const char * xmlFile,
                                         CTreeCtrl *  mfcTree)
{
  .
  DOMParser *parser;
  bool errorsOccured = false;
  CString error;
  try
  {
```

*continues*

Listing 6.2 **Continued**

```
  parser = new DOMParser;
  parser->setDoNamespaces(true);
  parser->parse(xmlFile);
}

catch (const XMLException& e)
{
  error.Format("%s\n%s",
          "An error occurred during parsing\n   Message: ",
          XTOC(e.getMessage()));
  errorsOccured = true;
}


catch (const DOM_DOMException)
{
  error.Format("%s \n",
          "A DOM error occurred during parsing\n");
  errorsOccured = true;
}


catch (...)
{
  error.Format("%s\n%s",
          "An error occurred during parsing\n   Message: ",
          "Undetermined");
  errorsOccured = true;
}

if(errorsOccured)
{
  AfxMessageBox(error,MB_OK);
}

DOM_Node doc = parser->getDocument();
DOM_NodeList aList = doc.getChildNodes();
DOM_Node aNode;
int i = 0;
// Find the first node element and present it.
do
{
      aNode  = aList.item(i++);
} while (aNode.getNodeType() != DOM_Node::ELEMENT_NODE);
// Now, simply call the construction method with the root element
constructTree(aNode,mfcTree,NULL);
}
```

The results of this tree traversal are, naturally, the visualization of a DOM tree into a Windows tree control. Further examples in the next chapter illustrate how the liaison between this view and the tree model can be maintained in order to provide user functions such as namespace checks. Figure 6.6 shows the result of opening an XML version of Macbeth in our editor.

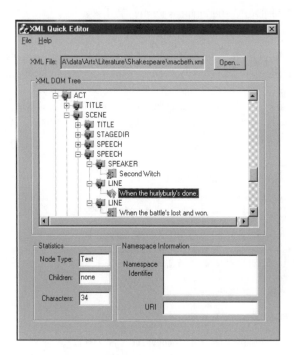

Figure 6.6    ConstructTreeView.cpp results.

# A Guide to Core Interfaces

In order to become proficient with DOM, you must have an exhaustive reference explanation of the key interfaces in the DOM and their C++-specific implications. This discussion has been saved for the CD (go to Chapter 6 in the main menu) in order to avoid unnecessary bloating in this chapter and to take advantage of hyperlinks for the API descriptions.

The CD's Chapter 6 section contains the Xerces API documentation, the complete collection of W3C standards and notes for DOM, and my commented version of the complete sample code for each interface.

For a higher-level discussion of other C++ issues with DOM and SAX, refer to Chapter 8.

# A Complete Example: An XML Editor

In this section we enhance the XML editor for Windows that we started before the formal explanation of the core interfaces. The tasks left (you already saw the construction of the model) are the following:

- Reflect in the DOM the changes in the GUI
- Save the DOM tree back to an XML file

Because of space limitations, I include here only the code required to save our DOM tree to the XML file (see Listing 6.3). Refer to the CD for the complete program code.

Note the elegance of the output implementation (an << operator overload), which allows you to simply say the following in order to write the file:

```
MyOutputFile << MyDomTree;
```

Listing 6.3  **Saving the Result Back to Disk**

```
// This operator is based on the original Xerces implementation of DOMPrint
ostream& operator<<(ostream& target, DOM_Node& toWrite)
{
    DOMString   nodeName = toWrite.getNodeName();
    DOMString   nodeValue = toWrite.getNodeValue();
    unsigned long lent = nodeValue.length();

    switch (toWrite.getNodeType())
    {
        case DOM_Node::TEXT_NODE:
        {
            gFormatter->formatBuf(nodeValue.rawBuffer(),
                                    lent, XMLFormatter::CharEscapes);
            break;
        }


        case DOM_Node::PROCESSING_INSTRUCTION_NODE :
        {
            *gFormatter << XMLFormatter::NoEscapes << gStartPI  << nodeName;
            if (lent > 0)
            {
                *gFormatter << chSpace << nodeValue;
            }
            *gFormatter << XMLFormatter::NoEscapes << gEndPI;
            break;
        }


        case DOM_Node::DOCUMENT_NODE :
        {
```

```
    DOM_Node child = toWrite.getFirstChild();
    while( child != 0)
    {
        target << child << endl;
        child = child.getNextSibling();
    }
    break;
}


case DOM_Node::ELEMENT_NODE :
{
    // The name has to be representable without any escapes
    *gFormatter   << XMLFormatter::NoEscapes
                  << chOpenAngle << nodeName;

    // Output the element start tag.

    // Output any attributes on this element
    DOM_NamedNodeMap attributes = toWrite.getAttributes();
    int attrCount = attributes.getLength();
    for (int i = 0; i < attrCount; i++)
    {
        DOM_Node  attribute = attributes.item(i);
        *gFormatter   << XMLFormatter::NoEscapes
                      << chSpace << attribute.getNodeName()
                      << chEqual << chDoubleQuote
                      << XMLFormatter::AttrEscapes
                      << attribute.getNodeValue()
                      << XMLFormatter::NoEscapes
                      << chDoubleQuote;
    }

    DOM_Node child = toWrite.getFirstChild();
    if (child != 0)
    {
        // There are children. Close start tag and output children.
        // No escapes are legal here
        *gFormatter << XMLFormatter::NoEscapes << chCloseAngle;

        while( child != 0)
        {
            target << child;
            child = child.getNextSibling();
        }

        *gFormatter << XMLFormatter::NoEscapes << gEndElement
                    << nodeName << chCloseAngle;
    }
    else
    {
```

*continues*

Listing 6.3  **Continued**

```
                  *gFormatter << XMLFormatter::NoEscapes << chForwardSlash
                              << chCloseAngle;
        }
        break;
    }


    case DOM_Node::ENTITY_REFERENCE_NODE:
        {
            DOM_Node child;
            for (child = toWrite.getFirstChild();
            child != 0;
            child = child.getNextSibling())
            {
                target << child;
            }
            break;
        }


    case DOM_Node::CDATA_SECTION_NODE:
        {
        *gFormatter << XMLFormatter::NoEscapes << gStartCDATA
                    << nodeValue << gEndCDATA;
        break;
    }


    case DOM_Node::COMMENT_NODE:
    {
        *gFormatter << XMLFormatter::NoEscapes << gStartComment
                    << nodeValue << gEndComment;
        break;
    }


    case DOM_Node::DOCUMENT_TYPE_NODE:
    {
        DOM_DocumentType doctype = (DOM_DocumentType &)toWrite;;

        *gFormatter << XMLFormatter::NoEscapes  << gStartDoctype
                    << nodeName;

        DOMString id = doctype.getPublicId();
        if (id != 0)
        {
            *gFormatter << XMLFormatter::NoEscapes << chSpace << gPublic
                << id << chDoubleQuote;
            id = doctype.getSystemId();
            if (id != 0)
```

```
        {
            *gFormatter << XMLFormatter::NoEscapes << chSpace
                << chDoubleQuote << id << chDoubleQuote;
        }
    }
    else
    {
        id = doctype.getSystemId();
        if (id != 0)
        {
            *gFormatter << XMLFormatter::NoEscapes << chSpace << gSystem
                << id << chDoubleQuote;
        }
    }

    id = doctype.getInternalSubset();
    if (id !=0)
        *gFormatter << XMLFormatter::NoEscapes << chOpenSquare
                    << id << chCloseSquare;

    *gFormatter << XMLFormatter::NoEscapes << chCloseAngle;
    break;
}


case DOM_Node::ENTITY_NODE:
{
    *gFormatter << XMLFormatter::NoEscapes << gStartEntity
                << nodeName;

    DOMString id = ((DOM_Entity &)toWrite).getPublicId();
    if (id != 0)
        *gFormatter << XMLFormatter::NoEscapes << gPublic
                    << id << chDoubleQuote;

    id = ((DOM_Entity &)toWrite).getSystemId();
    if (id != 0)
        *gFormatter << XMLFormatter::NoEscapes << gSystem
                    << id << chDoubleQuote;

    id = ((DOM_Entity &)toWrite).getNotationName();
    if (id != 0)
        *gFormatter << XMLFormatter::NoEscapes << gNotation
                    << id << chDoubleQuote;

    *gFormatter << XMLFormatter::NoEscapes << chCloseAngle << chCR
                << chLF;

    break;
}
```

*continues*

Listing 6.3  **Continued**

```
        case DOM_Node::XML_DECL_NODE:
        {
            DOMString  str;

            *gFormatter << gXMLDecl1 << ((DOM_XMLDecl &)toWrite).getVersion();

            *gFormatter << gXMLDecl2 << gEncodingName;

            str = ((DOM_XMLDecl &)toWrite).getStandalone();
            if (str != 0)
                *gFormatter << gXMLDecl3 << str;

            *gFormatter << gXMLDecl4;

            break;
        }


        default:
            cerr << "Unrecognized node type = "
                << (long)toWrite.getNodeType() << endl;
    }
    return target;
}
```

### An Introduction to the Paradigm Trade-Offs

The major cost when using DOM (and the model-driven approach in general) is memory consumption. The DOM can hold up to 15 times the size of the original document, thus making it very inefficient for a large number of problems. However, the ease of access and the ability to traverse it as many times as you want (as opposed to receiving events only once) make it a great tool for non-memory-critical applications.

Another serious implication of the DOM is its lack of problem-domain semantics. When you use DOM, you are using an object model of the XML document, not an object model of your data.

There is no hard rule to define which projects should be implemented with DOM and which with SAX. However, after seeing the mechanisms used in this chapter, as well as the guidelines in Chapters 7 and 8, you will be able to determine what is best for your projects.

# Summary

In this chapter, we explored the rationale and basic interfaces of DOM Level 2.0. Our guideline example was the creation of a simple XML editor for Windows.

The next chapter further refines the ideas presented here as well as alternatives for some of the implementations. We will pay special attention to design and implementation patterns as we construct a conceptual and programmatic layer on top of the basic DOM Level 2.0.

# Advanced C++ DOM Manipulation

T HIS CHAPTER DEALS FURTHER WITH THE DETAILS of DOM manipulation under C++. It is divided in two main parts. The first part discusses the construction and maintenance of program-specific models parallel to the DOM (such as visual representations). The second part deals with the most common and important mechanism of extending the DOM: visitors.

This chapter doesn't get into the basics, such as why low cohesion is undesirable in a class. Such themes are best left to introductory books. Instead, we will see how to best apply some high-level concepts to the problems of DOM manipulation.

## Binding the Document Model to a Native Model

The two most common high-order operations performed in nontrivial DOM applications are the creation and representation of models based on the DOM and the extension of DOM functionality via visitors.

This section deals with the first of these problems: the creation and successful maintenance of a parallel model based on the DOM. In this case, the dependent model will be the visual tree control of our simple XML editor.

## Defining the Problem

In the scope of our editor, the problem can be characterized as follows:

Every time the user clicks an element on the screen, statistics about the element should be visible to the user. As shown in Figure 7.1, such statistics include the number of subelements that it holds, the type of element, and so on. Ideally, you should take advantage of the fact that you know the tree and find the element in O(1) (see the following sidebar).

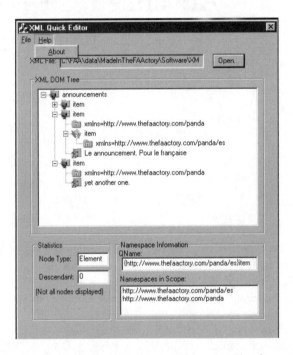

**Figure 7.1** Statistics and namespaces for a particular element.

**Big O Notation**

Big O notation indicates the complexity of an algorithm. It shows how sensitive an algorithm is to a change in the size of the data given to it.

For example, a particular implementation of a string might offer a function to look up a character on it. Every time the user asks for a character, the function goes through each character in the string. Because the time taken by the function grows proportionally with the size of the string ($n$), we say the function is O($n$).

On the other hand, replacing a particular character could be as easy as this:

```
myString[5] = 'R';
```

This is totally independent of the size of the string, so we say that the operation is performed in constant time or is O(1).

Other common complexities are O($n^2$) and O(log $n$). Even though this sidebar is sufficient for our discussion, you might find more about complexities in an algorithms or data structures book.

## The Problem

In the case of our editor, the answer to the problem is quite simple: Create a one-to-one relationship between the visual model and the document model by using an associative structure (an STL map) that, given the visual node, responds with the DOM node. Then use the given node for whatever purpose you see fit (such as counting the number of descendants or examining its namespaces).

Let's examine the previous paragraph in detail. The goal of this section is to associate visual nodes with DOM nodes. Let's begin with the former. Visual nodes are objects of the type HTREEITEM, defined in the Microsoft Foundation Classes (MFC). Whenever we inserted a new node into the visual tree, an HTREEITEM instance was returned. The following snippet shows the special case of inserting a visual representation of a DOM text node (the tree construction was shown in the previous chapter, and the complete code is on the CD):

```
HTREEITEM current;
case DOM_Node::TEXT_NODE:
        text = ((DOM_Text &)domNode).getNodeValue().transcode();
        text = trim(text);
        if(strlen(text))
        {
           current = mfcTree->InsertItem(text,
                1,3,parent == NULL ? TVI_ROOT: *parent);
        }
        delete[] text;
        break;
```

For the sake of completeness, Figure 7.2 shows a small point that may be relevant for non-seasoned visual C++ programmers—the use of ClassWizard (View->ClassWizard) to generate the tie code between the GUI events and the appropriate handler call.

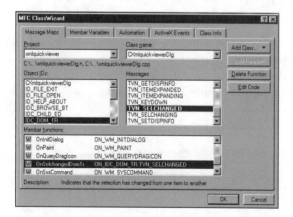

Figure 7.2    Using ClassWizard to bind the change selection event.

At this point of the program, you have both the visual node (current) and the DOM node (domNode). You put them together by using an STL (Standard Template Library) map, previously defined in the ConstructTreeVisitor class:

```
#include <map>

// Other includes go here. The point of the snippet is to show
// the necessary STL declarations. For the complete, documented
// class, please check the CD.
using namespace std;

class ConstructTreeVisitor {
 public:
  ConstructTreeVisitor();
  map<HTREEITEM ,DOM_Node > constructTree(const char * xmlFile,
                                   CTreeCtrl *  visualtree);


 protected:
 // This overloaded version of the constructTree method is used internally
 // to alter the map, without returning anything.
   void constructTree(DOM_Node &  domtree, CTreeCtrl *  mfcTree,
                  HTREEITEM * parent);
 private:
   map<HTREEITEM,DOM_Node > visual;
};
```

As you see (and as you know if you are familiar with STL), map is a parametric class that takes two types: the type of the keys and the type of the values.

A map is simply an associative array—one in which the indexes can be of any given type, not only integers. In this case, it is an array in which the values are DOM objects and the keys are MFC's HTREEITEMS.

In order to associate DOM nodes with visual nodes, you simply add an entry to the map every time you create a node:

```
visual[current] = domNode;
```

Querying the map and manipulating the results are the obvious complement of this part of the solution. You need to perform a search on the map every time the user selects a new node, so you bind the TVN_SELCHANGED of the tree control to the function shown in Listing 7.1. (Don't worry. You don't have to know the precise names of the events. The ClassWizard in Visual C++ or the QT/GTK documentation in Linux will help you.)

Listing 7.1  **The Tree Selection Change Handler Function**

```
void CXmlquickviewerDlg::OnSelchangedDomTr(NMHDR* pNMHDR, LRESULT* pResult)
{
     NM_TREEVIEW* pNMTreeView = (NM_TREEVIEW*)pNMHDR;
     *pResult = 0;
     HTREEITEM selected = pNMTreeView->itemNew.hItem;
     // If you are not familiar with STL, and iterators,
     // this is a good chance to check the STL appendix
      map<HTREEITEM,DOM_Node>::iterator result;
```

```
DOM_Node myNode;
if((result = visual.find(selected)) != visual.end())
{
    myNode = (*result).second;
    // In myNode, we have the original DOM node!
    // Now we can do whatever we want with it. In particular,
    // we will pass it to two analyzer objects (the sections on
    // visitors will explain this in detail)
    StatisticsVisitor *sv = new StatisticsVisitor(myNode);

    // Set the node type name
    m_TypeED.SetWindowText(sv->getNodeTypeAsString());

    // Set the children count
    char temp[6];
    m_ChildED.SetWindowText(itoa(sv->getChildrenCount(),temp,10));

    NamespacesVisitor *nv = new NamespacesVisitor(myNode);
    // Set the Qualified Name
    m_unameED.SetWindowText(nv->getQualifiedName());

    // Show the visible namespaces
    vector<char *> nms = nv->getVisibleNamespaces();
    m_namespaceLI.ResetContent();
    while(nms.size() > 0)
    {
        m_namespaceLI.InsertString(0,nms.back());
        nms.pop_back();
    }
}
}
```

Precisely what is done with the DOM node after you find it is the subject of the visitor sections in this chapter. Let's first reflect a bit on our solution and other similar problems that might arise and see how we can generalize the approach.

## Model and View Versus Model and Structure

In the previous example, we made a very valid application of DOM in the context of a model-versus-view relationship. Using the DOM in such situations is easy, natural, and convenient. (Imagine implementing the same editor using SAX and rereading the file every time the user selected an item.)

However, this case is often confused with the model/structure relationship, where what is really needed is an internal, semantically rich representation of the data in the XML file. In this case, the structure of the program *does not* require the XML representation of the data to be present in memory (DOM). It only requires the ability to create a good representation from the XML, and possibly the ability to write it back.

In almost every model/structure relationship, a SAX implementation is superior.

Whenever you discover yourself traversing the DOM tree just to create a parallel structure (instead of traversing it to create connections with a parallel structure), take a serious moment to analyze whether an event-oriented interface would be better.

## Generalizing the Approach

In our example, the one-to-one relationship between the model and the view makes it simple to maintain the data needed for its representation and logic. Namely, we delegated the logic to the visual client and the population of the representation to a constructor.

In other situations, the solution might not be as simple, and by not applying judicious scalability mechanisms, you might end up with a hard-to-maintain mess. Those situations are characterized by one or more of the following traits:

- There is more than one view of the same DOM.
- Views must be synchronized (a change in one view must be reflected in all others).
- The operations available in one view, as well as its restrictions, are dependent on other views. (In other words, if node X is selected in view A, that node can't be deleted in view B.)

In these cases, the best approach is to implement the modification logic in a special object, which knows every view, and the model, called a *controller* (or *mediator*). Figure 7.3 shows a controller, as traditionally defined in the patterns literature ("Design Patterns" by Gamma et. al).

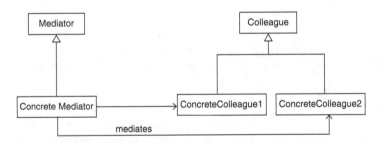

**Figure 7.3**   Controller/mediator.

All the views must be registered with the controller/mediator, and all the changes on them should be reported to it. By centralizing the common modification logic into this one class, you improve the maintenance and extensibility of the system.

Now that we have discussed the problem of finding an efficient way to bind our view with our DOM nodes, it is time to do something with them. The next sections deal with that challenge.

# Extending the DOM with Visitors

The easiest way to implement functionality over DOM is, of course, to implement it inside the client class (just as we did with the DOMPrint class). This might work fine with very simple, not highly reusable cases. However, simply augmenting the client creates an undesirably high coupling and is far from the ideal of reusability.

A better approach is to have extension classes in the form of *visitors*. A visitor is the implementation of a functionality extension in the form of an external class. It takes an instance of the DOM tree (or any other collection, in the general case) and goes through it, performing a particular operation.

Figure 7.4 shows the general structure of the visitor pattern.

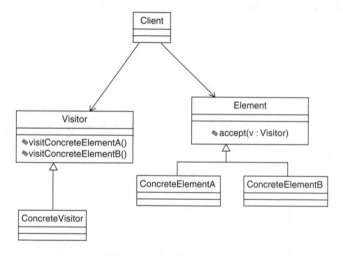

**Figure 7.4**   Visitor.

The main advantage of visitors is that they provide the necessary functionality extensions over collections without imposing the use of inheritance. To illustrate the point, we'll use them in our program to analyze the namespaces of a DOM subtree and to get its descendant count and other useful pieces of data not originally implemented in the DOM API. The following sections create visitors for statistics and namespace analysis.

## A Statistics Visitor

The first visitor implemented in our program is the statistics visitor. This simple class takes a node and counts all its descendants. It can also return a string identifying the type of node it is visiting.

This visitor was used after the selected DOM node was found in Listing 7.1. Listings 7.2 and 7.3 show the declaration (StatisticsVisitor.h) and implementation (StatisticsVisitor.cpp) of our visitor, omitting the DOC++ comments.

Listing 7.2  **StatisticsVisitor.h**

```
#include <DOM/DOM.hpp>
class StatisticsVisitor {
 public:
   /**@name Statistic Methods
    */
   //@{

   char *getNodeTypeAsString();

   unsigned int getChildrenCount(DOM_Node *node = 0);
   //@}


   /**@name Constructor Methods
    */
   //@{
   StatisticsVisitor(DOM_Node &dom);
   //@}
 private:
   DOM_Node myNode;
};
```

Listing 7.3  **StatisticsVisitor.cpp**

```
StatisticsVisitor::StatisticsVisitor(DOM_Node &dom) : myNode(dom)
{
}
char *StatisticsVisitor::getNodeTypeAsString()
{
  switch(myNode.getNodeType())
  {
  case DOM_Node::TEXT_NODE:
    return "Text";

  case DOM_Node::ELEMENT_NODE:
    return "Element";
```

```
  case DOM_Node::ATTRIBUTE_NODE:
    return "Attribute";

  case DOM_Node::ENTITY_REFERENCE_NODE:
    return "Entity Reference";

  case DOM_Node::CDATA_SECTION_NODE:
    return "CDATA";

  case DOM_Node::COMMENT_NODE:
    return "Comment";

  case DOM_Node::DOCUMENT_TYPE_NODE:
    return "Document Type";

  case DOM_Node::ENTITY_NODE:
    return "Entity";

  case DOM_Node::PROCESSING_INSTRUCTION:
    return "Processing Instruction";

  case DOM_Node::XML_DECL_NODE:
    return "XML Declaration";
  default:
    return "Unknown"; //Never happens. Included to avoid compilation warnings
  }
}

// Note that officially, the attributes are not counted as children of their
// containing element. That explains the difference between the visual number
// of children and the actual result of this method.
unsigned int    StatisticsVisitor::getChildrenCount(DOM_Node *node)
{
  if(node == 0)
  node = &myNode;
  unsigned int result = 0;
  DOM_NodeList aList = node->getChildNodes();
  result = aList.getLength();
  for(unsigned int i = 0; i < aList.getLength() ; i++)
  result += getChildrenCount(&aList.item(i));
  return result;
}
```

## A Namespace Visitor

The second visitor shows a different type of traversal. It takes a particular node and then walks up the tree, finding the namespaces of all the element's ancestors. It returns its results as an STL vector (see its manipulation in Listing 7.1).

Listing 7.4 shows the implementation of the namespaceVisitor class.

Listing 7.4  **NamespaceVisitor.cpp**

```cpp
#include "NamespacesVisitor.h"

NamespacesVisitor::NamespacesVisitor(DOM_Node &dom) : myNode(dom)
{
}
vector<char *> NamespacesVisitor::getVisibleNamespaces(DOM_Node *node)
{
  if(node == 0)
  {
    node = &myNode;
    ns.erase(ns.begin(),ns.end());
  }
  if(node->getNamespaceURI() != 0)
    ns.push_back(node->getNamespaceURI().transcode());

  if(node->getNodeType() == DOM_Node::DOCUMENT_NODE ||
  node->getParentNode() == 0)
    return ns;

  return getVisibleNamespaces(&node->getParentNode());

}

char * NamespacesVisitor::getQualifiedName()
{
  if(myNode.getNodeType() != DOM_Node::ELEMENT_NODE)
  return "Not an Element";
  char *result = new char[100];
  strcpy(result,"{");

  if(myNode.getNamespaceURI() != 0)
    strcat(result,myNode.getNamespaceURI().transcode());

  strcat(result,"}");
  strcat(result,myNode.getLocalName().transcode());

  return result;
}
```

This rounds out our treatment of DOM visitors in C++ and our XMLQuickViewer program. Make sure you read the source code provided on the CD, because it gives you additional insight into the construction of Windows XML C++ programs.

# Summary and Further Steps

This chapter discussed the general ideas and the practical application of the two most common and important activities with the DOM: creating connections with parallel models and extending the DOM in a reusable way.

The guiding thread in our practical examples was the XMLQuickViewer application, which we dissected completely. Its visitors, mediator data, and event mechanisms were all shown to give you a concise idea of the problems faced.

From here, in the realm of pure C++ SAX and DOM, three tasks are pending: the creation a framework for determining which type of parser to use in new C++ problems, the creation of tools to move smoothly from one model to another in C++, and the analysis of the major C++ implementation issues and factors in both SAX and DOM C++. These are the subjects of the next chapter.

# Advanced C++ Aspects
# of SAX and DOM

Previous chapters have discussed the theory and practice of C++ SAX and C++ DOM. Several issues regarding the structure and usage of these XML manipulation mechanisms were discussed. However, some important C++-specific issues such as memory management and char types were not discussed.

This chapter addresses the following key comparative (and cooperative) issues that touch both C++ SAX and C++ DOM:

- How to decide whether to go with DOM or SAX
- Techniques to integrate SAX and DOM in C++
- Memory management (and C++ garbage collection) in C++ SAX and C++ DOM
- Unicode character encodings and their C++ representation (and the choices used in the major parsers)

# C++ SAX Versus C++ DOM

One of the most recurrent and often oversimplified questions when developing XML applications is which criteria to use when deciding between SAX and DOM.

The most common answer to this question goes along the following lines: SAX is generally faster and requires less memory, because the footprint of creating new objects is not present. On the other hand, DOM provides random access to any point of the tree after the document has been read. There is basically a trade-off between memory consumption and fast multiple data accesses after parsing.

Even though the preceding sentences are the truth and nothing but the truth, they are far from being the whole truth. They are adequate for an entry-level discussion, because they address the nature of the interfaces, but they are unfit for our purposes, because they don't take into consideration the design of the applications in which these technologies will be used.

There are two dimensions to the decision of SAX versus DOM: One concerns performance, and the other focuses on system design quality. The following sections explain these issues in light of some facts.

## Performance

When reading and processing XML files, you can measure performance considerations in two dimensions: time and memory. Let's examine the consumption patterns for these resources in both SAX and DOM.

### Reading Time

The time to actually read the document using either SAX or DOM grows in linear proportion to the size of the XML source, as shown in Figure 8.1. However, DOM's line is much steeper than that of SAX, because all the objects for the document must be allocated (and eventually deleted), whereas in SAX, only simple strings are allocated and passed.

### Script for Calling Counting Programs

Figure 8.1 depicts the time taken by different versions of an element counter to handle long XML files. (There are four element-counter programs: SAX and DOM implementations using C++, and SAX and DOM implementations using Java.) The files have the following structure:

```
<tests>
<test anAttribute='avalue'>Some content</test>
<!-- ...repeat n times -->
<test anAttribute='avalue'>Some content</test>
</tests>
```

In this case, the test element gets repeated 5,000, 10,000,...,150,000 times.

The Perl script used to generate the files and call the counting programs is provided on the CD.

Even though the test of passing these big files and recording the time taken to process them is not a rigorous benchmark, it achieves the main goal: to give you a realistic idea of the growth of processing time in heavy-duty situations.

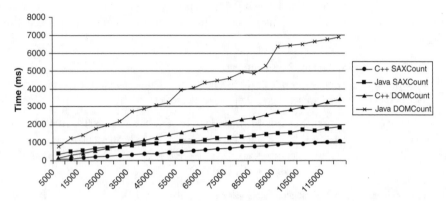

**Count Elements Benchmark**

**Figure 8.1**   Parsing large numbers of elements.

## Processing/Access Time

From the parsing time perspective, SAX seems to be a better approach than DOM. On the other hand, searches over the in-memory DOM tree are much faster than rereading the document. It is also important to mention that efficient random accesses to particular nodes of the document after it has been read are possible only using DOM (or an object model of your own). This was showcased in Chapter 7, "Advanced C++ DOM Manipulation," when you created an associative container to point to particular nodes in the tree, resulting in very fast access to elements.

If repeated access to arbitrary nodes is needed, an in-memory object model is always preferable to dealing with just events. However, this doesn't mean that "random access" equals "DOM," as you will see in the section "It's All About Design." (After all, you can always construct your own model, and sometimes you should.)

## Memory Consumption

DOM parsers create a whole object model automatically whenever they parse an XML document, whereas SAX merely holds simple strings for a few moments each time it calls a handler. Naturally, DOM consumes more memory than SAX. However, some details must be considered.

Old quick formulas for DOM memory consumption were very popular at the beginning of XML and still are in some introductory literature. They stated things such as, "The amount of memory used will be approximately 7 to 10 times the size of the document." These guidelines become more obsolete every day as DOM implementations get smarter by means of patterns such as "flyweight" (factorize data repeated in many objects and represent it only once) and "proxy" (wait to create an object until it is really needed).

Even though the old formulas might be less of a guideline nowadays, one thing is for sure: memory consumption in a DOM implementation is dependent on the size of the file, usually O(*n*). SAX memory consumption is largely a constant, independent of the document's size.

### The C++ Factor in Memory Consumption

One very appealing reason to stay with C++ in SAX/DOM programs is the excellent compromise between resource consumption and features. Consider the following anecdote:

While I was testing the benchmark script in the preceding section with a Pentium III 966Mhz computer running Windows 2000/XP with 256MB of RAM, the Java version of the DOMCount program consistently died with `java.lang.OutOfMemory`, except with files beyond 135,000 nodes. The C++ program performed fine (and significantly faster) for all test cases.

The programming effort to manipulate either version is virtually identical because of the C++ automatic garbage collection implemented in the Xerces toolkit (see the later section "Memory Management in C++ DOM").

This is just one of many examples of the pleasant (and sometimes antihype) facts you will encounter when developing C++ XML programs.


## It's All About Design

Even though performance issues are important, the main factors to decide between DOM and SAX remain a matter of design.

Table 8.1 enumerates the most common types of C++ XML modules and their constraints and provides guidelines (not a recipe, of course) for the SAX versus DOM decision.

Table 8.1   **Types of Problems and Their Implementation Strategies in C++ XML**

| Problem | Considerations | Implementation Strategy | Example |
|---|---|---|---|
| Construct numerous domain-specific objects based on a known vocabulary. | An object model is needed, but it must be one that is meaningful and rich for the program's problem, not a view of XML. | Use SAX handlers (or any event-oriented API, for that matter) as object builders, creating a hierarchy that is semantically rich for your program. Do not fall into the temptation of the "ready-made" hierarchy provided by DOM, because it is a terrible model for your problem and thus is a hard-to-maintain and inexpressive solution. | syntaxTree (see Chapter 3) |

| Problem | Considerations | Implementation Strategy | Example |
|---|---|---|---|
| Construct parallel representations of arbitrary XML documents (without knowing in advance their particular vocabulary). | This problem is faced by most general-purpose XML tools. There is no domain-specific knowledge, but there is sometimes the need to augment the DOM functionality. | Use DOM to represent the in-memory XML, and use Visitors over it in order to add the functionality required. | XML editor (see Chapters 6 and 7) |
| Manipulate another application's exported XML model. | In this case, apparently no decision needs to be made, because the external program exports a view of the XML (generally as a DOM tree). | In reality, there are two ways of adding functionality over the exported model: Work over it as it is originally provided (create Visitors over the DOM, as just discussed), or adapt the exported model so that it can be perceived as SAX events and work with it in an event-driven way (mainly for the reuse of existing SAX code). | Case 1: XPath programs for IE5.5 (see Chapter 10)<br><br>Case 2: SAX wrapper for DOM (see the next section of this chapter) |
| Filter XML input into an XML output. | Because multiple independent outputs may be connected, parallelism becomes a consideration. The partial output of a filter must be available as the input of the next one, before it finishes processing the whole document. | Because SAX provides natural interfaces for filter development, and also because of the parallelism contract, the best approach is to implement this type of program in terms of SAX. | SAXTrimmer (see Chapter 4) |
| Create XML-based extension languages for C++ applications. | Extension languages (languages for the power user to manipulate and extend C++ programs) are a special case of constructing custom-made hierarchies | Use SAX to create hierarchies or lists of commands (objects that encapsulate an action and provide an "undo" interface). | All the examples in Chapter 13 (Linux and COM+) |

| Problem | Considerations | Implementation Strategy | Example |
|---------|---------------|------------------------|---------|
|  | based on XML input. The main difference between these and the general case is that they must provide self-contained behavior, not only data. |  |  |
| Implement an XML view of other data sources. | When wrapping another data source (such as a database table) as XML, the decision between SAX and DOM must be driven by what your client expects. Chapter 15 expands on this, particularly for the problem of relational databases. | No inherently better approach. Totally driven by client preferences. | SAX view of databases (see Chapter 15) DOM view of databases (see Chapter 15) |

## About Patterns

The idea of this section is to create a good mental framework of the scenarios for the decision between C++ SAX and DOM. A related subject is that of design patterns. Even though you probably recognize parts of patterns in the list above, this list is not a patterns discussion. For more about XML patterns, refer to the following resources written by me:

- *XML Developer's Guide* (McGraw-Hill, 2000, ISBN 00702126485)

- *XML Patterns, Part I* (`www.xml.com/pub/a/2000/01/19/feature/index.html`, 1999)

- *XML Patterns, Part II* (`www.xml.com/pub/a/2000/02/16/feature/index.html`, 2000)

- *XMLable Pattern* (`www.thefaactory.com/ta/poa.ps`, Arciniegas and Casallas, 1998 [provided on the CD])

# C++ SAX Plus C++ DOM

The preceding sections discussed how to decide between SAX and DOM. This complementary section discusses the opposite problem: how to glue them together for the sake of reuse.

The notion of adapters is a key topic in object-oriented software engineering. Adapters are objects whose only purpose is to provide the interface that a client expects while delegating the actual work to an underlying, preexisting object that would otherwise be unfit to use.

The problem of gluing together SAX and DOM interfaces is common whenever preexisting pieces of software written for one model must be adapted to be used with the other.

## DOMAsSAX Adapter

Listing 8.1 is the source code of the DOMAsSAX adapter. It behaves like any other SAX source, except that its primary content is a DOM document (thus making the process invisible to the client). The edition shown here is based on the Linux version of Xerces 1.4.

> ### DOMAsSAX as COM
>
> DOMAsSAX is implemented in Listing 8.1. as a Linux program mainly because I try to keep platform variety in the examples. The code has also been ported to Windows and is available on the CD.
>
> For a COM version that implements similar functionality, please refer to the MSDN code center at
>
> `http://msdn.microsoft.com/code/default.asp?URL=/code/topic.asp?URL=/msdn-files/028/000/072/topic.xml`
>
> and download "XML Provider consumer" under the "XML DOM" item. This URL is not very likely to change, but if it does, this book's Web site will provide the new location.

Listing 8.1   **DOMAsSAX.h**

```
#ifndef DOMAsSAX_H
#define DOMAsSAX_H

#ifdef DO_DEBUG
#define DEBUG(x) cout << x
#else
#define DEBUG(x)
#endif


//-------------------------------------------------------------------
// Includes and Constants
//-------------------------------------------------------------------
#include <sax2/SAX2XMLReader.hpp>
#include <parsers/SAX2XMLReaderImpl.hpp>
```

*continues*

Listing 8.1   **Continued**

```
#include <util/PlatformUtils.hpp>
#include <util/XMLString.hpp>
#include <util/XMLUniDefs.hpp>

// Exceptions
#include <util/TranscodingException.hpp>
#include <util/IOException.hpp>
#include <dom/DOM_DOMException.hpp>
#include <dom/DOM.hpp>

#include <string.h>
#include <iostream.h>
//------------------------------------------------------------------
// Class definition
//------------------------------------------------------------------
/**
    Adapt a DOM Tree so it can be used as SAX events.
    @see DOMAsSAX
*/

class DOMAsSAX : public SAX2XMLReaderImpl

{
 public:
  /**
  Default constructor.
   */
  DOMAsSAX();

  /**
     Recursively traverse the given DOM node generating SAX events.
     Avoids multiple entrance
     @param n the node
   */
  void parse(const DOM_Node n);


 protected:
  /**
     Recursively traverse the given DOM node generating SAX events.
     @param n the node
   */
  void scanDOM(const DOM_Node n);


 private:
  bool fParseInProgress;
};
#endif DOMAsSAX_H
```

### Inheritance Versus Delegation in Adapters

You might notice an apparently small difference between the code shown here and the code provided on the CD. Here, the DOMAsSAX class inherits from SAX2XMLReaderImpl (the Xerces implementation of a SAX 2 parser), whereas the DOMAsSAX on the CD inherits directly from the pure virtual SAX2XMLReader.

Deriving from the implementation seems very convenient, because much behavior is readily available, and there is no need to go through the pain of defining all the pure virtual methods specified in SAX2XMLReader. However, it is a less-than-ideal choice from a design point of view, because it forces an unnecessary coupling between classes that conceptually should not have anything in common except their base class. (This is similar to the awkwardness of being adopted by your brother.)

A much more sensible approach in this case is the one taken in the complete code on the CD: Derive DOMAsSAX from the SAX2XMLReader interface, include a reference to a SAX2XMLReaderImpl member, and delegate functionality as needed.

Even though these two approaches might pay your bills, it is much better to ask your brother for a favor than to force him to adopt you as a son.

Listing 8.2 shows the implementation file for the DOMAsSAX program.

Listing 8.2 **DOMAsSAX.cpp**

```
#include "DOMAsSAX.h"


DOMAsSAX::DOMAsSAX() : SAX2XMLReaderImpl(),
                    fParseInProgress(false)
{

}

void DOMAsSAX::parse(const DOM_Node n)
{
    // Avoid multiple entrance
    if (fParseInProgress)
        ThrowXML(IOException, XMLExcepts::Gen_ParseInProgress);

    try
    {
        fParseInProgress = true;
        scanDOM(n);
        fParseInProgress = false;
    }

    catch (...)
    {
        fParseInProgress = false;
        throw;
    }
}
```

*continues*

Listing 8.2   **Continued**

```cpp
void DOMAsSAX::scanDOM(DOM_Node n)
{
  DOMString   nodeName = n.getNodeName();
  DOMString   nodeValue = n.getNodeValue();
  unsigned long len = nodeValue.length();

  // For the sake of readability
#define nn nodeName.rawBuffer()
#define nv nodeValue.rawBuffer()

  switch (n.getNodeType())
  {

  case DOM_Node::DOCUMENT_NODE :
    {

      startDocument();
      DOM_Node child = n.getFirstChild();
      while( child != 0) {
      scanDOM(child);
      child = child.getNextSibling();
      }
      break;
    }

  case DOM_Node::PROCESSING_INSTRUCTION_NODE :
    {
      docPI(nn,nv);
      break;
    }

  // ... and so on for each type of node.

  default:
    DEBUG("Unrecognized node type = " << (long)n.getNodeType());
  }
/**
What is happening on the base class:
void SAX2XMLReaderImpl::docPI( const   XMLCh* const    target
                      , const XMLCh* const    data)
{
    // Just map to the SAX document handler
    if (fDocHandler)
        fDocHandler->processingInstruction(target, data);

    //
    //  If there are any installed advanced handlers, let's call them
    //  with this info.
    //
    for (unsigned int index = 0; index < fAdvDHCount; index++)
        fAdvDHList[index]->docPI(target, data);
}
**/
}
```

Naturally, it is worth mentioning that the converse case of this code, a SAXAsDOM adapter, is also possible. Such an exercise in SAX handlers is not included, but you should be able to implement it after reading Chapter 4, "SAX C++," Chapter 5, "SAX C++ 2.0 and Advanced Techniques," and this chapter.

# Memory Management in C++ SAX

An always-important issue in C++ programs is memory management. Happily, the rules for memory responsibilities in all major C++ XML toolkits are quite well-defined. The following are the rules and guidelines for memory manipulation in C++ SAX.

## String Allocation and Release

C++ XML toolkits (MSXML 3.0, Xerces 1.4, Unicorn 1.0) are responsible for creating and destroying the strings they pass to the calling process. Other design issues might change in future versions of these tools, but deleting strings passed to your handler is something that will never be required.

Naturally, copies you make of the strings received in handlers are your responsibility and should be explicitly deallocated.

Strings in MSXML are represented as wchar arrays for the character data, plus a separate integer indicating their length. Strings in Xerces are represented as arrays of XMLCh and an unsigned integer for their length. In either case, the strings are not guaranteed to be zero-terminated and should never be read beyond the specified length.

> **Another Comparison: Features Recognized by Each Parser**
>
> Before I end all SAX-specific discussions in this chapter, you might want to check out the following information, which compares the features recognized by MSXML and Xerces. (See Chapter 5 for the definition of *feature* in SAX2.)
>
> The following are the features that are handled and recognized by the MSXML SAXXMLReader:
>
> - http://xml.org/sax/features/namespaces
> - http://xml.org/sax/features/namespace-prefixes
> - http://xml.org/sax/features/external-general-entities
> - http://xml.org/sax/features/external-parameter-entities
> - http://xml.org/sax/features/validation
> - normalize-line-breaks
> - server-http-request
>
> The following are the features that are handled and recognized by the Xerces SAX2XMLReaderImpl:
>
> - http://xml.org/sax/features/namespaces
> - http://xml.org/sax/features/namespace-prefixes
> - http://xml.org/sax/features/validation
> - http://apache.org/xml/features/validation/dynamic
> - http://xml.org/sax/features/validation feature (default)
> - http://apache.org/xml/features/validation/reuse-validator

# Memory Management in C++ DOM

DOM, having a much bigger memory footprint than SAX, must pay even closer attention to memory issues.

The idea of automatic memory management has been introduced in all major DOM implementations, and the notion of garbage collection by reference count in C++ is used in Xerces (and recent versions of MSXML).

Garbage collection by reference count is simple: As long as a node is accessible, either directly or via some other node, it stays in memory. As soon as the number of references to a node decreases to zero, the node is ready for automatic collection and is deleted. The most common case for automatic collection happens whenever a local DOM_Node variable goes out of scope, as shown in Listing 8.3.

Listing 8.3 **Garbage Collection and Scope**

```
void found(const DOM_Document& doc)
{
    DOM_Element a = doc.createElement("founder");
    a.setAttribute("surname",
                    "Durden");
    DOM_Element b = doc.createElement("company");
    a.setAttribute("name",
                    "The Paper Street Soap Company");
        d.appendChild(b);
} // a gets destroyed, as it goes out of scope
  // b stays, as it is accessible via doc
```

One important consequence of automatic garbage collection as implemented by Xerces is that the application is no longer allowed to create objects in the heap with new objects as it sees fit. Instead, the factory view of creation defined by the DOM interfaces (all the create methods in DOM_Document) is enforced, and all new nodes must be created either by a factory method in DOM_Document or by cloning, as shown in Listing 8.4.

Listing 8.4 **Cloning Versus the Factory Method**

```
void extend(const DOM_Document& doc)
{
    // Factory method in DOM_Document
    DOM_Element a = d.createElement("worker");
    a.setAttribute("name",
                    "Tyler");
    // Cloning
    // Note that the cloneNode has a boolean parameter. This indicates
    // whether a deep cloning should be performed (i.e. copy character
    // data) or not.
    DOM_Element b = a.cloneNode(false);

}
```

Given the conditions just mentioned, there is a risk of relaxing too much and becoming less than careful with memory and performance issues. In particular, it is not uncommon to see beginners passing and returning huge DOM objects by value. As an experienced and well-behaved C++ XML developer, you must avoid such situations and use references whenever possible.

## Character Encodings in C++

One very important aspect of C++ XML manipulation is a seemingly basic concept: characters. Characters, despite their ubiquitous use, are a surprisingly deep subject and deserve some careful attention. This section explains characters under C++ and their use in MSXML and Xerces.

Even though you can safely and profitably use the APIs without knowing much about Unicode or wchar_t, it is recommended that you read this section, because you can make performance and elegance improvements to your programs if you understand the inner workings of their character representation.

The following sections explain the relationship between characters, character codes, character encodings, and glyphs.

### Characters

Characters are abstract entities. They are defined (in the Unicode Standard) as "the smallest components of a written language that have semantic value." Abstract as they may be, you can assign a description to each character (pretty much the same process as naming "the number one"). A character description contains the character's name and other useful information, such as related characters or voicing. For example, the following entry has the character "v" in the Unicode Standard:

```
028C v LATIN SMALL LETTER V WITH HOOK
       = LATIN SMALL LETTER SCRIPT V
       voiced labiodental approximate
       -> 01B2 V latin capital letter v with hook
       -> 03C5 v greek small letter upsilon
```

### Character Codes

Just as you can assign a description to each character, you can assign it a unique universal value. This is the primary goal of the Unicode Standard: provide a 16-bit character code for each character in the world (this provides for 65,535 codes).

Character codes in Unicode are identified by a four-position hexadecimal number (four groups of 4 bits), such as the 028C in the example in the preceding section. (Now you know why you can insert Unicode characters in HTML documents using a reference such as &#x028C;.) In everyday use, people commonly call Unicode character codes Unicode characters. In print, it is also common to refer to a character with the notation U+*code*, such as U+0424.

Unicode character codes are organized in *blocks*—useful contiguous ranges of related characters. The following is the list of the first few blocks (the complete list is provided on the CD):

```
Start Code; End Code; Block Name
0000; 007F; Basic Latin
0080; 00FF; Latin-1 Supplement
0100; 017F; Latin Extended-A
0180; 024F; Latin Extended-B
0250; 02AF; IPA Extensions
02B0; 02FF; Spacing Modifier Letters
0300; 036F; Combining Diacritical Marks
0370; 03FF; Greek
0400; 04FF; Cyrillic
0530; 058F; Armenian
0590; 05FF; Hebrew
0600; 06FF; Arabic
0700; 074F; Syriac
0780; 07BF; Thaana
0900; 097F; Devanagari
0980; 09FF; Bengali
...    ...    ...
```

For the sake of extensibility, two surrogate blocks have been defined—D800-DBFF and DC00-DFFF. The idea is to expand the number of available points by identifying some Unicode characters as the combination of two codes: one in the surrogate block, and one outside it. These characters are currently not in use, and furthermore, they are illegal in XML, so there is no need to pay too much attention to them.

## Character Encodings

As a C++ programmer, you are not as surprised as others when somebody mentions that there are numerous ways to encode that 16-bit character value.

For instance, you might choose to use an unsigned `long int`, thus allowing the representation of each character in only one allocation unit. Also, you might recognize that the first block in Unicode coincides with ASCII and that a more-compact representation of English can be made: Use only 1 byte for Basic Latin and multiple bites for other characters.

Different considerations such as these (in terms of performance and aesthetics) have led to a myriad of machine character representations or encodings. The two most popular (and the only two required to be understood by every XML parser) are UTF-16 (the uniform 16-bit storage model described later) and UTF-8 (a multibyte representation suitable for ASCII and European characters but very expensive for Asian).

## Glyphs

We have gone from ideas (characters) to internal computer representation (encodings). Now it is time to present the encoded values to humans.

Characters are represented for humans as *glyphs*. A single character may have many glyphs, and more than two characters may be composed of only one glyph—such as when extension or composition characters such as an acute accent are applied, as shown in Figure 8.2.

| Character Description | Character Code | Encoded Character (UTF-8) | Glyph |
|---|---|---|---|
| Cyrillic Capital Letter ef<br>Combining acute accent<br>(modifier character) | U+0424<br>U+0301 | d0a4 cc81 3c2f 623e<br>(hex representation) | |

**Figure 8.2**  From characters to glyphs.

Characters are rendered by a displaying engine using fonts and typesetting rules. (This might seem obvious for English, but displaying languages such as Kannada is a challenge.)

### Representing UTF-16 and UTF-8 in C++

A UTF-8 character is represented as 1 to 3 bytes according to the following rules:

- Characters in the range U+0000 to U+007F in 1 byte: [0][bits 0 to 6]
- Characters in the range U+0080 to U+07FF in 2 bytes: [110][bits 7 to 10]10[bits 0 to 6]
- Characters in the range U+0800 to U+FFFF in 3 bytes: [1110][bits 12 to 15][10][bits 6 to 11][10][bits 0 to 5]

Even though both UTF-16 and UTF-8 are required to be read by a parser, all parsers represent their characters internally in a uniform way (normally, UTF-16).

UTF-16 is often represented by either a `wchar_t` (a wide char) or an unsigned integer. When using wide characters, you have three basic alternatives for string representation:

- Use an elegant implementation of strings defined by the C++ standard `basic_string`
- Rely on wide char C-style functions
- Use a custom-made string class

The `basic_string` class relies on the character representation definition given by the template `char_traits`, shown in Listing 8.5, to provide an efficient definition of a string.

Listing 8.5    **Char Traits**

```
struct char_traits<E> {
        //All the information needed by basic_string to elegantly and
        //efficiently implement a string made of this type of characters
    typedef E char_type;
    typedef T1 int_type;
    typedef T2 pos_type;
    typedef T3 off_type;
    typedef T4 state_type;
    static void assign(E& x, const E& y);
    static E *assign(E *x, size_t n, const E& y);
    static bool eq(const E& x, const E& y);
    static bool lt(const E& x, const E& y);
    static int compare(const E *x, const E *y, size_t n);
    static size_t length(const E *x);
    static E *copy(E *x, const E *y, size_t n);
    static E *move(E *x, const E *y, size_t n);
    static const E *find(const E *x, size_t n, const E& y);
    static E to_char_type(const int_type& ch);
    static int_type to_int_type(const E& c);
    static bool eq_int_type(const int_type& ch1, const int_type& ch2);
    static int_type eof();
    static int_type not_eof(const int_type& ch);
    };
```

This is elegant and convenient, but is unsupported by some compilers. None of the current major parsers rely on basic_string.

C-style functions (such as strlen) are available for wide characters in the library <cwchar>. MSXML 3.0, for the sake of efficiency, chooses to represent every string as an array of wchars and an integer for length. The usage of C-style functions for wide characters is thus common in projects using MSXML.

Finally, custom-made strings are also an option, especially when you're dealing with automatic garbage collection and other assorted trickery. This is more akin to the style chosen by Xerces. It defines its own XMLCh character type as an unsigned short (in most platforms) but also defines a series of manipulation methods around it in the form of its util and transcoding classes.

DOMString is implemented as a black box Unicode string that can be transformed into XMLCh* by means of the method rawBuffer.

### Practical C++ Tools for Translation and Display

Here are the four most useful tools I normally use for character display and transformation:

- emacs using mule and the UTF package for display (included with installation instructions on the CD).
- emacs using hexl mode for the inspection of particular codes for characters.

- saxprint with the -x switch. This Xerces utility produces a document using the specified encoding.
- The Unicode 3.0 Standard Book. This is a great tool and a total aesthetic pleasure. It contains sample glyphs for every code in the standard, plus detailed information on its implementation.

Figure 8.3 shows these tools in action.

**Figure 8.3**   Tools for translation and display.

## Programmatic Translation of UTF-16 and UTF-8 in C++

Even though the practical tools just discussed will prove very useful, sometimes you need programmatic access to conversions. The Listing 8.6 code snippet is based on the open-source program Cvtutf7 by Mark E. Davis and David Goldsmith. It shows how to translate from UTF-16 to UTF-8.

Listing 8.6   **Programmatic Conversion of UTF-16 to UTF-8**

```
typedef unsigned short    UTF16;
typedef unsigned char     UTF8;

// This code is embedded only as a guide to the look and feel of these
// transformations. Pointers to the commented code are given in the CD
// section for this chapter.
void ConvertUTF8toUTF16 (
        UTF8** sourceStart, UTF8* sourceEnd,
        UTF16** targetStart, const UTF16* targetEnd)
{
```

*continues*

Listing 8.6   **Continued**

```
ConversionResult result = ok;
register UTF8* source = *sourceStart;
register UTF16* target = *targetStart;
while (source < sourceEnd) {
        register UCS4 ch = 0;
        register unsigned short extraBytesToWrite =
        bytesFromUTF8[*source];
        if (source + extraBytesToWrite > sourceEnd) {
            result = sourceExhausted; break;
        };
        switch(extraBytesToWrite) {
            case 5:     ch += *source++; ch <<= 6;
            case 4:     ch += *source++; ch <<= 6;
            case 3:     ch += *source++; ch <<= 6;
            case 2:     ch += *source++; ch <<= 6;
            case 1:     ch += *source++; ch <<= 6;
            case 0:     ch += *source++;
        };
        ch -= offsetsFromUTF8[extraBytesToWrite];

        if (target >= targetEnd) {
            result = targetExhausted; break;
        };
        if (ch <= kMaximumUCS2) {
            *target++ = ch;
        } else if (ch > kMaximumUTF16) {
            *target++ = kReplacementCharacter;
        } else {
            if (target + 1 >= targetEnd) {
                    result = targetExhausted; break;
            };
            ch -= halfBase;
            *target++ = (ch >> halfShift) + kSurrogateHighStart;
            *target++ = (ch & halfMask) + kSurrogateLowStart;
        };
    };
    *sourceStart = source;
    *targetStart = target;
    return result;

}
```

# Summary

This chapter dealt with C++-specific issues, going from the highest-level design decision, SAX versus DOM, to the most basic and specific of concepts: characters.

Toolkits (MSXML and Xerces), paradigms (C++ DOM and SAX), techniques (filters versus builders), and implementations (`basic_string` versus `XMLCh*`, garbage collection versus manual management), were compared and unified to give you a better set of conceptual and physical tools to create advanced and efficient C++ XML applications.

This chapter concludes Part II of this book. The next chapters build on the concepts shown here in order to show programmatic applications in C++ of all the major XML-related technologies, such as XML Schema, XPointer, and XSLT.

# Using XML Related Standards with C++

# 9

# XML Schema, TREX, and Other Modeling Languages

THIS CHAPTER STARTS A NEW AND IMPORTANT PART of the book: a journey through the higher members of the XML family of specifications and the way they are programmatically treated in C++ projects.

This chapter deals with specifications related to advanced data modeling (see Chapter 2, "XML/C++ Overview," for a layout of the whole XML family) and the programmatic approaches needed to use these technologies with C++.

The following sections discuss three different languages that go beyond the expressive power of DTDs for advanced language modeling: W3C's XML Schema, ISO's RELAX, and OASIS's TREX. For each language, three sections are provided:

- A concise description of its rationale, concepts, and syntax

- Examples

- C++-specific techniques and tools for processing and embedding

Advanced Schema languages are still a matter of great discussion, and their implementations are not yet complete. However, this is an important topic that must be addressed and understood, because it will be ubiquitous in the future.

# XML Schema: The Language

The most visible of the advanced modeling languages for XML is *XML Schema*. XML Schema is the official W3C attempt to define a language that goes beyond the expressive power of plain DTDs.

The Normative XML Schema is divided in two parts: structures and datatypes. The following sections explore the most relevant characteristics and mechanisms of the language as a summarizing whole, not necessarily in the original order of the (hundreds of) pages of the candidate recommendation.

## XML Schema Basic Rationale

From the physical point of view, the first and most notable difference between XML Schemas and DTDs is the fact that schemas are written using XML documents.

From a more logical perspective, I consider the following three to be the most important differences found in XML Schemas:

- Separation of the idea of type from that of element
- Different encapsulation and reuse model (inheritance)
- XML Schema's capability to apply type-specific constraints (facets)

The following sections expand on these differences and their implementation.

## Types

XML Schemas are based on the notion of types and elements (similar to the way C++ defines classes and variables). Types may be either built-in or user-defined, they may be derived from other types (by using either extension or restriction), and they can be used to define elements (there is no one-to-one relationship between element names and types, as in traditional DTDs). To see all these points from a practical perspective, consider Listing 9.1, an annotated example showing a schema for the description of a set of computers.

Listing 9.1 **Computer Group Schema**

```
<?xml version="1.0"?>
<!-- This document is an XML Schema. It defines a class of documents by
     restricting the type, order, cardinality, etc. of their elements.
     Use the oracle schema_program or any other XML Schema-aware
     parser to validate a document against this definition. -->

<schema xmlns = "http://www.w3.org/1999/XMLSchema">

    <!-- A type definition -->
    <complexType name="computerDescription">
      <sequence>
      <element name="familiarName" type="string"/>
```

```
    <element name="ip"          type="string"/>
    <element name="owner"       type="string"  maxOccurs="*"/>
    <element name="purchaseDate" type="date"/>
    </sequence>
  </complexType>

  <!-- A type definition. Analog to a class or struct declaration in C++ -->
  <complexType name="computerGroup">
    <sequence>
    <!-- group is of type string (a built-in type) -->
    <element name="group"      type="string"/>

    <!-- computers is a sequence of 0 or more computer elements plus a
        group name -->
      <!-- computer is of type computerDescription, defined below -->
      <element name="computer" type="computerDescription"
                            maxOccurs="*"/>
    </sequence>
  </complexType>

  <!-- An element declaration. Analog to a variable declaration in C++ -->
  <element name="computers" type="computerGroup" />

</schema>
```

The document in Listing 9.2 shows an instance of document conformant with the preceding schema.

Listing 9.2   **Computer Group Instance**

```
<?xml version="1.0"?>
<computers xmlns:xsi="http://www.w3.org/1999/XMLSchema-instance"
        xsi:schemaLocation="computers.xsd">
  <group>FAA</group>
  <computer>
    <familiarName>Gatubela</familiarName>
    <ip>292.268.0.140</ip>
    <owner>Jim Pynchon</owner>
    <purchaseDate>15/10/2000</purchaseDate>
  </computer>

  <computer> <!-- Note that we use the element name, not the type name -->
    <familiarName>Yelena</familiarName>
    <ip>292.268.0.143</ip>
    <owner>Tom Pirandelli </owner>
    <owner>Luigi Morrison</owner>
    <purchaseDate>03/01/2001</purchaseDate>
  </computer>
  <!-- other computers here -->
</computers>
```

Even though this example gives you an idea of the look and feel of XML Schemas and shows you one of its powerful characteristics (the ability to separate types from element names), it does not show any of the constraining abilities that make this mechanism more expressive than DTDs. The following sections touch on the refinement and derivation of types.

## Complex Versus Simple Types

Simple types in XML Schemas can have only character data as content (no subelements) and cannot have attributes. Most of the built-in types (such as `boolean`, `binary`, and `float`) are simple atomic types. Declaring elements of simple built-in types is as simple as providing their names in the `type` attribute of the element declaration (see the `familiarName` element in Listing 9.1).

New simple types can be defined by the users, especially when restrictions must be applied to a particular simple type, as illustrated here (you'll read more about the restriction mechanisms in the "Type Restrictions: Facets" section):

```
<!-- Definition and Declaration (part of probabilities.xsd ) -->

<xsd:simpleType name="probability">
  <xsd:restriction base="xsd:float">
    <xsd:minInclusive value="0.0"/>
    <xsd:maxInclusive value="1.0"/>
  </xsd:restriction>
</xsd:simpleType>

<element name="defectRate" type="probability"/>

<!-- Instance (part of probabilities.xml ) -->

<defectRate>0.1</defectRate>
```

Besides the atomic types (`string`, `boolean`, `float`, `double`, `decimal`, `timeInstant`), there are two more simple types: lists and unions. Lists allow the value of an element to be a space-separated list of atomic values:

```
<!-- definition and declaration -->

<xsd:simpleType name="listOfProbabilities">
  <xsd:list itemType="probability"/>
</xsd:simpleType>

<element name="dices" type="listOfProbabilities"/>

<!-- instance -->
<dices>0.0 0.0 0.03</dices>
```

On the other hand, unions allow types to have a value that conforms with *one* of the provided types (much like unions in C++):

```
<!-- In our application, a finite set of probabilities can be expressed explicitly
or by providing a formula -->

<element name="formula"            type="string"/>

<xsd:simpleType name="finiteProbabilitySet">
  <xsd:union memberTypes="integer formula"/>
</xsd:simpleType>

<element name="responseRates" type="finiteProbabilitySet"/>
<!-- Both of the following elements are valid -->

<responseRates>0.1 0.2 0.3 0.4 0.5</responseRates>

<responseRates>x : x <= 0.5 && x > 0.0 && x*100 % 10 == 0</responseRates>
<!-- this only illustrates the union type. The interpretation of the formula
     would be part of the application logic (naturally) -->
```

From simple types (whether they are atomic or lists/unions), you can begin composing complex types. Complex types are analogous to structs in C: They provide the definition of a new data structure in terms of constituent components. Such components, in the case of XML Schema complex types, are subelements and attributes.

A complex type may be explicitly defined, as shown in Listing 9.3.

Listing 9.3   **Defining Named Complex Types**

```
<complexType name="Agent">
  <sequence>
    <element name="Name"       type="string"/>
    <element name="VoicePitch" type="agent:pitchType"/>
    <element name="VoiceSpeed" type="agent:speedType"/>
    <element name="Date"       type="date"/>
    <element name="Author"     type="string" maxOccurs="*"/>
  </sequence>
  <attribute name="language" type="string" use="default" value="English"/>
  <anyAttribute namespace="##local"/>
</complexType>
```

## Anonymous Types

Complex types, when they are not meant to be reused, but instead are particular to only one element, can also be defined anonymously, as shown in Listing 9.4.

Listing 9.4   **Defining Anonymous Complex Types**

```
<element name="AgentsCatalogue">
    <complexType>
        <sequence>
        <!-- note the usage of the agent namespace. This is the target
                namespace as defined in the next section -->
            <element name="Agent"
                    ref="agent:Agent" minOccurs="0" maxOccurs="*"/>

        </sequence>
    </complexType>
</element>
```

## Target Namespace

In order to differentiate between the elements that are part of XML Schema and those that are part of the language being defined, the specification provides the concept of target namespaces. The qualified names (using a namespace identical to the target) can be reused throughout the XML Schema document for derivation and element declaration purposes.

Listing 9.5 shows the syntax for declaring the target namespace used in Listings 9.3 and 9.4.

Listing 9.5   **Target Namespace**

```
<?xml version="1.0"?>
<schema xmlns = "http://www.w3.org/2000/08/XMLSchema"
        targetNamespace = "http://www.thefaactory.com/AgentDescription"
        xmlns:agent = http://www.thefaactory.com/AgentDescription
        elementFormDefault="qualified">

<!-- Include Listings 9.4 and 9.3 here -->

</schema>
```

## Type Restrictions: Facets

In order to constrain the values or aspects of simple types, you may apply facets. Facets are restrictions applicable to simple types that further shape their semantics and usability (such as the minExclusive facet for float and other number types).

Listing 9.6 shows the usage of facets in the description of the simple type pitchType, used in Listing 9.3. As you can see, it refines the basic integer type in order to allow only values in the range (1...25).

Listing 9.6 **Facets**

```
<simpleType name="pitchType">
   <restriction base="integer" >
      <minExclusive value = "1"/>
      <maxInclusive value = "25"/>
   </restriction>
</simpleType>
```

The CD that comes with this book (and `http://www.w3.org/TR/xmlschema-0/` `#SimpleTypeFacets`) contains the complete list of all the facets applicable to each type.

## More About the XML Schema Language

XML Schema is the longest and most complex of all the W3C initiatives regarding XML (a fact that has brought it many detractors). The explanation of every aspect and detail of the language is outside the scope of this chapter (and surely the matter of a whole book). Instead, we will next concentrate on the programmatic use of toolkits that implement the standard.

More about the language itself (including derivation and a complete list of facets) can be found at the following addresses:

`http://www.w3.org/TR/xmlschema-0`: XML Schema Part 0—Primer

`http://www.w3.org/TR/xmlschema-1`: XML Schema Part 1—Structures

`http://www.w3.org/TR/xmlschema-2`: XML Schema Part 2—Data Types

`http://xml.coverpages.org/schemas.html`: Robin Cover's pages on XML Schema

# C++ Tools for XML Schema

The usage of XML Schema inside a C++ project can take basically two forms:

- XML Schema validators used inside your project to replace the help of plain old DTD validation
- XML Schema inspection toolkits in order to programmatically manipulate and understand the structure of a class of documents

The following two sections discuss the relevant C++ tools (and their use) for each case.

## Embedding a Schema Validator in C++ Projects

Currently, the implementations of XML Schema are scarce (in every language, not just C++). The following example uses the Oracle XML Schema processor (publicly available from www.oracle.com, but not freely distributable). As more C++ processors for XML Schema become available, they will be listed on this book's Web site (http://www.thefactory.com/xmlcpp).

The Oracle Schema processor ships in a binary-only format (no source code) with the library files, DLLs, and includes files needed to develop against it. The distribution also includes a Windows NT application (which seems to work well under any flavor of Win32, actually) called *schema*, which allows the command-line verification of a document. Before using it, make sure you set the environment variable ORA_XML_MESG to the messages directory (as shown next). Otherwise, you will not get readable error messages.

```
SET ORA_XML_MESG=C:\programs\oracleschema\bin\mesg
schema patients.xml health_record.xsd
```

In order to embed the Oracle XML Schema parser in your application, use instances of the XMLParser and XMLSchema, as shown in Listing 9.7.

Listing 9.7 **Embedding the Oracle XML Schema Parser**

```cpp
// In order to successfully compile and link this file you'll need to download
// the (proprietary) Oracle XML Schema toolkit from http://www.oracle.com.
// Based on xsdtest.cpp as distributed by Oracle corporation in the Oracle
// XML Schema package.
// Copyright (c) Oracle Corporation 1999, 2000. All Rights Reserved.
//

#include <iostream.h>
#include <string.h>

# include <oraxml.hpp>
# include <oraxsd.hpp>

// The following macro added only to reduce verbosity in the book.
#define try_step(x) \
    if(ecode = x)\
    {\
        cout << "Failed with code: " << ecode;\
    }\

int main(int argc, char **argv)
{
    XMLSchema    schema;
    XMLParser    parser;
    xmlctx       *ctx;
    char         *doc, *uri;
    uword        ecode;
```

```
cout << "XML C++ Schema processor\n";

if ((argc < 2) || (argc > 3))
{
  cout << "usage: validate <xml document> [schema]\n";
  return -1;
}
doc = argv[1];
uri = (argc > 2) ? argv[2] : 0;

cout << "Initializing XML package...\n";
try_step(parser.xmlinit());

cout << "Parsing '" << doc << "'...\n";
try_step(parser.xmlparse((oratext *) doc, (oratext *) 0,
                XML_FLAG_DISCARD_WHITESPACE));

cout << "Initializing Schema package...\n";
try_step(schema.initialize(&parser));

cout << "Validating document...\n";
try_step(schema.validate(&parser, (oratext *) uri));

cout << "Document is valid.\n";
schema.terminate();

return 0;
}
```

## Accessing XML Schema Information

One desirable advanced feature of a validating parser (whatever the schema language might be) is the programmatic exposure of the components of the schema itself. Several XML 1.0 parsers include an API for the modeling and manipulation of DTDs. The C++ implementations of other validation languages such as TREX (discussed in the next section) also provide programmatic means to access the model. However, I'm unaware of any current XML Schema implementation that exposes explicit APIs for the schema manipulation.

# TREX: The Language

Useful and complete as it might be, XML Schema also has a reputation for excessive complexity. It has endured much serious criticism in advanced forums such as the xml-dev list (http://www.lists.ic.ac.uk/hypermail/xml-dev/). Many advanced XML programmers (let alone beginners) feel it must undergo simplification and further refinement before actually being the ultimate XML modeling language it attempts to be.

**The Debate Surrounding XML Schema**

Because I developed the first C++ implementation of a "competitor" language, my sometimes skeptic opinion of XML Schema should be taken with a grain of salt. However, although it remains a fact that XML Schema is highly important, it is also true that other serious alternatives must be evaluated and considered. The final decision will always be a matter of your requirements and comfort. Presenting the available C++ options is the only true goal of this chapter.

This section discusses one of the two major post-DTD alternatives to XML Schema (DTDs were discussed in Chapter 1, "XML: Constructs and Concepts"): the Tree Regular Expressions for XML (TREX).

TREX is a modeling language for XML created by James Clark. Since March of 2001, it has been developed and maintained by OASIS (Organization for the Advancement of Structured Information Standards).

TREX is based on the concept of patterns, is substantially more compact than XML Schema, and can be integrated with external datatype languages (such as XML datatypes themselves) for extension purposes. TREX addresses most of the limitations of DTD while maintaining a reasonable level of complexity (both for implementers and users).

The following sections explain the mechanisms and syntax of the TREX language, as well as the C++ tools and APIs available for TREX validation.

## Patterns

A TREX pattern (pretty much in sync with the traditional computer science term) is an expression (written as an XML file) that defines the set of possible structures and/or contents of a class of documents. Particular instances (documents) are matched against the pattern using a TREX interpreter or validator. The result of matching a document against a pattern is Boolean: it either complies or doesn't.

The example shown in Listings 9.8 and 9.9, an MP3 playlist, gives you a taste of TREX's syntax. The sections that follow discuss each language construct in detail.

Listing 9.8    **An MP3 Playlist TREX Pattern**

```
<?xml version="1.0"?>
<!-- A TREX Pattern for MP3 playlists -->
<!-- $Id: mtproxy.cpp,v 1.7 2001/03/17 03:56:36 LizardKing Exp $ -->

<element name="mp3playlist">
<oneOrMore>
  <element name="song">
    <element name="title">
    <anyString/>
    </element>
    <element name="file">
    <anyString/>
```

```
      </element>
    </element>
  </oneOrMore>
</element>
```

The document in Listing 9.9 introduces a valid document according to the TREX pattern shown in Listing 9.8.

Listing 9.9  **An MP3 Playlist Document**

```
<?xml version="1.0"?>
<mp3playlist>
  <song>
    <title>Pearl's girl</title>
    <file>music/underworld_PearlsGirl.mp3</file>
  </song>
  <song>
    <title>This is your life (featuring Tyler Durden)</title>
    <file>music/dustBrothers_ThisIsYourLife.mp3</file>
  </song>
</mp3playlist>
```

## Elements and Attributes

Listings 9.8 and 9.9 showed a representative yet very small example of the declaration of elements in a TREX schema (the term "schema" is also normally used to refer to a TREX pattern). The extension to the MP3 playlist shown in Listing 9.10 further shows the use of elements and introduces the syntax for attributes.

Listing 9.10  **An Attribute-Enhanced Playlist**

```
<?xml version="1.0"?>
<!-- A TREX Pattern for MP3 playlists -->
<element name="mp3playlist">
<oneOrMore>
  <element name="song">
    <!-- Note the addition of the year attribute -->
    <attribute name="year">
    <anyString/>
    </attribute>
    <attribute name="artist">
    <anyString/>
    </attribute>
    <element name="title">
    <anyString/>
    </element>
    <element name="file">
```

*continues*

Listing 9.10   **Continued**

```
      <anyString/>
      </element>
    </element>
  </oneOrMore>
</element>
```

Following the tradition of XML 1.0, the relative order of attributes in TREX is insignificant, but the order of elements is significant. Taking this into consideration, the two song elements shown in Listing 9.11 match the pattern in Listing 9.10.

Listing 9.11   **Relative Order Illustrated**

```
<?xml version="1.0"?>
<mp3playlist>
  <song year="1996" artist="underworld">
    <title>Pearl's girl</title>
    <file>music/underworld_PearlsGirl.mp3</file>
  </song>
  <!-- note the inverse order in the year/artist attributes -->
  <song artist="Dust Brothers" year="1997">
    <title>This is your life (featuring Tyler Durden)</title>
    <file>music/dustBrothers_ThisIsYourLife.mp3</file>
  </song>
</mp3playlist>
```

## Choices and Repetitions

Choices can be expressed in a TREX pattern using the choice element. Repetitions are marked using the elements optional, zeroOrMore, and oneOrMore. These elements are equivalent to the DTD wildcards ?, *, and +, respectively.

Listing 9.12 illustrates the usage of each choice and repetition element, expanding the MP3 playlist pattern to allow either complex or simple artist names. Note how the repetition elements can have both attributes and elements inside them, thus expanding the expressive power of patterns beyond that of DTDs. (There would be no way to specify in a DTD a type such as the one in Listing 9.12.)

Listing 9.12   **An Extended MP3 List (with Choices and Repetitions)**

```
<?xml version="1.0"?>
<!-- A TREX Pattern for MP3 playlists -->
<!-- $Id: mtproxy.cpp,v 1.7 2001/03/17 03:56:36 LizardKing Exp $ -->

<element name="mp3playlist">
<oneOrMore>
  <element name="song">
```

```
    <attribute name="year">
      <anyString/>
    </attribute>
    <choice>
      <!-- The artist name can be expressed either as a simple string in an
           attribute, or as a complex element, with subelements for each part
           of the name, etc -->
      <attribute name="artist">
      <anyString/>
      </attribute>
      <!-- Note that the artist element/attribute dichotomy could
           not have been accomplished in DTDs without an intermediate
           element. TREX patterns are indeed more expressive than DTDs. -->
      <element name="artist">
      <oneOrMore>
          <choice>
            <element name="group">
            <anyString/>
            </element>
            <element name="individual">
            <anyString/>
            </element>
          </choice>
      </oneOrMore>
      <zeroOrMore>
          <element name="featuring">
            <anyString/>
          </element>
      </zeroOrMore>
      </element>
    </choice>
    <element name="title">
    <anyString/>
    </element>
    <element name="file">
    <anyString/>
    </element>
  </element>
</oneOrMore>
</element>
```

Listing 9.13 shows the obligatory valid instance document.

Listing 9.13  **Enhanced Playlist Instance**

```
<?xml version="1.0"?>
<mp3playlist>
  <song year="1996" artist="underworld">
    <title>Pearl's girl</title>
    <file>music/underworld_PearlsGirl.mp3</file>
```

*continues*

Listing 9.13    **Continued**

```
    </song>
    <!-- note the inverse order in the year/artist attributes -->
    <song artist="Dust Brothers" year="1997">
      <title>This is your life (featuring Tyler Durden)</title>
      <file>music/dustBrothers_ThisIsYourLife.mp3</file>
    </song>
    <song year="1998"> <!-- no artist attribute, must have artist element -->
      <artist>
       <group>Depeche Mode</group>
       <featuring>The F.A.A. ensemble</featuring>
      </artist>
      <title>Barrel of a Gun</title>
      <file>music/BarrelOfAGun-Pafing_Swej-remix.mp3</file>
    </song>
  </mp3playlist>
```

### All About TREX

For a complete and updated list of TREX materials, including a formal description of the language, visit James Clark's site:

http://www.thaiopensource.com/trex/

For the latest version of Lorenza, the first (and only, at the time of this writing) C++ implementation of TREX, visit my site:

http://www.thefaactory.com/Lorenza or http://lorenza.sourceforge.net

## Interleaving

The interleave element allows its children to occur in any order. The pattern in Listing 9.14 shows its use in a document structure for comic book credits.

Listing 9.14    **Comic Book Credits**

```
<?xml version="1.0"?>
<!-- A TREX Pattern for comic books -->
<!-- $Id: interleave.trex,v 1.7 2001/03/17 03:56:36 LizardKing Exp $ -->
<element name="comic">
  <element name="title">
      <anyString/>
  </element>
  <interleave>
      <element name="script">
            <anyString/>
      </element>
      <element name="art">
            <anyString/>
```

```
        </element>
        <element name="lettering">
              <anyString/>
        </element>
    </interleave>
  </element>
```

The `interleave` element is particularly useful when you're modeling a mixture of character data (such as `anyString`) and other elements. As a matter of fact, it is so common that it has an abbreviation (the `mixed` element). The following snippet shows a replacement for the declarations inside `script`, `art`, or `lettering` in Listing 9.12:

```
<element name="lettering">  <!-- do the same for art and script -->
      <mixed>
              <element name="b">
                    <anyString/>
              </element>
      </mixed>
  </element>
```

The document in Listing 9.15 shows a valid instance of the complete comic book pattern.

Listing 9.15   **Comic Book Credits Instance**

```
<comic>
  <title>Black Widow - Breakdown 1</title>
  <art>Scott Hampton</art>
  <lettering>Wes (<b>RS &amp; COMICRAFT'S</b>) Abbott</lettering>
  <script>David Grayson &amp; Greg Rucka</script>
</comic>
```

Other aspects of TREX, such as named patterns and the modularization of patterns in different files, are best left for the advanced parts of the TREX tutorial included on the CD. Now that you have a working idea of the language, let's concentrate on how to use it inside a C++ program.

# C++ Tools for TREX: Lorenza

At the time of this writing, the only C++ implementation of TREX in C++ is an open source (GPL license) project called Lorenza. Lorenza is officially developed and maintained mainly only under Windows, but it has been known to successfully compile (at least once) in Linux systems.

The latest version of Lorenza can be downloaded from `lorenza.sourceforge.net` or `www.thefaactory.com/lorenza`.

## Running Lorenza as an Application

Lorenza can be run either as a command-line application (suited for easy portability) or as an adjunct program to Windows Explorer, allowing the right-click selection of the pattern file and the instance. The GUI interface for Lorenza displays a small window with either a success message or the list of errors (if any) after validation.

Emacs support for Lorenza and TREX has been started. Even though it most probably will not be available by the time this book is published, I recommend that you check for it in the future at this book's Web page (http://www.thefaactory.com/xmlcpp).

## Embedding Lorenza

In order to embed a copy of Lorenza in your C++ application, you must add lorenza.lib to your project and have the DLL in a path-visible place upon running.

In order to insert and use an instance of a TREX validator in your project, you must first create a `PatternBuilder` object that will create an in-memory representation of the pattern (including its semantics). Then you can use this pattern as the configuration of a validator, which will try to match document instances against it.

The code in Listing 9.16 is the C++ code needed to implement the procedure just described. As you can see, Lorenza is built on top of SAX 2. (Refer to Chapters 4 through 6 for more information on SAX 2.)

Listing 9.16  **Embedding a Lorenza Validator in Your C++ Program**

```cpp
// Lorenza includes
#include "PatternBuilder.h"
#include "Validator.h"
#include "Pattern.h"
// Other includes
#include <iostream>
#include <util/PlatformUtils.hpp>
#include <sax2/SAX2XMLReader.hpp>
#include <sax2/XMLReaderFactory.hpp>

#define usage lorenzaTest patternFile instanceFile
// Important: Lorenza uses namespaces; make sure you include it.
using namespace Lorenza;
using namespace std;

int main(char **argv,int argc)
{
  if(argc != 3)
    cerr << "usage" << endl;

    // Initialize the XML4C2 system
    try
    {
        XMLPlatformUtils::Initialize();
```

```
        }

        catch (const XMLException& toCatch)
        {
            cerr << "Error during Xerces initialization!" << endl;
            return 1;
        }

        // Create an XML Reader
        bool                            doNamespaces = true;
        SAX2XMLReader* parser = XMLReaderFactory::createXMLReader();
        parser->setFeature(XMLString::transcode(
                            "http://xml.org/sax/features/namespaces"
                                            ), doNamespaces);


        // Create a new Pattern Builder using the XML Reader
        PatternBuilder *pb = new PatternBuilder(parser);

        Pattern *p = NULL;
        Validator *v = NULL;
        string s(argv[1]);

        if(p = pb->buildPattern(s))
        {
          v = new Validator(p);
          if(v->Validate(argv[2]))
          cout << "Document is Valid" << endl;
        }
        else
          cerr << "Error creating Pattern. See log" << endl;


        // And call the termination method
        XMLPlatformUtils::Terminate();
        delete p; delete b; delete pb;
        return 0;


    }
```

# Getting Pattern Structure Information Programmatically

Even though the original intent of the `Pattern` classes in Lorenza was the representation of parser logic (that is, they contain methods used for the actual validation of documents), a pattern tree can also be used directly by the program as data, thus allowing the inspection and manipulation of document structure rules at runtime.

The `Pattern` interface in the C++ implementation of TREX is changing rapidly, so any printed reference would almost immediately be out of date. However, the ability to get lists of child patterns, add patterns, and push tokens is always guaranteed to be in the implementation (http://lorenza.sourceforge.net). Among the samples in the distribution is a Windows application that uses the `Pattern` interface to display a graph of the schema.

## RELAX and Schematron

Last but certainly not least in our exploration of advanced modeling languages (and their C++ implementations) are RELAX and Schematron.

RELAX (Regular Language Description for XML) is an ISO effort lead by Murata Makoto. It aims to be a complete and robust superset of the expressive capabilities of DTDs using a pure XML notation. RELAX predates TREX and is very similar to it in syntax and spirit, as shown in Listing 9.17.

Listing 9.17  **RELAX's Look and Feel: A Sample Grammar**

```
<!-- This file is included only as an example of the look and feel of the
language and its similarity to TREX. For space reasons, all explanations
of RELAX are left to the Makoto tutorial on the CD. -->
<module
      moduleVersion="1.2"
      relaxCoreVersion="1.0"
      targetNamespace=""
      xmlns="http://www.xml.gr.jp/xmlns/relaxCore">

  <interface>
    <export label="doc"/>
  </interface>

  <elementRule role="doc">
    <sequence>
      <ref label="title"/>
      <ref label="para" occurs="*"/>
    </sequence>
  </elementRule>

  <elementRule role="para">
    <mixed>
      <ref label="em" occurs="*"/>
    </mixed>
  </elementRule>

  <elementRule role="title">
    <mixed>
      <ref label="em" occurs="*"/>
    </mixed>
```

```
    </elementRule>

    <elementRule role="em" type="string"/>

    <tag name="doc"/>

    <tag name="para">
      <attribute name="class" type="NMTOKEN"/>
    </tag>

    <tag name="title">
      <attribute name="class" type="NMTOKEN"/>
      <attribute name="number" required="true" type="integer"/>
    </tag>

    <tag name="em"/>
  </module>
```

As shown, a set of RELAX structure rules (normally called modules) is known as a RELAX *grammar*. RELAX grammars dealing with elements, attributes, and choices are very readable (especially after you've read the TREX introduction in the preceding section). Grammars are not explained in this chapter, but instead are left to the RELAX tutorial.

A RELAX validator has been implemented in C++, and even though the examples are not transcribed here for space reasons, the companion CD includes the complete source code and Windows executables, along with the complete RELAX tutorial, courtesy of Murata Makoto.

At the time of this writing, the effort to merge RELAX and TREX is ongoing. The resulting implementation is expected to be implemented in C++ by a future version of Lorenza.

### Schematron

Finally, there is Schematron, a clever assertion language by longtime SGML/XML guru Rick Jelliffe. Schematron is based on XPath expressions, one of the topics in the next chapter. It also discusses Schematron and the advanced uses of XPath, after the theory behind the language has been introduced.

## Summary

This chapter explained the syntax, semantics, and C++ implementation of the major languages for the description of XML structures (also known as schemas or document classes). The main languages introduced were XML Schema and TREX. The high-quality work behind XML Schema was highlighted, its complexity was recognized, and alternatives were presented.

TREX was discussed—in particular, the Lorenza C++ implementation—and several code examples were given. Code, further tutorials (not included in the text for space reasons), and formal language specifications expanding on this chapter's concepts are included on the CD.

# 10

# XPath and XPointer in C++

THE XPATH LANGUAGE (SANCTIONED AS A W3C RECOMMENDATION) defines the syntax and semantics of expressions used to address a particular part of an XML document. Using XPath, you can create platform-independent "pointers" to specific locations in a document, thus making it possible for applications to refer unambiguously and portably to a particular portion of an XML document.

XPointer builds on XPath by adding a number of functions and allowing point and range expressions to be included in URI references.

XPath and XPointer are used heavily in XSLT and DOM manipulation, where they act as a simple and text-based way of constructing pointers to particular points or ranges in a document.

This chapter explores the syntax and semantics of both languages and their implementation as C++ classes. It also illustrates their use by showing a complete application example.

## XPath by Example

An XPath expression defines an unambiguous pointer to a position inside an XML document. The syntax of these expressions, although natural, can spawn some complex instances; so before we get into the formal aspects of the language, it will be useful to explore the usage of XPaths by example.

## Document

For the following examples, assume a `graphicNovel` document, an XML version of some of the elements of a graphic novel, such as chapters and descriptions of each frame. Other elements, such as the drawings themselves, could also be expressed as XML, using a vector language such as SVG, but I decided to leave these as external image files for the sake of simplicity.

### DTD

Listing 10.1 is the DTD governing the structure of `graphicNovel` documents. This file is included only for completeness and continuity with other chapters. It plays no role in the evaluation of the XPath expressions.

Listing 10.1    **DTD for a Graphic Novel**

```
<!--
    Typical use:

    <!DOCTYPE graphicNovel
      PUBLIC "Fabio Arciniegas A.//DTD graphicNovel V1.0//EN"
             "booknotes.dtd">
-->


<!--
*******************************************************************************
                    Modules
*******************************************************************************
-->
<!-- This file is included to re-use premade declarations of the date,
     and description elements, as well as for the default language value
     (english_def) used in some of the attribute lists.
-->

<!ENTITY % FAA-Standard SYSTEM "FAA-Standard-DTD.dtd">
%FAA-Standard;

<!-- Main Structure -->
<!ELEMENT graphicNovel    (title,by+,date,characters,chapter+)>
<!ELEMENT title           (#PCDATA|subtitle)*>
<!ELEMENT subtitle        (#PCDATA)>
<!ELEMENT by              (#PCDATA)>
<!ATTLIST by
          role            CDATA    #REQUIRED>

<!-- Characters -->
<!ELEMENT characters      (character+)>
<!ELEMENT character       (name,description)>
<!ATTLIST character
          id     ID        #REQUIRED>
```

```
<!ELEMENT name           (#PCDATA)>
<!ELEMENT description     (#PCDATA)>

<!-- Chapters and Frames -->
<!ELEMENT chapter         (title,frame+)>
<!ATTLIST chapter
          number          %number_att;     #REQUIRED>
<!ELEMENT frame           (description,img,speech?)>
<!ELEMENT speech          (line+)>
<!ELEMENT line            (#PCDATA)>
<!ATTLIST line
          annotation      CDATA      #IMPLIED
          speaker         IDREF      #REQUIRED
          %english_def;>
<!ELEMENT img             EMPTY>
<!ATTLIST img
          href    CDATA    #REQUIRED>
```

## Document Conformant

Listing 10.2 shows the document conformant with the preceding DTD, used for the XPath examples in the next section. It shows an abridged version of Chapter 5 of Alan Moore and David Lloyd's masterpiece, *V for Vendetta*.

Listing 10.2 **XML for *V for Vendetta*, Chapter 5**

```
<!DOCTYPE graphicNovel SYSTEM "dtd/graphicNovel.dtd">
<graphicNovel>
  <title>V for Vendetta</title>
  <by role="co-author">Alan Moore</by>
  <by role="publisher">D.C. Comics</by>
  <by role="co-author">David Lloyd</by>
  <date year="1982"/>
  <characters>
    <character id="V">
      <name xml:lang="en">V</name>
      <description>The masked Guy-Fawkes-like character, master mind and
      perpetrator of the Vendetta for individual freedom.</description>
    </character>
    <character id="leader">
      <name xml:lang="en">Adam Susan (The Leader)</name>
      <description>Fascist leader of post-war England.</description>
    </character>
    <character id="justice">
      <name xml:lang="en">Madam Justice (Statue)</name>
      <description>Statue of Justice, used in a monologue
      by V, in chapter 5, as if having a voice of her own -V simulating a
      woman's voice, answering his questions-</description>
    </character>
```

*continues*

Listing 10.2 **Continued**

```xml
</characters>
<!-- Other chapters here... -->
<chapter number="5">
  <title>Versions</title>
  <frame>
    <description>Black Title Frame</description>
    <img src="title.jpg"/>
  </frame>
  <frame>
    <description>Voice-off monologue in the car</description>
    <img src="car1.jpg"/>
    <speech>
    <line speaker="leader">My name is Adam Susan, I am the Leader.</line>
    <line speaker="leader">Leader of the lost, ruler of the ruins.</line>
    <line speaker="leader">I am a man, like any other man.</line>
    </speech>
  </frame>
  <!-- Rest of the leader's monologue to FAITH, praising fascism and his
       self-dubbed unworthy love.
    -->
  <frame>
    <description>Start of V's simulated dialog with Madam Justice (a statue)
    </description>
    <img src="justiceFromBelow1.jpg"/>
    <speech>
    <line speaker="V">Hello, dear lady</line>
    <line speaker="V">A lovely evening, is it not?</line>
    </speech>
  </frame>
  <!-- Rest of V's monologue to Justice, accusing her of betraying his love
       and driving him to the arms of a new lover: anarchy.
    -->
  <frame>
    <description>Final part of V and Justice's "dialog". V is about to leave.
    </description>
    <img src="vLeaving.jpg"/>
    <speech>
    <line annotation="voice simulated by V" speaker="justice">Sob! choke!"
      wh-who is she, V?</line>
    <line speaker="justice">What is her NAME?</line>
    <line speaker="V">Her name is ANARCHY. And she has taught me more as a
      mistress than you ever did!
      </line>

      <!-- next line originally in another frame. abbreviated for space
       reasons -->
    <line speaker="V" xml:lang="en">She hast taught me that justice is
      meaningless without freedom.</line>
    </speech>
```

```
    </frame>
      <!-- rest of V monologue and destruction of the statue with a heart-
        shaped bomb -->
    </chapter>
  </graphicNovel>
```

## Expressions and Their Values

The following list of expressions covers most of the syntax variations of XPath, show-casing most of its functionality. The XPaths here can be logically divided into two main groups: absolute and relative expressions. Each group is further divided into two more groups: abbreviated and unabbreviated expressions.

### Absolute Unabbreviated Expressions

An XPath expression is very similar in two respects to a filename in a hierarchical system:

- It is composed of steps, each refining a path through a hierarchical organization.
- It can be either absolute (starting with /) or relative to a current position.

The following are examples of unabbreviated valid absolute XPaths that address mean-ingful data in the document shown in Listing 10.2:

- `/child::graphicNovel/child::chapter`

  Returns the list of chapter nodes.

- `/child::graphicNovel/child::chapter/child::frame/ child::speech`

  Returns a list of all the speech elements in the document.

- `/child::graphicNovel/child::chapter/child::frame/child::img`

  Returns a list of images.

The result of evaluating an XPath (using a programmatic interface such as the one described in the section "C++ Manipulation of XPath") is a collection of nodes that match the expression. For example, the result of evaluating the last expression in the preceding list against our document is shown in Listing 10.3 (the root element output was manually added in order to have a well-formed document):

Listing 10.3 **Results of Applying an XPath Expression (as XML)**

```
<output>
 <img src="title.jpg"/>
 <img src="car1.jpg"/>
 <img src="justiceFromBelow1.jpg"/>
 <img src="vLeaving.jpg"/>
</output>
```

Unlike a filename path, an XPath can return more than one node as a result (as just shown) and have functional predicates (function expressions that constrain the node set, such as `position()>2`) for each step, further refining the results. (These predicates are enclosed in square brackets after each step.) These two points are illustrated in the following examples. Go through them intuitively; syntactical details will be explained soon:

- `/child::graphicNovel/child::chapter[1]/child::frame`

  Returns all frames of the first chapter element.

- `/child::graphicNovel/child::chapter/child::frame[1]`

  Returns the first frame of each chapter.

- `/child::graphicNovel/child::chapter/child::frame[position() > 1]/child::img`

  Returns the image elements of every frame but the first on each chapter.

- `/child::graphicNovel/descendant::img`

  Returns all image elements (note the descendant axis).

- `/child::graphicNovel/descendant::character/attribute::id`

  Returns the identifiers for all the characters in the novel.

### A Note About Formatting

Because of their length, some of these XPaths might appear on two lines. However, this is merely a formatting issue. All XPaths should be taken as if they are on one line.

### Absolute Abbreviated Expressions

As is obvious from the preceding examples, complex unabbreviated expressions can become too verbose for comfortable human manipulation. To abbreviate XPaths such as the ones just shown, you can omit the `child::` string when specifying a child element. Also, you can replace `attribute::` with `@`. More abbreviation rules will be specified as I introduce new concepts.

The following abbreviated expressions illustrate these rules:

- `/graphicNovel/chapter/frame/img/@href`

  Returns the URLs for all the images in Listing 10.2. Note that this is equivalent to the following unabbreviated expression:

  `/child::graphicNovel/child::chapter/child::frame/child::img/attribute::href`

- `/graphicNovel/by[@role = "co-author"]`

  Returns all the document's coauthors.

- `/graphicNovel/by[@role = "co-author"][1]`

  Returns the first `co-author` node (`<by role="co-author">Alan Moore</by>`).

- `/graphicNovel/by[@role = "co-author"][2]/text()`

  Returns the text inside the second `by` node with a role attribute equal to `co-author` (`David Lloyd`).

- `/graphicNovel/by[2][@role = "co-author"]/text()`

  Returns the text inside the second `by` node if it has the name `co-author`. (In this case, this is null, because the second `by` is a publisher.)

## Relative Expressions

XPath expressions can also be relative to a particular node. Such a node is known as the *context* and can also be determined by an XPath expression. For the following expressions (which show abbreviated and unabbreviated cases), assume the context `/graphicNovel/chapter[1]/frame[4]`.

- `.`

  Returns the whole fourth frame.

- `./descendant-or-self::line[@speaker="V"]`

  Returns all the lines spoken by V in the frame.

- `.//line[@speaker="V"]`

  Returns all the lines spoken by V in the frame.

- `./following-sibling::frame`

  Returns all the following siblings that are frames.

- `./following::line`

  Returns all the following nodes that are lines (all the lines from that point on).

- `./following-sibling::line`

  Returns all the following sibling nodes (that are at the same level on the tree) that are lines (null).

- `./*/text()`

  Returns the text for all the children of the node.

- `./descendant:*[@* = "justiceFromBelow1.jpg"]`

  Returns every node that has an attribute whose value is `justiceFromBelow1.jpg`.

# XPath, Formally

The list of sample expressions can be extended infinitely. Instead of doing so, it is time to look at XPath from a formal perspective, thus providing the ground for independent development.

## Model: Axis and Nodes

XPath works on a node representation of the XML document (not directly on the document syntax). This node-oriented view has seven types of nodes: root, element, text, attribute, namespace, processing instruction, and comment.

Figure 10.1 shows the graphic novel document example of Listing 10.2 as viewed in the XPath node model.

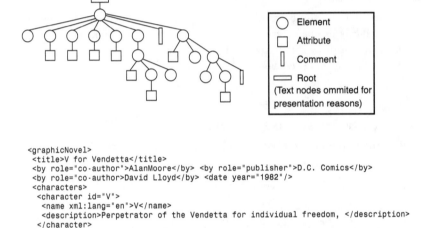

```
<graphicNovel>
 <title>V for Vendetta</title>
 <by role="co-author">AlanMoore</by> <by role="publisher">D.C. Comics</by>
 <by role="co-author">David Lloyd</by> <date year="1982"/>
 <characters>
  <character id="V">
   <name xml:lang="en">V</name>
   <description>Perpetrator of the Vendetta for individual freedom, </description>
  </character>
 </characters>
 <!-- Other chapters here... -->
 <chapter number="5"> <title>Versions</title>
  <frame> <description>Black Title Frame</description> < img src="title.jpg"/>
  </frame> <!-- Rest of the document abridged. -->
 </chapter>
</graphicNovel>
```

**Figure 10.1** XPath node model of an XML document.

At any given point in the document (that is, at any particular context node), there are 13 axes, or possible routes, that organize surrounding nodes according to their relationship with the context. To use an axis at any step of an expression, simply include its name and two colons, as shown in the previous examples (such as `descendant::`).

The following is the complete list of axes: child, parent, ancestor, following-sibling, preceding-sibling, following, preceding, attribute, namespace, self, descendant-or-self, and ancestor-or-self. Note that a particular axis might be empty, depending on the context—for example, the attribute axis in a comment context node.

The semantics of each axis are very intuitive and are not discussed in detail here. Figure 10.2 shows three cases of the organization of nodes along axes. For a more in-depth explanation, refer to section 2.2 of the specification (`http://www.w3.org/TR/xpath#axes`) and/or experiment with the code in this chapter.

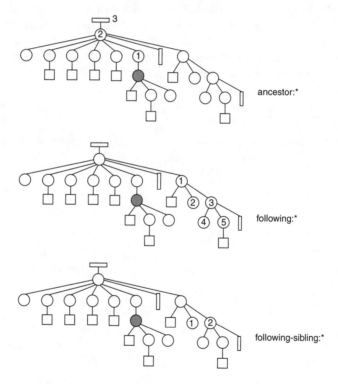

**Figure 10.2**  Representation of Listing 10.2.

## Predicates

Predicates are expressions evaluated to boolean values. They can be applied after a node selection in order to further refine it. Predicates are enclosed in square brackets. Only the nodes for which the predicate is true are returned.

The following are two more examples of the use of predicates:

```
.//line[@speaker = "justice"]  (// abbreviates the axis descendant
-or-self)

.//line[@speaker = "justice"][position() > 1]
```

## Functions

In order to make richer predicates, XPath defines a set of core functions. Table 10.1 lists them. The usage of each function is not discussed here, because most of the functions are self-explanatory, and such a discussion falls out of the scope of this text. (You can refer to http://www.w3.org/TR/xpath#corelib for detailed descriptions.) We conclude here our view of the XPath language per se and prepare to jump into its C++ manipulation.

Table 10.1  **XPath Functions**

| Return Type | Name | Arguments |
| --- | --- | --- |
| | NODE FUNCTIONS | |
| number | last | — |
| number | position | — |
| number | count | node-set |
| node-set | id | object |
| string | local-name | node-set? |
| string | namespace-uri | node-set? |
| string | name | node-set? |
| | STRING FUNCTIONS | |
| string | string | object? |
| string | concat | string,string,string* |
| boolean | starts-with | string,string |
| boolean | contains | string,string |
| string | substring-before | string,string |
| string | substring-after | string,string |
| string | substring | string,number,number? |
| number | string-length | string? |
| string | normalize-space | string? |
| string | translate | string,string,string |

| Return Type | Name | Arguments |
|---|---|---|
| | BOOLEAN FUNCTIONS | |
| boolean | boolean | object |
| boolean | not | boolean |
| boolean | TRUE | — |
| boolean | FALSE | — |
| boolean | lang | string |
| | NUMERIC FUNCTIONS | |
| number | number | object? |
| number | sum | node-set |
| number | floor | number |
| number | ceiling | number |
| number | round | number |

# C++ Manipulation of XPath

The Apache Project, Microsoft, and Unicorn all present similar C++ interfaces for XPath representation and manipulation. Namely, they share two components: an XPath class that is capable of returning a set of nodes given a particular expression and a document, and the necessary classes to represent XPath nodes and collections of them.

Even though pointers to the Unicorn and Microsoft equivalents are given on the CD (see "Resources" for this chapter), the code shown here is written against Xalan (Apache's implementation). The main reasons for this choice are as follows:

- Xalan is free, and the redistribution of your commercial and free programs using this toolkit is far more flexible than with other toolkits.

- I'm personally satisfied with the toolkit's performance, stability, documentation, and features, and I find it the best candidate for the following examples.

## XPath Classes in Xalan

Xalan (the Apache Project's implementation of XSLT) contains a fairly complete implementation of the XPath specifications, embodied mostly in the form of the XPath class.

The XPath class relies on several implementation decisions and details that might not be obvious at first and that are better hidden from most projects. This being the case, our work in this section is twofold: First, present and understand the native classes forming the Xalan API for XPath, and then make an abstraction layer on top of them to make a natural, simplified interface for future projects.

Figure 10.3 shows the UML class diagram for the main XPath–related classes in Xalan. The classes shown are only the most relevant ones in the toolkit. A complete program needs a number of other auxiliary classes to run properly (as shown later in Listing 10.6).

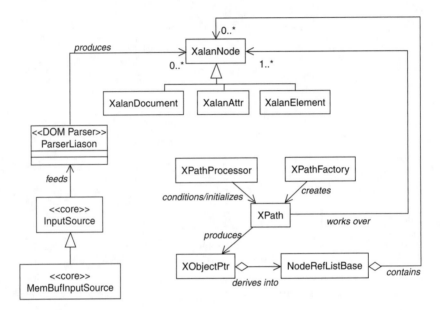

**Figure 10.3**  Xalan XPath class diagram.

## XPath Classes: Roles and Interaction

Before jumping into the code, let's take the time to briefly examine the role of each key XPath class and its interaction with others. I will describe the process of finding the value of an expression, from the reading of the XML file to the application of the XPath and the presentation of the results. In Listing 10.6, where XPathWrapper is presented for future projects, we will convert this prose into code.

The complete process can be seen as a three-stage affair: DOM parsing, XPath allocation and evaluation, and node list processing.

### The DOM Parsing Part of the Process

The XML DOM processor receives its input from an instance of one of the classes implementing `InputSource`. `InputSource` provides a unified API to the DOM so that it can unknowingly access things as varied as a file, a network connection, or a memory buffer. The particular class used for the latter case is called `MemBufInputSource`.

The result of parsing an XML document with a DOM-oriented processor is (as discussed in Chapters 6 and 7) a tree of DOM nodes: elements, attributes, and a root document element, all complying with the node interface. In the case of Xalan, the basic class of DOM nodes is `XalanNode`, from which all other types of nodes are derived (`XalanDocument`, `XalanElement`, and `XalanAttr`).

### XPath Object Allocation and Execution

When the nodes are ready, an XPath object must be constructed in order to search the tree with an expression. Because of Xalan's memory management model (based on reference counts), the creation of the XPath class instance is not a direct *new*; instead, you must ask an `XPathFactory` to create the object, which is then part of its count and should never be explicitly deleted by the user.

After the XPath is created, it must be registered with an `XPathProcessor`, a partner class that takes care of the initialization of the XPath and will later help (internally) when you finally execute an expression.

Finally, the `execute` method in the XPath object is called with two main arguments: the desired expression and the `XalanNode` for the root of the tree to search.

### Node List Manipulation

The result of executing an expression is a pointer to an `XObject`. `XObject`—an admittedly ample name—is a class used to represent and encapsulate the node list, especially in the context of being the result of an XPath. By calling the `nodeset` method on the resulting `XObject`, you get an instance of a `NodeRefListBase`: a collection of `XalanNodes` representing the result of the query. From this point on, it is a matter of DOM node manipulation (explained in Chapters 7 and 8) in order to present and manipulate the results.

## Implementing XPath Interaction

The code in Listing 10.4 serves a double purpose. First, it documents the process just described. Second, it provides a wrapper class so that the complete process from now on is reduced to one function call.

Listing 10.4    *XPath Wrapper*

```
// This code is provided by the Apache Software Foundation.
// Only Windows-specific keywords were stripped out; all the
// logic remains as in the original XPathWrapper.cpp
#include <cassert>
#if defined(XALAN_OLD_STREAM_HEADERS)
#include <iostream.h>
#else
#include <iostream>
#endif
#include <framework/MemBufInputSource.hpp>
```

*continues*

Listing 10.4  **Continued**

```cpp
#include <framework/URLInputSource.hpp>
#include <parsers/DOMParser.hpp>
#include <util/PlatformUtils.hpp>

#include <XalanDOM/XalanDocument.hpp>
#include <XalanDOM/XalanElement.hpp>
// other includes
#include <XalanSourceTree/XalanSourceTreeParserLiaison.hpp>

#if !defined(XALAN_NO_NAMESPACES)
using std::cerr;
using std::endl;
using std::vector;
#endif

// the implementation class that does all calls to XPath and Xerces
class XPathWrapperImpl
{
public:
  XPathWrapper::CharVectorTypeVectorType
  evaluate(
    const CharVectorType&     xml,
    const CharVectorType&     context,
    const CharVectorType&     expr)
  {

    try
    {
      XMLPlatformUtils::Initialize();
    }
    catch(const XMLException&)
    {
      cerr << "XMLPlatformUtils::Initialize() failed!" << endl;
      throw;
    }

    XPathWrapper::CharVectorTypeVectorType     theResultList;
    {
      XPathInit                              theInit;
      XalanSourceTreeDOMSupport              theDOMSupport;
      XalanSourceTreeParserLiaison           theLiaison(theDOMSupport);
      theDOMSupport.setParserLiaison(&theLiaison);
      XalanElement*                          rootElem = 0;

      try
      {
      MemBufInputSource inStream((XMLByte*)c_str(xml), xml.size(), "foo", false);

      XalanDocument* const     doc = theLiaison.parseXMLStream(inStream);
```

```
assert(doc != 0);
rootElem = doc->getDocumentElement();
assert(rootElem != 0);
}
catch(const XMLException&)
{
cerr << "Caught XMLExecption..." << endl;
throw;
}
XPathEnvSupportDefault          theEnvSupport;
XObjectFactoryDefault           theXObjectFactory;
XPathExecutionContextDefault    theExecutionContext(theEnvSupport,
                                                    theDOMSupport,
                                                    theXObjectFactory);

XPathFactoryDefault             theXPathFactory;
XPathProcessorImpl              theXPathProcessor;

try
{
XPath* const                    contextXPath = theXPathFactory.create();
theXPathProcessor.initXPath(*contextXPath,
                        TranscodeFromLocalCodePage(context),
                        ElementPrefixResolverProxy(rootElem,
                                                   theEnvSupport,
                                                   theDOMSupport),
                    theEnvSupport);

XObjectPtr   xObj = contextXPath->execute(rootElem,
                    ElementPrefixResolverProxy(rootElem, theEnvSupport,
                                               theDOMSupport),
                                theExecutionContext);
const NodeRefListBase&    contextNodeList = xObj->nodeset();
const unsigned int        theLength = contextNodeList.getLength();
if (theLength == 0)
{
cerr << "Warning -- No nodes matched the location path \""
        << context         << "\"."        << endl
        << "Execution cannot continue..."    << endl
     << endl;
}
else
{
  if (theLength > 1)
  {
    cerr << "Warning -- More than one node matched the location path \""
        << context    << "\"."    << endl
        << "The first node matched will be used as the context node."
        << endl       << endl;
  }

  XPath* const     xpath = theXPathFactory.create();
```

*continues*

Listing 10.4  **Continued**

```cpp
theXPathProcessor.initXPath(*xpath,
                    TranscodeFromLocalCodePage(expr),
                    ElementPrefixResolverProxy(rootElem,
                                          theEnvSupport,
                                          theDOMSupport),
                    theEnvSupport);

xObj = xpath->execute(contextNodeList.item(0),
                    ElementPrefixResolverProxy(rootElem,
                                          theEnvSupport,
                                          theDOMSupport),
                    theExecutionContext);

switch (xObj->getType())
{
case XObject::eTypeNodeSet:
  {
    const NodeRefListBase& nodeset = xObj->nodeset();
    size_t len = nodeset.getLength();
    for (size_t i=0; i<len; i++)
    {
    XalanNode* const    node = nodeset.item(i);
    XalanDOMString      str;

    const int theType = node->getNodeType();

    if (theType == XalanNode::COMMENT_NODE ||
        theType == XalanNode::PROCESSING_INSTRUCTION_NODE)
      str = node->getNodeValue();
    else if (theType == XalanNode::ELEMENT_NODE)
      str = node->getNodeName();
    else
      DOMServices::getNodeData(*node, str);

    theResultList.push_back(TranscodeToLocalCodePage(str));
    }
    break;
  }
  default:
  {
    theResultList.push_back(TranscodeToLocalCodePage(xObj->str()));
    break;
  }
  }
}
}
catch(const XMLException&)
{
cerr << "Caught XMLExecption..." << endl;
throw;
```

```
      }
      XMLPlatformUtils::Initialize();
    }
    return theResultList;
  }
};
// The public XPathWrapper methods just delegate to our impl class
XPathWrapper::XPathWrapper() :  pImpl(new XPathWrapperImpl()){ }
XPathWrapper::~XPathWrapper() {  delete pImpl; }
XPathWrapper::CharVectorTypeVectorType
XPathWrapper::evaluate(
                    const CharVectorType&    xml,
                    const CharVectorType&    context,
                    const CharVectorType&    path)
{
  return pImpl->evaluate(xml, context, path);
}
```

# XPointer

XPointer is an extension of XPath developed to be the language for fragment identifiers in URI references to XML resources. In other words, given a URI such as `http://[web site]/index.xml#[expression]`, the expression fragment will be an XPointer.

XPointer introduces two new key concepts on top of those of XPath: point and range. It also introduces a small number of extra functions and a dose of syntactic sugar for the concise expression of some frequent cases. The following sections address these concepts and their implementation in C++.

## Points

Points extend the notion of location defined in XPath (that is, nodes) by providing the concept of a nonnegative index associated with a node. In the case of nodes with mere character data content, the index represents the location preceding an individual character. In the case of a node with children (such as an element node), the index indicates the zero-based position of the particular child node.

The concept of points is particularly useful in human-intervening applications where arbitrary points such as the middle of a phrase rendered on a page (such as the position X of the content of a text node) are subject to selection.

## Ranges

A range is simply defined as the span between two points in a document. It is a concept different from that of a node list (represented by a `NodeRefListBase` object, as seen previously), because some nodes might be included only partially.

Ranges are useful when the program exhibits the ability to select or modify arbitrary portions of XML data that might not correspond neatly with complete nodes. (For example, a future version of Mozilla could allow the user to highlight and replace the range between the third letter of a heading and the end of a paragraph.)

## Location Sets

Just as locations extend the notion of position in order to refer to both nodes and points, location sets are the natural extension of node sets. They include the possibility of points and ranges as the result of an XPointer expression (whereas node sets allow only nodes).

## Additional Functions

Table 10.2 enumerates the functions added by XPointer to the XPath collection. For details on their semantics, refer to the specification (`http://www.w3.org/TR/ xptr#b2d250b5b9`).

Table 10.2 **XPointer Functions**

| Return Type | Name | Arguments |
| --- | --- | --- |
| location-set | range-to | location-set |
| location-set | string-range | locationset,string,number?,number? |
| ADDITIONAL RANGE-RELATED FUNCTIONS | | |
| location-set | range | location-set |
| location-set | range-inside | location-set |
| location-set | start-point | location-set |
| location-set | end-point | location-set |
| location-set | here | — |
| location-set | origin | location-set |

## Syntactic Sugar

In order to simplify the syntax of very common expressions, XPointer provides the following three varieties for its expressions.

### Full XPointer

The first version is a collection of steps (valid XPath expressions) enclosed in parentheses and preceded by the word `xpointer`:

```
xpointer(/graphicNovel/) xpointer(characters[2]/name)
```

Because XPointers are meant to be used as part of URLs, they must undergo URL character escaping before being used as fragment identifiers. For example, the preceding pointer when used in a URL would look like this:

```
http://www.foo.bar/doc.xml#xpointer(/graphicNovel/)%20xpointer(characters
[2]/name)
```

Also, when used inside XML documents, XPointers must escape the & and < characters to avoid turning the document into a malformed instance. The following escaped XPointer shows an example:

```
<a href =
"http://www.foo.bar/doc.xml#xpointer(/graphicNovel/)%20xpointer(characters
[position()&lt;3]/name)"
> The names of the first two characters in the story </a>
```

### Bare Names

When dealing with the value of ID attributes, you may abbreviate the expression ID (name) for the plain string name. This somewhat resembles the name mechanism for internal links in HTML. The following example shows two equivalent XPointer expressions:

```
mason/dixon
xpointer(id("mason")) xpointer(id("dixon"))
```

### Child Sequences

Last, but not least, a child sequence abbreviates as a series of integers the positions of the children in a particular path. The following example shows two equivalent expressions to access the name attribute of the third daughter of the second daughter of the current element:

```
./2/3/@name
```

```
xpointer(*[position() = 2]/*[position() = 3]/@name)
```

# C++ Manipulation of XPointer

Now that you have seen the extensions provided to XPath by XPointer, it's time to examine the state of the art in C++ XPointer support.

Unfortunately, currently the support for XPointer in some C++ toolkits is limited. MSIE has no direct support for XPointer spans, but Xalan has a limited representation. The following sections briefly describe what is available in Apache's Xalan. Then the chapter concludes with a complete application.

# The XPointer Class

Xalan provides a limited XPointer representation implemented in the classes XPointer and XSpan. The XPointer class methods, presented in Listing 10.5, provide the means to retrieve a range (XSpan) from an expression.

Listing 10.5   **Xalan 1.1 *XPointer* Class**

```
class XALAN_XPATH_EXPORT XPointer
{
public:

        static XSpan*
        getNode(const XalanDOMString&      xpointer);

        static XSpan*
        getNode(XPath&      xpath);
};
```

The XSpan class simply augments the traditional node set by implementing the offset integers needed to mark the start and end points. Listing 10.6 shows the code.

Listing 10.6   **Xalan 1.1 *XSpan* Class**

```
class XALAN_XPATH_EXPORT XSpan : public XNodeSet
{
public:

        XSpan(BorrowReturnMutableNodeRefList&      value);
        XSpan(const XSpan&      source);
        virtual
        ~XSpan();

        virtual XSpan*
        clone(void*      theAddress = 0) const;

        virtual int
        getStart() const;

        virtual void
        setStart(int      start);

        virtual int
        getEnd() const;

        virtual void
        setEnd(int      end);
```

```
        virtual void
        setSpan(
                    int      firstNodeOffset,
                    int      lastNodeOffset);
    private:
        int        m_start;
        int        m_end;
    };
```

For the complete files, refer to the samples directory of the Xalan source distribution, included on the CD.

## The Graphic Novel Browser

To close this chapter, we will create a Windows application to browse the images of graphic novels conformant with the DTD of Listing 10.1.

This application does the following:

1. Reads the document and creates a list of the frames in the novel using an XPath expression. (As an exercise, the example can be extended to use the XPointer classes.)

2. When the user selects a description for the list, the application comes up with an XPath expression to fetch the value of the image filename associated with it.

3. Given the result of the expression in point 2, the application retrieves the image and displays it.

Note how the mapping between user interface and XML elements reappears, just as in the XML editor created in the DOM chapters (7 and 8), except this time we use XPath expressions instead of C++ pointers to DOM objects.

This approach (using XPath internally as a form of pointer) might prove valuable for distributed applications, preferences and state persistence, and many other complex uses, because it decouples pointing from memory representation. Using the XPath-as-pointers approach, you could seamlessly plug in a DOM representation that loads into memory only a subset of the tree (usually called lazy allocation or proxy allocation). This would be very hard to maintain using pointers, because the positions of nodes in memory could not be mapped in advance.

### Reading the Frame Descriptions

Listing 10.7 is tied to the Open button in the GraphicNovelBrowser dialog. It gets the value of the descriptions by evaluating an XPath expression, whose result is returned as strings that are displayed in a windows list control.

Listing 10.7 **Reading Descriptions**

```
void CGraphicNovelBrowserDlg::OnOK()
{
  CFileDialog dlg(TRUE,"xml","*.xml");

  // Open a modal dialog to select the name of the file
  if(dlg.DoModal()==IDOK)
  {
    m_filename.SetWindowText(dlg.GetPathName().GetBuffer(MAXPATH));
    m_description_list.DeleteAllItems();
  }
  else return;


  CharVectorType xmlContext, xmlPath;

  ifstream in(dlg.GetPathName().GetBuffer(MAXPATH));

  // Read the file into a vector (so we can use it with the XPathWrapper)
  char c;
  theXML.clear();
  while(in.get(c))
    theXML.push_back(c);
  theXML.push_back('\0');

  try
  {
    CharVectorType xmlContext, xmlPath;
    xmlContext = str2vector("/");
    xmlPath = str2vector("graphicNovel/chapter/frame/description/text()");

    // call evaluate, passing in the XML string,
    // the context string and the xpath string
    const XPathWrapper::CharVectorTypeVectorType result =
                  helper.evaluate(theXML, xmlContext, xmlPath);

    size_t len = result.size();

    // Put each result into a temporary char array and add it to the
    // visual list of descriptions (see Figure 10.4)
    for (size_t i=0; i<len; i++){
      char asmo[200];
      int j = 0;
      for(const char * l = result[i].begin(); l < result[i].end() ; l++)
      asmo[j++] = *l;
      m_description_list.InsertItem(i,asmo,0);
    }
  }
  catch(const XMLException&)
  {
    cerr << "Exception caught!  Exiting..." << endl;
  }
}
```

## Fetching and Showing the Images

Every time the user clicks an item in the list, the correct image must be displayed. Listing 10.8, instead of traversing a DOM tree or having a SAX handler, creates a simple XPath expression that results in the name of the correct image. Using it, you can load the bitmap file and display it in the lower part of the window.

Listing 10.8   **Fetching and Showing the Correct Image**

```
// The selection on the list of frames changed; fetch the correct image
// name using XPath and pass it to the displayBMP
void CGraphicNovelBrowserDlg::OnClickFrameList(NMHDR* pNMHDR, LRESULT* pResult)
{
  // The 0-based index of the selected item in the list
  int selected = m_description_list.GetSelectionMark();
  char selectedAsString[4];
  // Note that we add 1 to the selection: XPath node indexes are 1-based
  itoa(m_description_list.GetSelectionMark()+1,selectedAsString,10);
  // We now construct the XPath expression for the image name,
  // based on the frame index X:
  // /graphicNovel/chapter/frame[X]/img/@src

  char imageExpression[100];
  strcpy(imageExpression,"graphicNovel/chapter/frame[");
  strcat(imageExpression,selectedAsString);
  strcat(imageExpression,"]/img/@src");

  CharVectorType xmlPath = str2vector(imageExpression);
  try
  {

    CharVectorType xmlContext;
    // Todo: encapsulate this copy as a macro, or a function.
    xmlContext = str2vector("/");
    // Call evaluate, passing in the XML string,
    // the context string and the xpath string
    const XPathWrapper::CharVectorTypeVectorType result =
              helper.evaluate(theXML, xmlContext, xmlPath);

    // We know the result is only one node, with the name of the file
    char asmo[200];
    int j = 0;
    for(const char * l = result[0].begin(); l < result[0].end() ; l++)
      asmo[j++] = *l;

    #ifdef DEBUG
    // In debug mode you can see the value of the expression as
    // a pop-up dialog
    AfxMessageBox(imageExpression);
    #endif
  displayBMP(asmo);
```

*continues*

Listing 10.8   **Continued**

```
    }
    catch(const XMLException&)
    {
      cerr << "Exception caught!  Exiting..." << endl;
    }

    *pResult = 0;
  }
```

Figure 10.4 shows the application (all the code and binaries are available on the CD) running with storyboards for the short film "Dreaming of Castel," marked up as the images for a `graphicNovel` document.

**Figure 10.4**   GraphicNovelBrowser.

# Summary

XPath and XPointer provide the syntax and semantics for pointing and qualifying nodes in an XML document. XPath and XPointer work on a node view of the document, allowing the query and search of nodes by means of intuitive expressions. This chapter explored the syntax and semantics of both languages and their implementation as C++ classes. It also illustrated their use with a reusable XPath wrapper and an application that uses XPath expressions as a means of maintaining pointers to images in a document.

# 11

# XSLT Transformations

THIS CHAPTER PRESENTS THE XML STYLESHEET Language Transformations (XSLT). The presentation is divided into two parts. The first part presents a practical introduction to the language, and the second part presents its implementation in C++ and shows how these technologies can be embedded in your C++ applications.

## XSLT

XSLT is the transformation language portion of the XSL specification (http://www.w3.org/xsl). XSLT defines the syntax and semantics of documents called XSLT stylesheets (or transformations), which include declarative rules for transforming one XML tree into another.

The underlying model for XSLT is that of XPath, explained in Chapter 10, "XPath and XPointer in C++." The syntax of the language is, of course, XML-based. The following sections present the most common instructions in XSLT—especially how to use C++ to interpret them, in the context of both standalone applications and surrogate modules.

## Transformation Process

XSLT stylesheets are not procedural programs such as those of C. An XSLT stylesheet is not written in terms of sequential calls to objects and methods, but instead is a collection of rules (also called templates). An XSLT processor walks the source tree, trying to match the nodes in the source with rules in the stylesheet. This is illustrated in Figure 11.1.

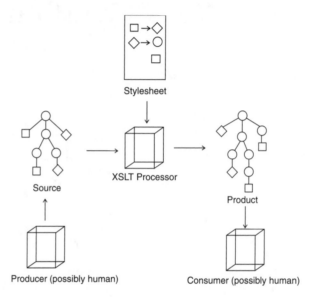

**Figure 11.1**   Overview of the XSLT process.

Each rule in an XSLT stylesheet is divided into two parts: an XPath expression that selects which nodes in the tree the rule applies to, and the body of the rule.

The body of a rule may be composed of two types of elements: those inside the XSLT namespace, and those outside it. Elements in the XSLT namespace are called XSLT instructions. We will explore them in the following sections. Elements outside the XSLT namespace are taken as simple literals that should be copied into the final result.

To illustrate, Listing 11.1 shows an XSLT stylesheet with one template, which applies to all H1 elements of a document (the selection part of the rule is expressed in the value of the match attribute). The body of the rule (expressed as the contents of the template) is simple: Include a literal element p, and inside it, put the value of the original element.

Listing 11.1 **A Simple XSLT Stylesheet**

```xml
<?xml version="1.0"?>
<xsl:stylesheet xmlns:xsl="http://www.w3.org/1999/XSL/Transform">

  <xsl:template match="h1">
      <p> <!-- not in the xsl namespace, so it is copied to the output -->
         <xsl:value-of select="."/> <!-- an xsl instruction asking the
                                          value of the current node
                                          (see Chapter 10 for XPath
                                          syntax) -->
      </p>
  </xsl:template>

  <!-- If this stylesheet would be applied to a document such as:
        <html>
           <h1>foo</h1>
           <h1>bar</h1>
           <h1>foobar</h1>
        </html>

      The result would be:
         <p>foo</p>
         <p>bar</p>
         <p>foobar</p>
   -->
</xsl:stylesheet>
```

As soon as you understand the basics of XPath (see Chapter 10), learning and using XSLT involves getting used to the language's different instructions and its declarative nature. Throughout the examples in the following sections, I will illustrate both of these aspects.

## Source Document

The following sections use the document shown in Listing 11.2, an XML rendering of some of the elements of a graphic novel. In Chapter 10, we used the C++ implementations of XPath and XPointer APIs directly to create a browsing application for documents of this type. In this chapter, we will instead use XSLT as a higher-level transformation language, which we will interpret using C++ modules.

Listing 11.2 **Graphic Novel**

```xml
<?xml version="1.0" encoding="iso-8859-1" ?>
<graphicNovel>
  <title>V for Vendetta</title>
  <by role="co-author">Alan Moore</by>
  <by role="publisher">D.C. Comics</by>
```

*continues*

Listing 11.2   **Continued**

```xml
<by role="co-author">David Lloyd</by>
<date year="1982"/>
<characters>
  <character id="V">
    <name xml:lang="en">V</name>
    <description>The masked Guy-Fawkes-like character, master mind and
    perpetrator of the Vendetta for individual freedom.</description>
  </character>
  <character id="leader">
    <name xml:lang="en">Adam Susan (The Leader)</name>
    <description>Fascist leader of post-war England.</description>
  </character>
  <character id="justice">
    <name xml:lang="en">Madam Justice (Statue)</name>
    <description>Statue of Justice, used in a monologue
    by V, in chapter 5, as if having a voice of her own -V simulating a
    woman's voice, answering his questions-</description>
  </character>
</characters>
<!-- Other chapters here... -->
<chapter number="5">
  <title>Versions</title>
  <frame>
    <description>Black Title Frame</description>
    <img src="title.jpg"/>
  </frame>
  <frame>
    <description>Voice-off monologue in the car</description>
    <img src="car1.jpg"/>
    <speech>
    <line speaker="leader">My name is Adam Susan, I am the Leader.</line>
    <line speaker="leader">Leader of the lost, ruler of the ruins.</line>
    <line speaker="leader">I am a man, like any other man.</line>
    </speech>
  </frame>
  <!-- Rest of the leader's monologue to FAITH, praising fascism and
      his self-dubbed unworthy love.
    -->
  <frame>
    <description>Start of V's simulated dialog with Madam Justice (a statue)
    </description>
    <img src="justiceFromBelow1.jpg"/>
    <speech>
```

```
    <line speaker="V">Hello, dear lady</line>
    <line speaker="V">A lovely evening, is it not?</line>
  </speech>
</frame>
<!-- Rest of V's monologue to Justice, accusing her of betraying his love
     and driving him to the arms of a new lover: anarchy.
  -->
<frame>
  <description>Final part of V and Justice's "dialog". V is about to leave.
  </description>
  <img src="vLeaving.jpg"/>
  <line annotation="voice simulated by V" speaker="justice">Sob! choke!"
  wh-who is she, V?</line>
  <line speaker="justice">What is her NAME?</line>
  <line speaker="V">Her name is ANARCHY. And she has taught me more
    as a mistress than you ever did!
    </line>

    <!-- next line originally in another frame. abbreviated for space
    reasons -->
    <line speaker="V" xml:lang="en">She hast taught me that justice is
      meaningless without freedom.</line>
    </speech>
  </frame>
      <!-- rest of V monologue and destruction of the statue with a
      heart-shaped bomb -->
  </chapter>
</graphicNovel>
```

## Expected Result

The following sections introduce one by one the necessary concepts to create (from Listing 11.2) an XHTML file such as the one shown in Figure 11.2. The code for the final result shown in the figure (vashtml.xml on the CD) will become evident as we go through each section.

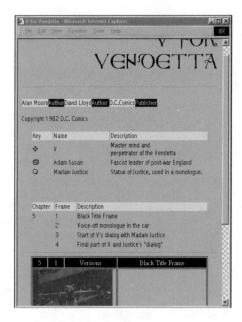

**Figure 11.2**    Final XHTML result.

## Inserting Data in the Result

There are two basic ways to insert data into the result. The first and most common is the inclusion of literal data. The second is the use of `xsl:value-of` in order to collect the string value of an XPath expression.

> **A Note About Completeness**
>
> Even though the summary of XSLT presented here is fairly complete, it naturally omits several instructions and options. For a comprehensive explanation of XSLT, please refer to either the specification (included on the CD) or a specialized book, such as my book *XSLT* (Sams Publishing).

The first mechanism is shown in all the HTML tags of Listing 11.3; these are simply copied to the output. The second mechanism is shown in the extraction of values such as the title. The `xsl:value-of` instruction has one attribute, `select`, which receives the XPath expression.

Relative XPaths such as `title` use the matched node (in this case, the one root element) as their context.

Listing 11.3  **Creating a Skeleton by Inserting Literals**

```xml
<?xml version="1.0"?>
<xsl:stylesheet xmlns:xsl="http://www.w3.org/1999/XSL/Transform">

  <xsl:template match="/graphicNovel">
    <html>        <!-- literal -->
      <head>      <!-- literal -->
        <title>  <!-- literal -->
            <xsl:value-of select="title"/>  <!-- XSLT instruction -->
        </title>
      </head>
      <body bgcolor="#C0C0C0">
      <p align="right">
        <font size="7" face="Anglo-Saxon Caps">
        <xsl:value-of select="title"/>
      </font>
      </p>
      <hr/>
          <!-- XXX : we will fill in here the rest of the content -->
      </body>
    </html>
  </xsl:template>

</xsl:stylesheet>
```

### Running an XSLT Processor

There are two basic ways to run XSLT processors. The first is the command line. The syntax for the Xalan processor is simply

```
xalan -IN <xml source> -XSL <xslt stylesheet>
```

The latest version of Xalan can be downloaded from www.apache.org. The CD contains version 1.1.

The second way to run an XSLT processor is by using a visual front end to it. XML editors such as XMLSpy (www.xmlspy.com) include such front ends. Later in this chapter, we will create a visual front end to Xalan so that you can use the Send To menu in Windows Explorer to invoke the processor.

## Flow of Control

By adding new templates, we begin constructing the rest of the content. For example, the revised version of our stylesheet, shown in Listing 11.4, contains a rule for by elements.

Listing 11.4 **Adding the *by* Template**

```
<?xml version="1.0"?>
<xsl:stylesheet xmlns:xsl="http://www.w3.org/1999/XSL/Transform">

  <xsl:template match="/graphicNovel">
   <!-- same as in Listing 11.3 -->
  </xsl:template>

  <xsl:template match="by">
    <font face="Abadi MT Condensed" size="3">
        <span style="background-color: #FFFF00">
            <xsl:value-of select="."/>
        </span>
        <span style="background-color: #000000
                      foreground-color: #FFFF00">
            <xsl:value-of select="@role"/>
        </span>
    </font>
  </xsl:template>


</xsl:stylesheet>
```

Even though there is a rule for managing by elements, if you run Listing 11.4 against Listing 11.2 (xalan -IN v.xml -XSL gn2html-02.xsl), you will get only the results shown in Listing 11.5 (the by elements are never processed).

Listing 11.5 **The Result of Running Listing 11.4 Against Listing 11.2**

```
<html>
<head>
<title>V for Vendetta</title>
</head>
<body bgcolor="#C0C0C0">
</body>
</html>
```

The problem is that nothing inside the rule for /graphicNovel instructs the XSLT tool to continue processing the children of the current node. In order to remedy the situation, we include the instruction xsl:apply-templates at the point where we want the parser to process other nodes. xsl:apply-templates has an optional attribute, select, which receives an XPath expression for the nodes to be processed. If no value for select is given, the children of the current node are assumed. Listing 11.6 shows the necessary changes in the /graphicNovel template.

Listing 11.6 **Using** *apply-templates*

```
<xsl:template match="/graphicNovel">
  <html>          <!-- literal -->
    <head>        <!-- literal -->
      <title> <!-- literal -->
          <xsl:value-of select="title"/>  <!-- XSLT instruction -->
      </title>
    </head>
    <body bgcolor="#C0C0C0">
    <p align="right">
      <font size="7" face="Anglo-Saxon Caps">
      <xsl:value-of select="title"/>
    </font>
    </p>
    <hr/>
    <xsl:apply-templates select="by"/>
      <!-- add other xsl:apply-templates here as needed -->
    </body>
  </html>
</xsl:template>
```

## Conditionals

Conditionals in XSLT are created using the xsl:if instruction. xsl:if has only one attribute: test, which is an XPath that gets evaluated to a boolean value. Using xsl:if and the expressions presented in Chapter 10, you can create templates such as those shown in Listing 11.7, where only the first frame of each chapter gets an entry in the chapter number column (this produces the second table in Figure 11.2).

Listing 11.7 **Using Conditionals**

```
  <!-- this template generates a table row (tr) for each frame -->
<xsl:template match="frame">
  <tr>
    <td width="13%">
      <xsl:if test="position() = 1">
        <xsl:value-of select="../@number"/> <!-- chapter number -->
      </xsl:if>
    </td>
    <td width="12%">
      <xsl:value-of select="position()"/>
    </td>
    <td width="75%">
      <xsl:value-of select="description"/>
    </td>
  </tr>
</xsl:template>
```

Naturally, to produce the correct results, this template must be instantiated inside a table. Listing 11.8 shows the necessary additions to the /graphicNovel template.

Listing 11.8   **The Surrounding Table for the Frame Template**

```
<xsl:template match="/graphicNovel">
    <!-- all the rest as in previous listings -->
    <hr/>
    <xsl:apply-templates select="by"/>
        <center>
      <table border="0" width="90%">
        <tr>
          <td>Chapter</td> <td>Frame</td><td>Description</td>
          </tr>

          <!-- now, for each frame add a row -->

          <xsl:apply-templates select="chapter/frame"/>

      </table>
        </center>
    </body>
    <!-- all the rest as in previous listings -->
</xsl:template>
```

## Loops

Because XSLT is a declarative language with no modifiable variables, loops in XSLT are mostly restricted to iterations through collections of nodes (not arbitrary whiles). Listing 11.9 shows how to iterate through all the frames again to produce a table for each one with the image and the lines of each character involved in the scene.

Listing 11.9   **An Addition to /graphicNovel Using Loops**

```
<xsl:template match="/graphicNovel">
  <html>
   <!-- All the rest as in previous listings -->
      <table border="1" width="90%" bordercolor="#000000">

        <xsl:for-each select="chapter/frame">
        <tr>
         <td width="9%" bgcolor="#000000" align="center">
           <font color="#FFFFFF">
             <xsl:value-of select="../@number"/> <!-- chapter number -->
           </font>
         </td>
         <td width="9%" bgcolor="#000000" align="center">
           <font color="#FFFFFF">
```

```
                    <xsl:value-of select="position()"/>
                  </font>
              </td>
              <td width="30%" bgcolor="#000000" align="center">
                <font color="#FFFFFF">
                  <xsl:value-of select="../title"/> <!-- chapter title -->
                </font>
              </td>
              <td width="52%" bgcolor="#000000" align="center">
                <font color="#FFFFFF">
                  <xsl:value-of select="description"/>
                </font>
              </td>
          </tr>
          <tr>
              <td width="48%" colspan="3">
                <xsl:copy-of select="img"/>
              </td>
              <td width="52%" valign="top">
                <xsl:for-each select="speech/line">
                  <!-- exercise: use if to change the icon according with
                        each character -->
                  <font face="Wingdings">a</font>
                  <font face="Abadi MT Condensed">
                   <xsl:value-of select="."/>
                  </font><br/>
                </xsl:for-each>
              </td>
          </tr>
      </xsl:for-each>
    </table>
    </center>
  </body>
</html>
</xsl:template>
```

This concludes our overview of the most important instructions of XSLT. Follow the extra resources mentioned in the sidebar titled, "A Note About Completeness," for more information about XSLT as a language (named templates, recursion, and so on). In the remainder of this chapter, you will see the implementation options for embedding XSLT processors in C++ programs and the development of two applications around them.

# XSLT in C++

All the major C++ XML toolkits—Oracle, Microsoft, Xalan, and Unicorn—currently include XSLT 1.0 support. They all expose a similar interface—namely, a high-level interface for filename-oriented transformation (basically, an API call that resembles a call to the command line) and a low-level interface that permits the fine adjustment of configuration options for a particular transformation.

The following examples use the Xalan toolkit (part of the Apache project), because it illustrates all the capabilities in a free and open-source implementation, and because it supports the compilation of stylesheets.

## "Low-Level" API

The "low-level" API for XSLT transformations allows the use of arbitrary sources (XML InputSources were used in Chapter 10 when processing XPath expressions) for the transformation, but it imposes a bigger setup process. However, the setup process is always similar and can easily be copied and adapted from the code in this chapter and the examples in the Xalan distribution.

The code in Listing 11.10, shown in a moment, illustrates the following nine steps to follow each time you embed a Xalan processor in your application:

1. Include Xerces headers

2. Initialization

    2.1. Initialize Xerces

    2.2. Initialize the Xalan XSLT

3. Create sources and support and bind them together

4. Create processor

5. Create execution contexts (Xalan-specific)

6. Create input sources

7. Define output

8. Invoke process

9. Terminate Xerces

Before seeing these nine steps in code, let's see the higher-level API that reduces them to a simpler, friendlier, cleaner application.

## "High-Level" API

The higher-level API in Xerces takes the form of the XalanTransformer object, which receives the DOM trees or filenames of the XML to transform and the XSL stylesheet in one method (transform), returning the result in an out parameter (see Listing 11.10).

Listing 11.10    **Using *XalanTransformer***

```
// [1] Initialize
#include <util/PlatformUtils.hpp>
#include <XalanTransformer/XalanTransformer.hpp>
```

```
void main() {
// [2] Initialize
XMLPlatformUtils::Initialize();
XalanTransformer::initialize();

// [3 - 6]  Implicit when using XalanTransformer
XalanTransformer theXalanTransformer;

// [8] Invoke transfomer
const char* xmlIn    = "in.xml";
const char* xslSheet = "transformation.xsl";
const char* xmlOut   = "out.xml";
int theResult = 0;
theResult =  xaltransform.transform(xmlIn,xslSheet,xmlOut);

// [9] Terminate XalanTransformer and Xerces
XalanTransformer::Terminate();
XMLPlatformUtils::Terminate();
}
```

For more options when invoking `XalanTransformer`, see the Xalan documentation on the CD or go to `http://xml.apache.org/xalan-c/usagepatterns.html`.

### A Note About Performance

XSLT is great for quick and easy development. Its syntax is quite simple, and you can get simple and medium-sized stylesheets in minutes. However, you must keep in mind that SAX (and even DOM) programs with equivalent functionality are bound to be significantly faster and less memory-hungry than any XSLT stylesheet.

Some performance-oriented, heavy-load systems might use XSLT for prototyping and direct SAX for the actual implementation.

## Sample Application: vxslt

The following MFC application creates a program that implements the nine steps just discussed in order to allow the easy Windows invocation of XSLT transformations.

The program's behavior is as follows: When invoked with the name of a file that has an .xsl extension, the program adds it to a list of recent stylesheets. When invoked with a file that has an .xml extension, it displays a window so that the user can choose which stylesheet to apply and the name of the output file.

Figure 11.3 shows the application at work, when invoked through the Send To menu in Windows Explorer.

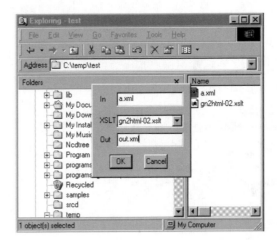

**Figure 11.3**   vxslt.

Listing 11.11 shows the XSLT-relevant part of the application, when the names for the input, XSLT, and output have been collected and the nine steps must be applied.

Listing 11.11   **XSLT Parts of vxslt**

```
// [1] Includes

#include <util/PlatformUtils.hpp>
#include <PlatformSupport/DOMStringHelper.hpp>
#include <DOMSupport/DOMSupportDefault.hpp>
// other includes in the .h
#include <XalanSourceTree/XalanSourceTreeDOMSupport.hpp>
#include <XalanSourceTree/XalanSourceTreeParserLiaison.hpp>

//code based in simpleTransfomr.cpp by apache project
#include "vxslt.h" //using namespace std;

void vxslt::transform(char *in, char *xslt, char*out)
{
    try
    {
      // [2.1] Initialize Xerces
      XMLPlatformUtils::Initialize();

      {
      // [2.2] Initialize the Xalan XSLT
      XSLTInit init; //just declaring it is enough

      // [3] Create sources and support and bind them together
      XalanSourceTreeDOMSupport       domSupport;
      XalanSourceTreeParserLiaison    parserLiasion(domSupport);
```

```
      domSupport.setParserLiaison(&parserLiasion);

      XSLTProcessorEnvSupportDefault    processorEnvSupport;
      XObjectFactoryDefault             xobjectFactory;
      XPathFactoryDefault               xpathFactory;


        // [4] Create processor
      XSLTEngineImpl   processor(parserLiasion,
                       processorEnvSupport,
                       domSupport,
                       xobjectFactory,
                       xpathFactory);

      processorEnvSupport.setProcessor(&processor);

      // [5] Create execution contexts (Xalan-specific)
      StylesheetConstructionContextDefault
         constContext(processor,processorEnvSupport,
                      xpathFactory);

      StylesheetExecutionContextDefault
          exContext(processor,processorEnvSupport,
                    domSupport,xobjectFactory);

      // [6] Create input sources
      const XalanDOMString xmlfn(in);
      const XalanDOMString xslfn(xslt);

      XSLTInputSource   inputSource(c_wstr(xmlfn));
      XSLTInputSource   ssSource(c_wstr(xslfn));

      // [7] Define output
      const XalanDOMString   outfn(out);
      XSLTResultTarget       rTarget(outfn);

      // [8] Invoke process
      processor.process(inputSource,
                        ssSource,
                        rTarget,
                        constContext,
                        exContext);
    }
    // [9] Terminate Xerces
    XMLPlatformUtils::Terminate();
  }
  catch(...)
  {
    //exception handling here
  }
 }
}
```

## More Examples

XSLT is one of the most widely applicable XML technologies. I don't have enough space to show you all the examples I could. The custom-made examples not included here for space reasons (as well as those in the Xalan toolkit)can be found on the CD and on the Web site (`http://www.cppxml.com`). You are encouraged to read them and reuse them.

One particularly interesting example is the extended Apache XSLT module, which allows the construction of ultrafast custom-made modules for Apache based on pre-compiled XSLT stylesheets. The development of this code involves a good deal of Apache knowledge (which would derail you from your C++ XML study) and thus has been included only as an extra application tutorial on the Web site (`http://www.cppxml.com`).

### Other Transformation Languages: DSSSL

XSLT is not the only transformation language that has good C++ support.

The Document Style Semantics and Specification Language (DSSSL) is a powerful pre-XML language (it was released in 1996, and it works on top of SGML) that can be used for many of the transformation tasks that XSLT can do.

One interesting feature of DSSSL is the ability of its processors to output directly to an intermediate format that can be processed into RTF, TeX, or HTML.

The discussion of DSSSL and its most important C++ implementation, OpenJade, falls outside the scope of this book, because it is mainly an SGML technology. However, in case you are interested, several resources, including OpenJade's binaries and source code, have been included on the CD, in this chapter's extras directory.

# Summary

XSLT is a powerful alternative to direct SAX or DOM manipulation. It provides a template-based language that allows the transformation of XML documents by means of simple XSLT instructions and literal XML elements. This chapter has shown the syntax and semantics of XSLT, as well as how to embed an XSLT processor in a C++ application. The code presented can easily be reused, at either a code or binary level, and it provides a quick jump-start for the development of your own applications, from lightning-fast server-side transformation of documents to desktop applets.

# 12

# Toolkit Features and Implementation Frameworks

THE PREVIOUS CHAPTERS COVERED THE MAIN COMPONENTS of the XML family individually, from the point of view of C++ application development. In order to do so, we have concentrated on the technology at hand (SAX, DOM, XPath, XPointer, XSLT), using different choices for the toolkits and libraries in which the examples were implemented.

This chapter reverts the focus and concentrates on the toolkits we have been using and shows ways to modularize common activities with them. In this chapter, you analyze and build reusable code frameworks to improve your experience with each library.

This chapter is organized by toolkit/library (MSXML, Xerces, Xalan), briefly listing for each one its level of support for each XML technology and providing one or more implementation frameworks for improving their use in common C++ development cases.

### About the Toolkit Information

From the point of view of toolkit listing, this chapter is mainly a quick-lookup reference, and a good portion of its contents can be found throughout this book. If you are not particularly interested in creating templates for future projects at this time, you can safely consider skimming through this chapter. Be sure, however, to see the frameworks added here, because they might provide you with time saving techniques in your own projects.

# Xerces/Xalan

Xerces and Xalan are the key components of the Apache XML Project (http://
xml.apache.org). Xerces provides the C++ implementations for the key APIs for
XML processing (SAX versions 1.0 and 2.0 and DOM Level 2.0), as well as a number
of interesting features such as beta support for XML Schema. Xalan provides an XSLT
implementation (along with all the classes for XPath and XPointer, as used in Chapter
10, "XPath and XPointer in C++").

## Platforms and License

Xerces (currently version 1.4) has precompiled distributions for the following
platforms:

- Win32
- Red Hat Linux (6.1, egcs-2.91.66, and glibc-2.1.2-11)
- AIX 4.3
- HP-UX 11
- Solaris 2.6

### xml4c and Xerces

It is not uncommon to hear questions about the relationship between IBM's xml4c toolkit and Xerces.
The relationship is simple: xml4c has evolved into Xerces, thanks to the donation of the base code
from IBM to the Apache project. xml4c, however, is still available from the alphaworks site
(http://alphaworks.ibm.com).

If you have developed applications for xml4c, you might be interested in migrating to Xerces.
The official Xerces documentation includes a good page on the subject:
http://xml.apache.org/xerces-c/migrate.html.

Xalan (currently version 1.4) is available for the following platforms:

- Win32
- Red Hat Linux (6.1 and up)
- AIX 4.3
- HP-UX 11
- Solaris 2.6

Xerces and Xalan are distributed under the Apache Software license (see any Xerces-
based example on the CD for the complete text). This is a fairly liberal license that
allows the use, redistribution, and modification of the toolkits as long as reasonable
license redistribution is kept and the name "Apache" is reasonably used. The quality of
the implementation (portability, robustness, coverage) and the fact that it is open
source, free, and is under the Apache license are why this book tends to favor Xerces
C++ and Xalan C++ as its most-used toolkits.

## Technologies Supported

The following is a list of XML technologies supported by Xerces and Xalan. (Xalan, even though it is distributed separately, relies heavily on Xerces and is considered here in conjunction with it.)

- SAX 1.0 (see Chapter 4, "SAX C++," and Chapter 8, "Advanced C++ Aspects of SAX and DOM").
- SAX 2.0 (see Chapter 5, "SAX C++ 2.0 and Advanced Techniques," and Chapter 8). Even though there is no SAX C++ standardization yet, Xerces provides a complete implementation that complies in functionality and design spirit with the Java SAX 2.0 standard.
- DOM 1.0 (see Chapter 6, "DOM Level 2.0," and Chapter 8). Uses a reference-count library that greatly simplifies memory management.
- DOM 2.0 (see Chapter 7, "Advanced C++ DOM Manipulation," and Chapter 8).
- XPath and XPointer (see Chapters 8 and 10).
- XSLT (see Chapter 11, "XSLT Transformations").

## Where to Obtain It

Xerces and Xalan C++ for all the platforms just mentioned are provided on the CD, in both binary and source forms. The latest versions can always be obtained from `http://xml.apache.org`.

## What Is a Framework?

The word "framework" is used here in the general software engineering sense of a "prefabricated software building block that programmers can use, extend, or customize for specific computing solutions." Such prefabricated pieces of software can take a myriad of forms, including programming templates, visual components, and programming wizards. A particular framework can be classified according to the intended nature of the system that results from its use (application, domain, support) and/or according to the type of programming the user must perform to extend it (composition versus inheritance).

The frameworks in this chapter take the form of code templates and code wizards, both resulting in derived classes for general-purpose XML manipulation.

## XMLableFR (XMLable Framework)

The XMLable pattern defines the structure of a general and simple XML reading mechanism for arbitrary classes. The structure, shown in Figure 12.1, could be described as follows: for each class you want to read from XML ("product"), you define a partner "builder" class associated with it. This builder class works on behalf of a "client" who will ultimately use the product.

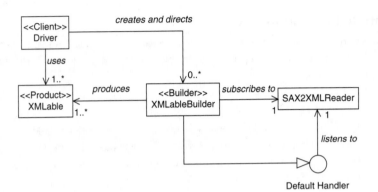

**Figure 12.1**   XMLable pattern.

It is the responsibility of the user to define the particular implementation of the builder as a SAX handler. (Unlike in "marshaling" products, XMLable has no preconceived mapping between data members and their XML representation.)

XMLable is a design pattern (see my original 1999 article introducing XMLable in Chapter 8's extras directory on the CD), but it is common and concise enough to be coded as a small framework.

The input of the XMLable framework is the name of the product class, and its output is the skeleton for the builder, plus a test client (who receives the name of the file in the command line).

XMLableFR can be executed either by calling the batch file XMLable (Windows) or directly through the Perl script XMLableFR.pl:

```
perl  XMLableFR.pl [name of the product class] [-NOCLIENT]
```

**Perl**

In order to generate files using XMLableFR, you need Perl 5 or higher.

Perl can be downloaded from one of the following:

- http://www.activestate.com (Windows)

- http://www.perl.com

If you are running any modern UNIX flavor (such as Linux), chances are you already have this tool installed.

## XMLableFR Example

Listings 12.1 and 12.2 present the result of running XMLableFR with the following command:

```
perl XMLableFR.pl Stats
```

The first file is StatsBuilder.h, the interface for the class, which reads an XML file and creates a Stats object from it.

Listing 12.1 **StatsBuilder.h**

```
//Comments omitted for space reasons. See file on the CD.

#include "Stats.h"

class StatsBuilder   : public DefaultHandler
{
 public:

   StatsBuilder(SAX2XMLReader &parser);
   StatsBuilder();

   ~StatsBuilder();

   Stats *build(const char* url);

   const long getDuration();

 private:
  SAX2XMLReader *mobjParser;
  Stats          *mobjProduct;
  long           mlngDuration;
  bool           mblnIndependent;
};


class StrX
{
  public :
    StrX(const XMLCh* const toTranscode)
    {
      fLocalForm = XMLString::transcode(toTranscode);
    }

  ~StrX()
    {
      delete [] fLocalForm;
    }

  const char* localForm() const
    {
      return fLocalForm;
    }

  private :
    char*   fLocalForm;
};
```

*continues*

Listing 12.1 **Continued**

```
inline ostream& operator<<(ostream& target, const StrX& toDump)
{
  target << toDump.localForm();
  return target;
}
```

The second file (Listing 12.2) is the implementation of the builder, a skeleton for a derivative of DefaultHandler. The logic of the reading will be provided by implementing the functions in which you have interest (see the list of SAX2 functions in Chapter 5).

Listing 12.2 **StatsBuilder.cpp**

```
//Again, comments elided for space reasons. See CD for commented code.
#include "StatsBuilder.h"

StatsBuilder::StatsBuilder(SAX2XMLReader &parser)
{
  mblnIndependent = false;
  mobjParser = &parser;
  mobjProduct = NULL;
}

StatsBuilder::StatsBuilder()
{
  mblnIndependent = true;
  mobjProduct = NULL;
  // Initialize the XML4C2 system
  try
  {
    XMLPlatformUtils::Initialize();
  }

  catch (const XMLException& toCatch)
  {
    cerr << "\nError during initialization! Message:\n"
         << StrX(toCatch.getMessage()) << endl;
    throw(toCatch);
  }

  mobjParser = XMLReaderFactory::createXMLReader();
  mobjParser->setFeature(
            XMLString::transcode("http://xml.org/sax/features/validation"),
        true);
  mobjParser->setFeature(
```

```
XMLString::transcode("http://apache.org/xml/features/validation/dynamic"),
      true);

  mobjParser->setContentHandler(this);
  mobjParser->setErrorHandler(this);
  // If your builder implements any other type of handler (uncommon),
  // register it here.
}


StatsBuilder::~StatsBuilder()
{
  if(mblnIndependent)
    XMLPlatformUtils::Terminate();
}

Stats *StatsBuilder::build(const char* file)
{
  try
  {
    const unsigned long startMillis = XMLPlatformUtils::getCurrentMillis();
    mobjParser->parse(file);
    const unsigned long endMillis = XMLPlatformUtils::getCurrentMillis();
    mlngDuration = endMillis - startMillis;
  }

  catch (const XMLException& e)
  {
    cerr << "\nError during parsing " << endl;
    if(mblnIndependent)
      XMLPlatformUtils::Terminate();
    throw(e);
  }

  catch (...)
  {
    cerr << "\nUnexpected exception during parsing '" << endl;
    if(mblnIndependent)
      XMLPlatformUtils::Terminate();
    return NULL;
  }

  return mobjProduct;
}

Stats *StatsBuilder::build(const vector<char>)
{
  return NULL;
}
```

*continues*

Listing 12.2 **Continued**

```
const long StatsBuilder::getDuration()
{
  return mlngDuration;
}

// *Apache license here*
```

Finally, the Test program is generated, as shown in Listing 12.3.

Listing 12.3 **StatsTestDriver.cpp**

```
#include "StatsBuilder.h"

void usage()
{
    cout << "\nUsage:\n"
            "     <XML file>\n\n"
            "This program tests the XML Builder for creating Stats "
            "instances.\n\n";
}

int main(int argc, char* argv[])
{
  if (argc < 2)
  {
    usage();
    return 1;
  }

  StatsBuilder builder;
  Stats *product = builder.build(argv[1]);

  cout << product;

  return 0;
} //that's all!
```

In order to implement the logic of the builder, we implement a brief Stats class, as shown in Listing 12.4.

Listing 12.4 **Declaring the Stats Class**

```
#include <iostream>

class Stats
{
```

```
public:
      Stats();
      int charCount;
};

inline Stats::Stats() : charCount(0) {}

inline ostream& operator<<(ostream& s,Stats const *m)
{
      return s << m->charCount << "\n";
}
```

Then we make two alterations to the builder so that it constructs our product correctly: Change the constructor so that instead of initializing mobjProduct to NULL, it calls the Stats() constructor, and add a handler for characters, as shown here:

```
void StatsBuilder::characters(const    XMLCh* const    chars,
                              const unsigned int    length)
{
  mobjProduct->charCount+=length;
}
```

And that is all. The following is the output of running the test program (StatsTestDriver test.xml):

```
1257 characters in 0 milliseconds (and 5 minutes of code).
```

Naturally, in order to run the program, you must compile it with the Xerces include files and link it with the Xerces library. The test directory under XMLableFR provides a sample project doing just that, plus the executable.

### Small Speed Anecdote

Without being a benchmark, the result of running StatsTestDriver (a program that took 5 minutes to write) versus its Java equivalent is interesting. For the same 154,489-character file, the debug version (no particular optimization) of StatsTestDriver took 99 milliseconds on my laptop, and the Java equivalent took 490.

## Other Highly Reusable Xerces/Xalan Software

In previous chapters, we created or used other highly reusable pieces of software based on Xerces and Xalan. They are listed here, because they are implementations that can be considered (or extended into) frameworks similar to the one we just developed:

- XSLT as an Apache module (see Chapter 11)
- DSSSL as a reusable C++ component (see Chapter 11)
- XPath wrapper (see Chapter 10)

- DOM C++ visitors (see Chapters 7 and 8)
- Postgres table2xml (see Chapter 15, "XML and Databases with C++ (ODBC and DAO)")

# MSXML

Microsoft's XML Toolkit (called MSXML or MSXML3 because of its current version), despite its proprietary nature, is one of the fastest, more robust, and more complete XML tools available. Its latest incarnation (currently version 3) supports every major core XML technology and fixes the main characteristics that could have given it a bad reputation in the past—namely, its nonconformance to the latest XSLT standard and the use of its own XSL dialect.

### MSXML and MSXML3

The names MSXML, MSXML3, and some capitalization variations such as msxml3 are common across the literature and Web sites. The name of the product is MSXML, and its current version is 3. The names can be used interchangeably.

As we explored key technologies in past chapters, I tried to keep the amount of MSXML3 code somewhat low (even though some MSXML3 versions of the programs were given) so that we could concentrate on the technologies and the pure C++ aspects of them, as opposed to the Windows-specific and COM+ issues that msxml3 brings along. All the principles shown, however, are valid and portable to Xerces (and libxml2 or any other toolkit for that matter).

In case you need to sacrifice the portability and openness of Xerces/Xalan for the sake of an MSXML feature, I have included pointers to several Microsoft tables and documents with the APIs and conventions of their product in this chapter's extras directory on the CD.

## Platforms and License

MSXML3 is available under the different Win32 platforms (95, 98, NT, 2000, Me, and XP). MSXML3 is especially oriented toward COM, but this book does not expect any particular COM knowledge, so it isolates the COM issues as much as possible, leaving these and other Windows-specific explanations to other books. That being said, if you are a COM programmer, you will still find the techniques and examples in this chapter useful, and you will be able to apply them to your COM components. Also, several pointers to COM-specific examples are provided in this chapter's extras directory on the CD.

The MSXML3 Software Development Kit is distributed under the Microsoft EULA (End User License Agreement), which means you must agree to certain conditions regarding liability and format when distributing the MSXML package. In all fairness (and I'm not much of a Microsoft advocate), these restrictions are considerably more reasonable than those imposed by other commercial companies.

I will end this legal-details thread by merely referring you to the MSXML site, where you can find precise license information: `http://msdn.microsoft.com/xml/default.asp`.

## Technologies Supported

The following is the list of XML technologies supported by MSXML3:

- SAX 1.0 (see Chapters 4 and 8)
- SAX 2.0 (see Chapters 5 and 8)
- DOM 1.0 (see Chapters 6 and 8)
- DOM 2.0 (see Chapters 7 and 8)
- XPath and XPointer (see Chapter 10)
- XSLT (see Chapter 11)

The functionality, techniques, and rationale of MSXML3's implementation of each of these technologies are very similar to that of Xerces. However, it maintains the naming, calling, and code structure conventions of Microsoft's COM programming (for example, all the SAX interface names are preceded by a capital I, as in `IContentHandler`). See the API tables and examples on the CD for more on this subject.

## Where to Obtain It

The MSXML3 SDK is not included on the CD. It can be downloaded from `http://msdn.microsoft.com/xml/default.asp`.

## Reusable Design and Code: DOM Walkers

As seen in Chapters 7 and 8, one of the main techniques for DOM programming is the use of visitors (also known as *walkers*), which iterate through the document as a collection of DOM nodes, performing a particular manipulation.

Figure 12.2 shows the structure of our `Walker` classes, as implemented in the following examples.

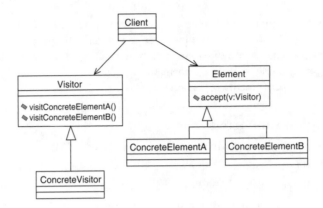

**Figure 12.2** DOMWalker class diagram.

Most of the aspects of walkers are instances of reusable design as much as they are of reusable code. After all, a DOM walker will always perform the following implementable actions:

1. Check the current node for its type, and decide what to do accordingly.

2. Decide whether it wants to continue exploring the tree.

3. Decide and implement how to explore the tree (implement a particular form of traversal: preorder, inorder, postorder, and so on).

Also, each walker (I use the terms walker and visitor interchangeably in this section) has a client, supplying the DOM node from which the traversal begins. This client must be implemented repeatedly every time a walker is constructed, in order to do unit tests.

By this time, you no doubt have guessed the nature of our next framework: the automatic creation of DOM walkers using MSXML3.

### A Particular Walker: BlockWorldRenderer

Before jumping into the creation of the framework (implemented as a Visual Studio Project Wizard), let's look at an example of the type of application we want to generate.

Listing 12.5 shows the DTD for defining 3D figures in a world made of blocks. A block is identified by its position (three integers, one for each coordinate) and color. Groups of blocks can be rotated arbitrarily, encapsulating them in a rotation element.

Our 3D worlds may also have additional information regarding the model's author, and other data that will be ignored by the rendering engine (a DOM walker we will create named BlockWorldRenderer).

Listing 12.5  **BlockWorld.dtd**

```
<!ELEMENT blockworld (head?,world)>
<!ELEMENT head        (author?,name,version?)>
<!ELEMENT author      (#PCDATA)>
<!ELEMENT name        (#PCDATA)>
<!ELEMENT version     EMPTY>
<!ATTLIST version
          release     CDATA       #REQUIRED
          build       CDATA       #REQUIRED>

<!ELEMENT world       (rotation¦block)*>

<!ENTITY % color      "white¦red¦blue¦green¦purple¦black">

<!ELEMENT block       EMPTY>
<!ATTLIST block
          x           CDATA       #REQUIRED
          y           CDATA       #REQUIRED
          z           CDATA       #REQUIRED
          color       (%color;)   #REQUIRED>

<!ELEMENT rotation    (rotation¦block)*>
<!ATTLIST rotation
          angle       CDATA       #REQUIRED
          axis        (x¦y¦z)     #REQUIRED>
```

A simple blockworld, a 3D cross, is defined as shown in Listing 12.6 using an XML document conformant with Listing 12.5.

Listing 12.6  **3DCross.xml**

```
<?xml version="1.0"?>
<!DOCTYPE blockworld SYSTEM "blockworld.dtd">
<blockworld>
  <head>
    <name>A 3D Cross</name>
    <version release="1" build="0"/>
  </head>
  <world>
    <block x="0" y="1" z="0" color="red"/>
    <block x="0" y="0" z="0" color="red"/>
    <block x="0" y="-1" z="0" color="red"/>
    <block x="1" y="0" z="0" color="red"/>
    <block x="-1" y="0" z="0" color="red"/>
    <block x="0" y="0" z="-1" color="red"/>
    <block x="0" y="0" z="1" color="red"/>
  </world>
</blockworld>
```

The result of processing the preceding file must be the display of the 3D blocks in a screen. For this purpose, we use OpenGL, the industry library standard for 3D graphics. We will program a walker that goes through the DOM tree, generating the appropriate OpenGL function calls as it encounters block elements.

Figure 12.3 shows the final result to achieve (with the exception that in the program the cross is constantly rotating).

**Figure 12.3** BlockWorld C++ running.

### The *BlockWorldDOMWalker* Class

The `BlockWorldDOMWalker` class is a typical visitor that goes over a collection of nodes by analyzing them one at a time and then calling itself recursively for each child node.

Listing 12.7 shows the implementation of the class. Note how a helper class has been defined and is used to read the file from disk into an `IXMLDOMNodePtr` (that is, an MSXML3 pointer to a DOM node). A simple inspection reveals that the structure and principles of MSXML3 DOM manipulation are the same as those used previously with Xerces, but some names vary. In order to get familiar with the naming conventions, I recommend that you read the help file associated with MSXML3 (it gets installed under \Program Files\Microsoft XML Parser SDK\docs\xmlsdk20.chm).

Listing 12.7 **BlockWorldWalker**

```
include "BlockWorldXMLWalker.h"

/**
    recursive method used to navigate the tree
 */
```

```
void BlockWorldXMLWalker::visit(IXMLDOMNodePtr n)
{
      if(n->nodeType == NODE_ELEMENT)
      {
            if(!strcmp(n->nodeName,"block"))
            {
                  // Get the values for each coordinate
                  IXMLDOMNodePtr x,y,z,strColor;
                  color cubeColor = black;
                  n->attributes->get_item(0,&x);
                  n->attributes->get_item(1,&y);
                  n->attributes->get_item(2,&z);
                  n->attributes->get_item(3,&strColor);
                  if(!strcmp(strColor->text,"red"))
                        cubeColor = red;
                  if(!strcmp(strColor->text,"white"))
                        cubeColor = white;
                  if(!strcmp(strColor->text,"green"))
                        cubeColor = green;
                  if(!strcmp(strColor->text,"blue"))
                        cubeColor = blue;
                  if(!strcmp(strColor->text,"purple"))
                        cubeColor = purple;
                  putCube((int)atoi(x->text), //x, y, and z are bstrs.
                                    // They are converted to ints
                        (int)atoi(y->text),
                            (int)atoi(z->text),
                            cubeColor);
                  return; // No interest in looking at the
                        // children of a block (none!)
            }

            else if(!strcmp(n->nodeName,"rotation"))
            {
                  // Get the values for each coordinate
                  IXMLDOMNodePtr axis,angle;
                  n->attributes->get_item(0,&angle);
                  n->attributes->get_item(1,&axis);
                  if(!strcmp(axis->text,"x"))
                      glRotatef((int)atoi(angle->text), 1.0f,
                                0.0f, 0.0f);
                  else if(!strcmp(axis->text,"y"))
                      glRotatef((int)atoi(angle->text),
                                0.0f, 1.0f, 0.0f);
                  else
                      glRotatef((int)atoi(angle->text),
                                0.0f, 0.0f, 0.0f);

                  // Now traverse the rest of the tree,
                  // looking for more nodes or rotations
```

*continues*

Listing 12.7 **Continued**

```
                          for(int i = 0; i < n->childNodes->length ;i++)
                              visit(n->childNodes->item[i]);
                          // Now put us back where we started
                  if(!strcmp(axis->text,"x"))
                              glRotatef(-(int)atoi(angle->text),
                                        1.0f, 0.0f, 0.0f);
                          else if(!strcmp(axis->text,"y"))
                              glRotatef(-(int)atoi(angle->text),
                                        0.0f, 1.0f, 0.0f);
                          else
                              glRotatef(-(int)atoi(angle->text),
                                        0.0f, 0.0f, 0.0f);
                          return; // Already processed its children!
                  }
            }
      // Now traverse the rest of the tree, looking for more nodes or rotations
        for(int i = 0; i < n->childNodes->length ;i++)
              visit(n->childNodes->item[i]);
}

IXMLDOMNodePtr BlockWorldXMLWalker::Helper::readXMLFile(const char *name)
{
  try
  {
    IXMLDOMDocumentPtr docPtr;

    // init
    docPtr.CreateInstance("msxml2.domdocument");

    // load a document
    _variant_t varXml(name);
    _variant_t varOut((bool)TRUE);
    varOut = docPtr->load(varXml);
    if ((bool)varOut == FALSE)
      throw(0);
    return docPtr; // remember, a document Node is also a Node
  } catch(...)
  {
    MessageBox(NULL, "Exception occurred! Malformed or inexistent file",
               "Error", MB_OK);
  }
        return NULL;
}
```

Even though it is not necessary to know OpenGL to see the XML points of this example, Listing 12.8 shows the OpenGL code, just in case you are curious about it.

Listing 12.8 *putCube:* **OpenGL–Related Functions**

```
/**
   put a cube with color col in a particular point of the world(x,y,z)
   Included here for readability purposes
 */
void putCube(int x,int y,int z,enum color col)
{

  switch(col)
  {
  case black:
    glColor3f(BLACK);
    break;
  case red:
    glColor3f(RED);
    break;
  case blue:
    glColor3f(BLUE);
    break;
  case green:
    glColor3f(GREEN);
    break;
  case purple:
    glColor3f(PURPLE);
    break;
  default:
    glColor3f(WHITE);
    break;
  }

  glTranslatef((float)x*2,(float)y*2,(float)z*2);
  // Draw the sides of the cube
  glBegin(GL_QUAD_STRIP);
  glNormal3d(0.0, 0.0, -1.0); // Normal A
  glVertex3d(1, 1, -1);       // Vertex 1
  glVertex3d(1, -1, -1);      // Vertex 2
  glVertex3d(-1, 1, -1);      // Vertex 3
  glVertex3d(-1, -1, -1);     // Vertex 4
  glNormal3d(-1.0, 0.0, 0.0); // Normal B
  glVertex3d(-1, 1, 1);       // Vertex 5
  glVertex3d(-1, -1, 1);      // Vertex 6
  glNormal3d(0.0, 0.0, 1.0);  // Normal C
  glVertex3d(1, 1, 1);        // Vertex 7
  glVertex3d(1, -1, 1);       // Vertex 8
  glNormal3d(1.0, 0.0, 0.0);  // Normal D
  glVertex3d(1, 1, -1);       // Vertex 9
  glVertex3d(1, -1, -1);      // Vertex 10
  glEnd();

  // Draw the top and bottom of the cube
```

*continues*

Listing 12.8  **Continued**

```
glBegin(GL_QUADS);
glNormal3d(0.0, 1.0, 0.0);
glVertex3d(-1, -1, -1);
glVertex3d(1, -1, -1);
glVertex3d(1, -1, 1);
glVertex3d(-1, -1, 1);

glNormal3d(0.0, 1.0, 0.0);
glVertex3d(-1, 1, -1);
glVertex3d(1, 1, -1);
glVertex3d(1, 1, 1);
glVertex3d(-1, 1, 1);
glEnd();
glTranslatef((float)-x*2,(float)-y*2,(float)-z*2);


}
```

### The Visual Studio DOMWalkerWizard

Now that you have a clear idea of how DOM visitors are implemented with
MSXML3, you can factorize the programming portions common to all visitors so that
you can reuse them and concentrate on the DOM visitor logic instead of writing the
same XML-handling code repeatedly.

The previous framework (XMLableFR) was implemented with an open-source
UNIX system in mind (even though it is runnable and generates correct code for
Windows too). It is based on a free library, it has a command-line interface, it is written in Perl, and it makes no assumptions about your development environment. The
next framework, DOMWalkerWizard, is the other side of the coin: It assumes you are
using a commercial product (MSXML3) under Windows and that you are programming using Visual Studio. Both poles are valid, and chances are you have to develop in
both of them. I hope you find the broad mix of technologies useful.

### What to Factorize?

By inspecting the BlockWorld example, as well as the visitors introduced in Chapters
7 and 8, you can see the following common programming elements in all walkers:

- Decide how to traverse the tree (preorder, postorder, or inorder).
- Decide what types of nodes to take into consideration (for example, treat only
  elements).
- Sometimes create a helper class to read the DOM tree from an external source
  (generally a file).

Our task is to implement this common behavior in the most reusable way, congruent
with MSXML and the Visual Studio mechanisms.

## Implementing DOMWalkerWizard

Visual Studio provides the ability to create applications by using *wizards,* step-by-step dialogs that help create the skeleton of an application by means of simple user input. The following sections show how to implement a wizard for creating generic DOM walkers.

A custom application wizard is composed of three things:

- **Visual interface.** The dialogs in which the user makes his or her selections.
- **Templates.** The actual templates for the files on the generated project.
- **Configuration files.** Instruct Visual Studio about the template files and how they should be mapped to the generated project.

Let's inspect the implementation of DOMWalkerWizard in terms of these three components. After this, you will be able to extend this wizard to fit your needs better and even create your own.

### Interface: The Custom Dialogs

The DOMWalkerWizard project has two dialog classes (see the CD). They implement a simple GUI for the user to enter his or her preferences about traversal, helper generation, and node types. Figure 12.4 shows both dialogs.

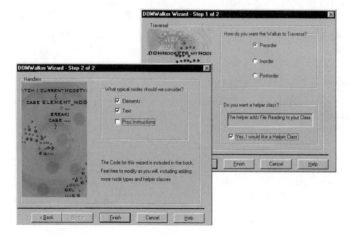

**Figure 12.4** The DOMWalkerWizard GUI.

In order to remember the user's preferences, the values represented by the widgets are entered in a dictionary. This is done in the function OnDismiss(), as shown in Listing 12.9.

Listing 12.9    *OnDismiss* **Function for DOMWalkerWizard**

```
BOOL CCustom2Dlg::OnDismiss()
{
     if (!UpdateData(TRUE))
          return FALSE;
     if(m_elements)
          DOMWalkerWizardaw.m_Dictionary["WANT_ELEMENTS"] = "YES";
     else
          DOMWalkerWizardaw.m_Dictionary["WANT_ELEMENTS"] = "";
     if(m_text)
          DOMWalkerWizardaw.m_Dictionary["WANT_TEXT"] = "YES";
     else
          DOMWalkerWizardaw.m_Dictionary["WANT_TEXT"] = "";
     if(m_pis)
          DOMWalkerWizardaw.m_Dictionary["WANT_PIS"] = "YES";
     else
          DOMWalkerWizardaw.m_Dictionary["WANT_PIS"] = "";
     return TRUE;  // return FALSE if the dialog shouldn't be dismissed
}
```

## Templates

The main part of the Wizard are the templates. The templates are processed according to the values set in the dictionary, creating the files in the generated project. For this case, we define two templates (Listings 12.10 and 12.11)—one for the interface and one for the implementation of our walker class.

Listing 12.10    **DOMWalker.h**

```
// The variable root is automatically set to the name of the project
#ifndef $$root$$XMLWALKER_H
#define $$root$$XMLWALKER_H

#include <windows.h>

#import "msxml3.dll"
using namespace MSXML2;

class $$root$$Walker
{
  public:
  /**
     recursive method used to navigate the tree
   */
  void visit(IXMLDOMNodePtr n);
$$IF(WANT_HELPER)
//*****************************************************************************
//     Internal Helper Class
//*****************************************************************************
```

```
     class Helper
        {
        public:
               static IXMLDOMNodePtr readXMLFile(const char *name);
        };
$$ENDIF
};
#endif
```

Listing 12.11   **DOMWalker.cpp**

```
#include "$$root$$Walker.h"

void $$root$$Walker::visit(IXMLDOMNodePtr n)
{
$$IF(INORDER)
  // INORDER: visit the left child, then the rest
  if(n->childNodes->length > 0)
    visit(n->childNodes->item[0]);
$$ENDIF
$$IF(POSTORDER)
  // POSTORDER: visit the children, then the current node
  for(int i = 0; i < n->childNodes->length ;i++)
      visit(n->childNodes->item[i]);
$$ENDIF
$$IF(PREORDER)
   // PREORDER: visit this node, then visit its left child, then the rest
   // Treat the node here first
$$ENDIF
$$IF(WANT_ELEMENTS)
  if(n->nodeType == NODE_ELEMENT)
  { // handle the element here
    // At this point you may want to look for the name of the
    //   element with:
    // if(!strcmp(n->nodeName,"foo"))
    //  {
    //    and perhaps get an attribute with:
    //       IXMLDOMNodePtr att;
    //       n->attributes->get_item(0,&att);
    //    (these are not the only mechanisms)
    //  }
  }
$$ENDIF
$$IF(WANT_TEXT)
  if(n->nodeType == NODE_TEXT)
  { // handle the text here
  }
$$ENDIF
$$IF(WANT_PIS)
```

*continues*

Listing 12.11 **Continued**

```
  if(n->nodeType == NODE_PROCESSING_INSTRUCTION)
  { // hanlde the P.I. here
  }
    // The Source for the wizard itself is included with the
    // book's CDROM, so you can enhance this file with other cases
    // for other node types.

$$ENDIF
$$IF(INORDER)
  // we already visited the first child
  for(int i = 1; i < n->childNodes->length ;i++)
      visit(n->childNodes->item[i]);
$$ENDIF
$$IF(PREORDER)
  // go through the rest of children
  for(int i = 0; i < n->childNodes->length ;i++)
      visit(n->childNodes->item[i]);
$$ENDIF
}

$$IF(WANT_HELPER)
IXMLDOMNodePtr $$root$$Walker::Helper::readXMLFile(const char *name)
{
  try
  {
    IXMLDOMDocumentPtr docPtr;
    // Init
    docPtr.CreateInstance("msxml2.domdocument");

    // load a document
    _variant_t varXml(name);
    _variant_t varOut((bool)TRUE);
    varOut = docPtr->load(varXml);
    if ((bool)varOut == FALSE)
      throw(0);
    return docPtr;
  } catch(...)
  {
    // ... log, show a window, rethrow, whatever you prefer.
    return NULL;
  }
}
$$ENDIF
```

## Configuration Files

The configuration files for the project simply record the message that is shown to the user when the process is completed and the association is made between templates and the names of the files in the generated project. Listing 12.12 shows only the file association. You can see the message file either in the templates directory or by simply running the wizard.

Listing 12.12 **newproj.inf for DOMWalkerWizard**

```
$$// newproj.inf = template for list of template files
walker.cpp    $$root$$Walker.cpp
walker.h      $$root$$Walker.h
```

## Final Result

The final result of compiling our project is a wizard file (extension.awx) that is placed under %MSDEVDIR%\TEMPLATES. Now, you can generate a DOMWalker by selecting File, New, Project and clicking the DOMWalkerWizard, as you would do with any other application type in Visual Studio.

Figure 12.5 shows a project generated with our tool, including a correct preorder DOMWalker for elements and text, and a helper class to read the DOM from disk.

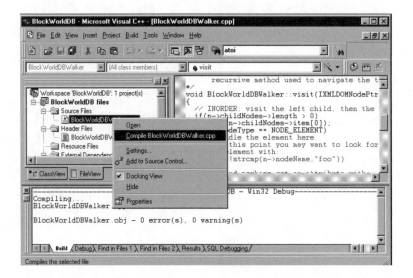

**Figure 12.5**   Project generated with DOMWalkerWizard.

**Toolkits/Frameworks Updates**

C++ XML is a rapidly evolving field. For daily information on Xerces, MSXML, libmxml, and other toolkits, refer to this book's Web site: `http://www.cppxml.com`.

# Summary

In this chapter you turned your attention to reutilization mechanisms for some of the major C++ toolkits available. I discussed the frameworks themselves, along with the rationale for their creation and use, and I highlighted the major features of MSXML and Xerces.

Two diametrically opposed frameworks were developed: one for SAX class factories using Xerces, and one for DOM visitors, using MSXML3, in a Visual C++ custom wizard. Two applications were constructed with these tools: an XMLable factory for a simple user-defined data type, and an OpenGL interpreter for XML files describing 3D worlds.

# IV

# Integrating Well-Known C++ Modules

# Creating XML-Based Extension Languages for C++ Programs

**13**

ONE PARTICULARLY INTERESTING APPLICATION OF THE TECHNIQUES and technologies seen in previous chapters is the creation and interpretation of XML extension languages for C++ programs.

In a way, this topic is a transitional one: It connects traditional C++ XML processing with elements of distributed applications—namely, the interpretation of messages encoded as XML documents. Thus, this chapter can be seen as a preparation from the applications you have developed so far to those you will develop when SOAP and XML-RPC are introduced.

In other ways, this chapter can be seen as totally independent. The creation of little XML languages for the expression of behavior in C++ programs is becoming as popular as the usage of XML for maintaining its data. The study of the alternatives for implementing these languages deserves a separate space.

There are several ways to create an interpreter for an extension language based on XML in your C++ application. This chapter covers the two I consider most common and relevant:

- Creation of a self-executing object representation of the program
- Transformation of the XML into a preexistent extension language

This chapter covers the principles and applications of these two mechanisms by implementing a language and an interpreter for each one. The first is a scripting language for a custom-made image manipulation program in Windows (built on top of postgraphy classes), and the second is an XML scripting language for the popular Linux graphics program The Gimp. The first mechanism, being new material in this book, is fully described in this chapter. The transformation of XML documents into scheme scripts is merely an exercise in XSLT (covered in Chapter 11, "XSLT Transformations") and has been left only as code for the CD.

# Creating Program Tree Objects from XML

The first mechanism for implementing your own scripting (or extension) XML languages on top of C++ applications is the creation of an interpreter for the XML format into your program. The theory and implementation options behind writing an interpreter can be overwhelming. We will stick with a clean and proven (if not the most efficient in every case) pattern called "little language."

The first brush with little language was introduced in Chapter 3, "Event-Driven Processing," where you created an XML format for arithmetic expressions. As you might remember, the XML file could contain primitives such as add and subtract (called nonterminals) and numbers (at the leaves of the tree) such as 4 and 5 (called terminals).

The following sections take this idea further, adding concepts such as variables and control flow structures to an XML language for scripts to a program that manipulates images.

### Why Use XML for Extension Languages?

Some platforms already define mechanisms for programs to expose interfaces so that scripting languages can manipulate them. Furthermore, XML syntax can be verbose, so why create extension languages based on XML?

The answer is twofold. First, from the user's perspective, writing scripts in XML can be much more pleasant and safe than writing Lisp, Visual Basic, or some other scripting language. The user already has the tools to do it, knows the conventions and underlying syntax, and can use a multitude of readily-available free tools to generate and audit his scripts. Second, from the developer's perspective, using XML brings the promise of portability, transparency, the possibility of easily implementing cross-platform extension hooks without relying on any particular platform or middleware (such as CORBA or COM), and many chances for code reuse and robustness. (For example, you no longer need to write a low-level parser for the language. You already have SAX to do that.)

## Overview of the Mechanism

Without getting into the details of programming language theory, it can be said that an expression or program can be seen as a tree, where each element can be evaluated to a certain value, either because it is an atomic *terminal* (such as the number 5 in an arithmetic example) or because it can be evaluated by applying the semantics of the *nonterminal* to its children. (For example, the result of an add element is determined by adding its two children.) Figure 13.1 further illustrates this point.

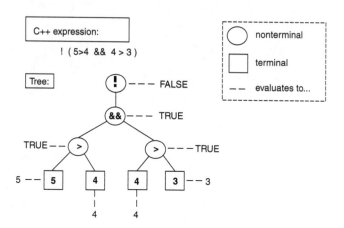

**Figure 13.1**  An expression as a tree.

In addition, the evaluation of some nodes might produce side effects. For example, a call to printf produces an output according to its arguments.

An XML document (as you well know) is a tree, so programs can be represented using XML documents, where nonleaf nodes represent functions and control structures and leaves represent atomic values. The interpretation of these files results in object hierarchies that can be evaluated at runtime.

## Designing the Language

The testImage program is a powerful set of tools to do all sorts of image manipulation, including dozens of effects. It also has support for many file types. The winConvert application is a Windows front end to testImage that adds the ability to visually select the files to treat and the options to use. Figure 13.2 shows winConvert running.

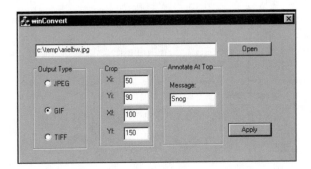

**Figure 13.2**  winConvert.

As you can see, winConvert exposes only a very small subset of the core program's functionality. Namely, it allows the transformation of the file into three output formats, cropping to a particular rectangle, and adding a message at the top of the image. winConvert is limited, but our goal is to define XML extension languages, not comprehensive image manipulation, so it will serve our purposes well. (For more about all the possibilities of the testImage program and image manipulation software related to it, go to http://www.postgraphy.com.)

The goal of this section is to create an XML scripting language for applying winConvert functions to several files automatically.

### Real-World Examples

The code included in this chapter, and the components it links, are the base of real products. The script manipulation techniques shown here and the core image manipulation engine are the foundations of some of the products of my own company, postgraphy.

### Philosophy

The first step in creating the language is making high-level decisions about what functionality to expose and the paradigm used to do it. In particular, it is important to decide whether the XML will reflect the underlying API or provide higher-level abstractions.

In this case, the underlying API is basically that of the CImage object (see Figure 13.3). We could very well expose its methods directly as XML elements, but we instead prefer to expose a higher-level view of the language. For example, Image objects provide a method to change their own output format, but instead of saying "Save this image as JPG," you want to say "All the save operations from this point on should be done using JPG format." The language must reflect such decisions.

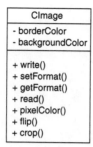

**Figure 13.3** The CImage object.

## Primitives

Following our philosophy for this language, we come to the following basic primitive functions:

- Set the output format
- Crop the image
- Annotate the image

In order to provide a way to specify the input filename, we will provide a treat element, which can contain both crop and annotate instances. Turning the functions just discussed into a DTD, we obtain Listing 13.1.

Listing 13.1 **convertScript_0_1.dtd**

```
<!ELEMENT convertScript   (setOutputFormat|treat)*>
<!ELEMENT setOutputFormat EMPTY>
<!ATTLIST setOutputFormat
          to              (JPEG|TIFF|GIF)     #REQUIRED>
<!ELEMENT treat           (crop?,annotate?)>
<!ATTLIST treat
          file            CDATA               #REQUIRED>

<!ELEMENT crop            (x,y,xf,yf)>
<!ELEMENT x               (#PCDATA)>
<!ELEMENT y               (#PCDATA)>
<!ELEMENT xf              (#PCDATA)>
<!ELEMENT yf              (#PCDATA)>

<!ELEMENT annotate        (#PCDATA)>
```

Using this language, you can already define somewhat interesting scripts, such as the one shown in Listing 13.2.

Listing 13.2 **script_0_1.xml**

```
<?xml version="1.0"?>
<!DOCTYPE convertScript SYSTEM "convertScript_0_1.dtd">
<convertScript>
  <setOutputFormat to="JPEG"/>
  <treat file="c:\temp\Leira.gif">
    <crop>
      <x>0</x><y>0</y>
      <xf>102</xf><yf>49</yf>
    </crop>
  </treat>
  <treat file="c:\temp\Et.tif">
    <annotate>second file</annotate>
  </treat>
  <treat file="c:\temp\Oeluc.gif">
  </treat>
  <setOutputFormat to="GIF"/>
  <!-- treat some more images here....-->
</convertScript>
```

## Variables and Operators

It would be interesting to be able to define variables in our language (that is, to reuse an annotation). Listing 13.5, shown in a moment, expands the convertScript DTD to allow the assignment and retrieval of values to and from variables (namely, the assign and variable elements). The equal, greaterThan (>), and plus operators are also introduced. The improved DTD is shown in Listing 13.3.

Note that I keep the number of operands at a minimum for space and complexity reasons, but the language can be easily extended with other primitives if you so desire.

Listing 13.3 **Adding Variables and Operators to the Language**

```
<!ELEMENT convertScript     (assign|setOutputFormat|treat)*>

<!ENTITY % operator          "equal|plus|greaterThan">
<!ELEMENT variable          EMPTY>
<!ATTLIST variable
          name              CDATA      #REQUIRED>
<!ELEMENT assign            (variable,value)>
<!ELEMENT value             (#PCDATA|variable|%operator;)*>
<!ELEMENT equal             (operand,operand)>
<!ELEMENT plus              (operand,operand)>
<!ELEMENT greaterThan       (operand,operand)>

<!ELEMENT operand           (#PCDATA|variable)*>

<!ELEMENT setOutputFormat EMPTY>
<!ATTLIST setOutputFormat
```

```
                 to              (JPEG|TIFF|GIF)     #REQUIRED>
<!ELEMENT treat                  (crop?,annotate?)>
<!ATTLIST treat
           file                  CDATA               #REQUIRED>


<!-- now the values of crop can also be complex expressions -->
<!ELEMENT crop                   (x,y,xf,yf)>
<!ELEMENT x                      (#PCDATA|variable|%operator;)*>
<!ELEMENT y                      (#PCDATA|variable|%operator;)*>
<!ELEMENT xf                     (#PCDATA|variable|%operator;)*>
<!ELEMENT yf                     (#PCDATA|variable|%operator;)*>


<!ELEMENT annotate               (#PCDATA|variable|%operator;)*>
```

## Control Structures

Finally, we want to illustrate support for a control structure, so we add the `while` statement. (Again, syntactic sugar such as `for`, and other control structures such as `if`, can be added at your leisure.)

The `while` element has two children: a condition and a body. Much in the C tradition, the contents of the condition are ultimately evaluated to a value; in case the value is 0, the condition is taken to be false. In any other case, the condition is true. Listing 13.4 shows the final version of the language.

Listing 13.4   **convertScript_1_0.dtd**

```
<!ELEMENT convertScript   (while|assign|setOutputFormat|treat)*>

<!ENTITY % operator        "equal|plus|greaterThan">
<!ELEMENT variable         EMPTY>
<!ATTLIST variable
           name            CDATA     #REQUIRED>

<!ELEMENT assign           (variable,value)>
<!ELEMENT value            (#PCDATA|variable|%operator;)*>
<!ELEMENT equal            (operand,operand)>
<!ELEMENT plus             (operand,operand)>
<!ELEMENT greaterThan      (operand,operand)>

<!ELEMENT while            (condition,body)>
<!ELEMENT condition        (#PCDATA|variable|%operator;)*>
<!ELEMENT body             (while|assign|setOutputFormat|treat)*>

<!ELEMENT operand          (#PCDATA|variable)*>

<!ELEMENT setOutputFormat EMPTY>
<!ATTLIST setOutputFormat
           to              (JPEG|TIFF|GIF)     #REQUIRED>
```

*continues*

Listing 13.4 **Continued**

```
<!ELEMENT treat                (crop?,annotate?)>
<!ATTLIST treat
           file                CDATA                 #REQUIRED>

<!ELEMENT crop                 (x,y,xf,yf)>
<!ELEMENT x                    (#PCDATA|variable|%operator;)*>
<!ELEMENT y                    (#PCDATA|variable|%operator;)*>
<!ELEMENT xf                   (#PCDATA|variable|%operator;)*>
<!ELEMENT yf                   (#PCDATA|variable|%operator;)*>

<!ELEMENT annotate             (#PCDATA|variable|%operator;)*>
```

Listing 13.5 shows a script that uses all the constructs we generated in order to generate multiple crops with different sizes from a single file.

Listing 13.5 **script_1_0.xml**

```
<?xml version="1.0"?>
<!DOCTYPE convertScript SYSTEM "convertScript_1_0.dtd">
<!-- the following script would be equivalent to the following c++ pseudo-code:
     setOutputFormat(JPEG)
     j = 0;
     while(300 > j)
     {
        f = treatFile("c:\\temp\\face.gif");
        f.crop(0,0,j,j);
        j = j + 50;
     }
-->
<convertScript>
  <setOutputFormat to="JPEG"/>
  <assign>
      <variable name="j"/>
      <value>0</value>
  </assign>
  <while>
    <condition>
      <greaterThan>
          <operand>300</operand>
          <operand><variable name="j"/></operand>
      </greaterThan>
    </condition>
    <body>
      <treat file="c:\temp\face.gif">
      <crop>
        <x>0</x>
        <y>0</y>
```

```
        <xf><variable name="j"/></xf>
        <yf><variable name="j"/></yf>
      </crop>
      </treat>
      <assign>
      <variable name="j"/>
      <value>
          <plus>
          <operand><variable name="j"/></operand>
          <operand>50</operand>
          </plus>
      </value>
      </assign>
    </body>
  </while>
</convertScript>
```

This language, as you can see, can already throw somewhat interesting results. Executing this script (with the objects we will create in the next section) results in the files shown in Figure 13.4.

**Figure 13.4** Results of interpreting script.xml.

## Creating the Object Structure

In order to interpret the programs just shown, we will reuse the logic of Chapter 3: construct hierarchies, where every object exposes an `eval()` method, implementing the logic associated with it. (For example, the `eval` method of `plus` returns the addition of its two operands.)

The complete script is represented by a tree of Term (the base class for Treat, Crop, and all other possible members of the tree). When the eval() method in the root is called, it recursively calls eval() on its children (and so on), finally evaluating the whole program. The following sections show the implementation of the different types of terms.

### Modeling the Primitives

The treat, crop, setOutputFormat, and annotate primitives are modeled by making calls to a global CImage variable, as illustrated in Listing 13.6. Because we are allowing the one-time setting of the output format via the setOutputFormat element, we must also keep track of the format value. But, the Image object is being updated constantly, so every time treat is called, it can set the Image format to the correct value.

Listing 13.6  **Crop Implementation**

```
class crop : public Term {
public:

   crop(int nx,int ny,int nxf,int nyf) : x(nx), y(ny), xf(nxf), xy(nyf){ }

   int eval()
   {
       globalImage.crop(x,y,xf,yf);
   }

private:
   int x,y,xf,yf;
};
```

Listing 13.7 shows the implementation of the Treat object, which reads the file, applies all the children underneath it, and then writes it back, appending a random number to the filename (in an imperfect way to avoid rewrites when a loop forces the same file to be treated more than once).

Listing 13.7  *Treat* **Implementation**

```
#include <vector>
#include <string.h>

using namespace std;

class  : public Term {
public:

   void setName(char* newName)
   {
       strcpy(name,newName);
```

```
    }

    void addTerm(Term *t)
    {
        children.push_back(t);
    }

    int eval()
    {
        globalImage.read(name);
        // This method sets the output format
        globalImage.Format(format); // format is a global variable,
                                    // set by the eval method ofsetOutputFormat
        // now, process all the children, thus modifying the image
        for(int i = 0; i < children.size();i++)
            children[i]->eval();
        // the modifications are complete; save
        char randomPostfix[15];
    globalImage.save(strcat(name,itoa(rand()%100,randomPostfix,10)));
        return 1;
    }

private:
    vector<Term*> children;
    char name[90];
};
```

## Modeling the Control Structures

The implementation of while objects also falls compactly into the term-based scheme we have been using. Listing 13.8 shows the eval() method for this class.

Listing 13.8   *while::eval( )*

```
int eval()
{
  while(condition->eval() != 0)
      for(int i = 0; i < children.size();i++)
          children[i]->eval();
  return 1;
}
```

Finally, in order to keep the value of variables, we maintain a map of names versus values (for simplicity, all variables are integers):

```
static vars<string,int>;
```

The eval() method of the Variable object fetches values from this table, and the eval() method of Assign updates it.

### Constructing the *Term* Tree

Using the XMLableFR framework from Chapter 12, "Toolkit Features and Implementation Frameworks," we can easily write the SAX2 skeleton class, which will act as our object hierarchy builder. Filling it out is a matter of creating instances of Crop, Treat, and so on according to an element name. For space reasons (and because you saw this technique in Chapters 3 and 6), the builder code for Term trees is omitted.

## Summary

With the techniques shown here, we have extended the concepts introduced in Chapter 3 so that you can implement any custom scripting language, including control structures, variables, and domain-specific primitives. This chapter discussed a simplified version of a real commercial product, innovating with the concepts from previous chapters. Using Chapter 12's XMLableFR and the classes of this chapter as a template, you can significantly decrease the development time for your own XML scripting languages.

# 14

# Distributed C++ XML Applications: SOAP and XML-RPC

**M**OST OF THE IMPORTANT XML-RELATED APPLICATIONS written in C++ are a system's performance-driven components. The previous chapters discussed the techniques for making standalone C++ XML applications and extending existing C++ applications using XML languages. This chapter discusses distributed applications written in C++ and communicating via XML-based protocols—especially the creation of high-performance custom servers that can be easily integrated with other languages and platforms by means of XML messaging.

This chapter examines the two preeminent technologies for XML-based RPC (Remote Procedure Calls) in distributed applications: SOAP and XML-RPC. Most of the explanations and discussion will revolve around Simple Object Access Protocol (SOAP), because it is the more complex of the two, but complete examples of both, using exclusively C++, are given.

## An Introduction to the Problem

The problem that SOAP and XML-RPC attempt to solve is conceptually simple: A server program in a particular machine exhibits a service that is required by a client in another environment. A call must be issued remotely, from the client to the server, and a response must be sent back. The format and conventions for remotely invoking the service and getting the response, as well as all other related issues, such as memory management, reference/value passing, and error signaling, are the subject of specifications such as SOAP and XML–RPC. The following sections show the logic behind them, as well as their C++ implementations and examples.

# SOAP 1.1

SOAP 1.1 is an XML message-exchanging mechanism that is endorsed by Microsoft, IBM, and other big companies in the distributed applications arena. SOAP is divided into three parts:

- Definition of an XML representation for interapplication messages
- A set of conventions for expressing instances of application-defined datatypes
- Definition of an XML representation for RPC

The following sections discuss the theory and isolated examples of each of these parts before jumping into the creation of a complete remote service and its client.

## Envelopes

An envelope is the top element of a SOAP message. (For all practical purposes, an envelope *is* the message, so I use the terms interchangeably.) It belongs to the namespace `http://schemas.xmlsoap.org/soap/envelope` and contains two things: a body with the values for the parameters of a call (or the value for the response), and an optional header, with somewhat advanced data, which I will not discuss in this chapter.

An envelope must always have the element name `Envelope` and be tied to the namespace `http://schemas.xmlsoap.org/soap/envelope`. Listing 14.1 is an example of a SOAP request for a movie service. It returns the average recommendation (from 1 to 10) for a movie, given its title. Granted, this is not the most computationally intensive of exercises, so the use of C++ to process it would be only an aesthetic choice, but it will serve our purposes.

Listing 14.1   **SOAP Envelope for a Movie-Recommendation Request**

```
<soap:Envelope xmlns:soap="http://schemas.xmlsoap.org/soap/envelope/"
               soap:encodingStyle="http://schemas.xmlsoap.org/soap/encoding/">
    <soap:Body>
        <GetMovieRating>
            <name>Shadow of the Vampire</name>
        </GetMovieRating>
    </soap:Body>
</soap:Envelope>
```

Similarly, a SOAP message to encode the result of the operation would take the form shown in Listing 14.2.

Listing 14.2    **SOAP Envelope for a Movie-Recommendation Response**

```
<soap:Envelope xmlns:soap="http://schemas.xmlsoap.org/soap/envelope/"
               soap:encodingStyle="http://schemas.xmlsoap.org/soap/encoding/">
    <soap:Body>
        <GetMovieRatingResponse>
            <rating>10</rating>
        </GetMovieRatingResponse>
    </soap:Body>
</soap:Envelope>
```

Two important additional details become apparent after you see these samples. The first one is the use of the SOAP attribute encodingStyle. The second is the apparent lack of specification for a mechanism to connect messages and responses (nothing in the two messages themselves identifies one as the answer for the other).

**Encoding Style**

The encodingStyle attribute explicitly indicates a URL that identifies the set of rules for data representation used to encode the envelope's contents (the idea being that you can send SOAP messages using data representations other than that suggested by the specification). In most cases, the value of this attribute is the following:

```
http://schemas.xmlsoap.org/soap/encoding
```

In this case, the encoding is that defined in the SOAP specification and explained in the section "SOAP Encoding."

**A Word on SOAP as RPC**

An explanation about the second mentioned characteristic of Listings 14.1 and 14.2 is too long to fit in this paragraph, but a note about it and pointers to the solution are worth the space.

Apparently, there is no connection between Listings 14.1 and 14.2 as semantically rich tokens in an RPC conversation. However, once you understand the mechanisms outlined in the sections "RPC Conventions" and "SOAP HTTP," it will become evident that SOAP manages to convey the status and semantics of calls by means of conventions over the body of the message itself and the protocol with which it is communicated.

# SOAP Encoding

Independent of whether you use an envelope as an RPC call or response (or perhaps for another activity totally unrelated to RPC), the use of SOAP encoding makes it possible to express a graph of complex and simple types and values as an XML representation. The SOAP encoding style is a generalization of the notion of basic type versus struct found in many languages, including C and C++.

In SOAP encoding, a type may be simple or compound. A simple type may be any of the built-in datatypes of XML Schema, described in Chapter 9, "XML Schema, TREX, and Other Modeling Languages." The values of the type are represented with a string, as illustrated in Listing 14.3.

Listing 14.3   **Simple Types: Definition and Instances**

```
<element name="numPages" type="int"/>
<element name="length" type="float"/>
<element name="cheese">
  <simpleType base="xsd:string">
    <enumeration value="Cheddar"/>
    <enumeration value="Edam"/>
    <enumeration value="Lipta"/>
    <enumeration value="Limburger"/>
  </simpleType>
</element>

<numPages>45</numPages>
<length>5.9</length>
<cheese>Blue</cheese>
```

A compound type is a collection of simple types, each identified by an accessor. A compound type may be one of two kinds: struct or array. In the struct case, the accessors are the names of the components, while with arrays it is simply a nonnegative integer index.

The value of a compound type is represented by an element whose name is that of the type and that contains a collection of subelements—namely, the accessors for the complex type. Listing 14.4 illustrates this with a simple struct definition and a particular value conforming to it.

Listing 14.4   **Complex Types: Definition and Instances**

```
<element name="artist">
 <complexType>
    <element name="name"      type="xsd:string"/>
    <element name="surname"   type="xsd:string"/>
    <element name="school"    type="xsd:string"/>
      <element name="favoriteCheese"> <!-- :) -->
      <simpleType base="xsd:string">
        <enumeration value="Cheddar"/>
        <enumeration value="Edam"/>
        <enumeration value="Swiss"/>
        <enumeration value="Limburger"/>
      </simpleType>
    </element>
  </complexType>
</element>
```

```
<artist>
  <name>Leni</name>
  <surname>Riefenstahl</surname>
  <school>Mountain</school>
  <favoriteCheese>Swiss</favoriteCheese>
</artist>
```

It is important to note that even though the types of the elements are taken from part 2 of the XML Schema specification, the definition of the types can be done in any other schema language (such as TREX or RELAX). The fact that I have adhered to XML Schema notation is merely to keep continuity with the examples on the specification of SOAP itself (http://www.w3.org/TR/SOAP) in case you have to refer to it.

For practical purposes, the notion of a SOAP type being either simple or compound (either array or struct), plus the examples just given, will be enough to get you started. If you need to refer to more formal rules of type definition, see section 5, "SOAP Encoding," of the specification.

## RPC Conventions

Our primary interest in SOAP is RPC. For this purpose, the SOAP specification defines a set of conventions, so the rules of SOAP encoding just defined can be used to represent calls and responses. These rules are described in the following sections.

### Procedure Invocation Conventions

The conventions for representing a method invocation in terms of the SOAP encoding are as follows:

- A method invocation is modeled as a struct.
- The method invocation is viewed as a single struct containing an accessor for each parameter. The struct is both named and typed identically to the method name.
- Each parameter is viewed as an accessor, with a name corresponding to the name of the parameter and a type corresponding to the type of the parameter. These appear in the same order as in the method signature.

An example of these rules is Listing 14.5, which presents a SOAP invocation of the ldexp function (math.h).

Listing 14.5 **SOAP Invocation of** *ldexp*

```
<SOAP-ENV:Envelope
  xmlns:SOAP-ENV="http://schemas.xmlsoap.org/soap/envelope/"
  SOAP-ENV:encodingStyle="http://schemas.xmlsoap.org/soap/encoding/"/>
  <!-- ldexp(3.5,4) -->
  <SOAP-ENV:Body>
      <ldexp>
        <x>3.5</x>
        <exp>4</exp>
      </ldexp>
  </SOAP-ENV:Body>
</SOAP-ENV:Envelope>
```

## Procedure Response Conventions

The conventions for representing a method response in terms of SOAP encoding are as follows:

- A method response (see Listing 14.6) is modeled as a struct.
- The method response is viewed as a single struct containing an accessor for the return value and each "out" or "in/out" parameter. The first accessor is the return value followed by the parameters in the same order as in the method signature.
- Each parameter accessor has a name corresponding to the name of the parameter and a type corresponding to the type of the parameter. The name of the return–value accessor is insignificant. Likewise, the name of the struct is insignificant. However, a convention is to name it after the method, with the string "Response" appended.

Listing 14.6 *ldexp* **Response**

```
<SOAP-ENV:Envelope
  xmlns:SOAP-ENV="http://schemas.xmlsoap.org/soap/envelope/"
  SOAP-ENV:encodingStyle="http://schemas.xmlsoap.org/soap/encoding/"/>
  <SOAP-ENV:Body>
      <ldexpResponse>
        <!-- response -->
        56.00
      </ldexpResponse>
        <!-- no out or in/out parameters -->
  </SOAP-ENV:Body>
</SOAP-ENV:Envelope>
```

# SOAP HTTP

A final subject in the study of SOAP is that of the carrying mechanism and how SOAP relies on it for semantics about the call invocation.

SOAP is not inherently tied to HTTP or any other protocol, but the use of HTTP is pervasive and is a standard choice for SOAP exchanges.

### SOAP Features Not Addressed

For the sake of brevity and simplicity, some features of SOAP are not discussed here. The two most important that you might want to review in the specification itself are fault messages and headers.

# MS C++ SOAP Implementation

The Microsoft SOAP implementation (MS SOAP Toolkit 2.0) contains support for C++. It can be downloaded from `http://msdn.microsoft.com/xml/default.asp`. It contains support for WSDL (Web Service Definition Language) in order to bind SOAP services to Web servers. It also has a number of tools to help you define interfaces and implementations for your own services. However, currently the development of applications with the Microsoft SOAP toolkit is highly coupled with Microsoft-specific components—namely, WSML—so the code shown here is abridged to showcase only the look and feel of the SOAP implementation. Microsoft-specific explanations are left for the additional material (see the file soap.chi that gets installed in C:\Program Files\Common Files\MSSoap for more information).

### Calculator Server (Abridged)

Listing 14.7 shows the most relevant portions of the client calculator. Additional WSML bindings to call this service from ASPs are provided with Microsoft SOAP 1.1.

Listing 14.7  **Calculator Server**

```
#include "stdafx.h"
#include "CalcSvcRpcCpp.h"
#include "Calc.h"
// Copyright Microsoft
STDMETHODIMP CCalc::Add(double A, double B, double *Result)
{
     *Result = A + B;
     return S_OK;
}

STDMETHODIMP CCalc::Subtract(double A, double B, double *Result)
{
     *Result = A - B;
     return S_OK;
}
```

*continues*

Listing 14.7   **Continued**

```
STDMETHODIMP CCalc::Multiply(double A, double B, double *Result)
{
    *Result = A * B;
    return S_OK;
}

STDMETHODIMP CCalc::Divide(double A, double B, double *Result)
{
    *Result = A / B;
    return S_OK;
}
```

### Calculator Client (Abridged)

Listing 14.8 shows the most relevant portions of the client calculator. Additional GUI wrappings for methods such as OnSubtract are provided with Microsoft SOAP 1.1.

Listing 14.8   **Calculator Client**

```
// Copyright Microsoft
// Execute Subtract
void CCalcCliRpcCppDlg::OnSubstract()
{
    Execute(L"Substract");
}

// Execute the specified method.
void CCalcCliRpcCppDlg::Execute(OLECHAR *pMethodName)
{

    if(Connect())
    {

        HRESULT hr;
        DISPID dispid;
        DISPPARAMS dispparams;
        VARIANTARG params[2];
        VARIANT result;
        CString ParamText;
        EXCEPINFO ExceptInfo;

        // Get dispatch ID corresponding to method name.
        hr = m_pSoapClient->GetIDsOfNames(IID_NULL, &pMethodName, 1,
                                          LOCALE_SYSTEM_DEFAULT,
                                          &dispid);
        if(FAILED(hr))
        {
            DisplayHResult(_T("Cannot get dispatch id of calc method."),hr);
            return;
```

```
        }

        // Set B parameter.
        VariantInit(&params[0]);
        params[0].vt = VT_R8;
        m_BCtl.GetWindowText(ParamText);
        params[0].dblVal = atof(ParamText);

        // Set A parameter.
        VariantInit(&params[1]);
        params[1].vt = VT_R8;
        m_ACtl.GetWindowText(ParamText);
        params[1].dblVal = atof(ParamText);

        // Initialize DISPPARAMS structure.
        dispparams.cArgs = 2;
        dispparams.cNamedArgs = 0;
        dispparams.rgdispidNamedArgs = NULL;
        dispparams.rgvarg = params;

        // Prepare result variant.
        VariantInit(&result);

        // Invoke the specified method.
        hr = m_pSoapClient->Invoke(dispid, IID_NULL,
                              LOCALE_SYSTEM_DEFAULT,
                              DISPATCH_METHOD, &dispparams,
                              &result, &ExceptInfo, NULL);
        if(FAILED(hr))
        {
            DisplayFault(_T("Invoke of calc method failed."));
        }
        else
        {

            // Convert result to a string.
            VariantChangeType(&result, &result, 0, VT_BSTR);

            // Display result.
            m_ResultCtl.SetWindowText(CString(result.bstrVal));

        }

        // Clean up variants.
        VariantClear(&result);
        VariantClear(&params[0]);
        VariantClear(&params[1]);

    }

}
```

### Other C++ SOAP Implementations

For a complete and updated listing of all SOAP implementations (41 at the time of this writing), visit `http://soap.weblogs.com`. C/C++ client and server implementations are clearly marked.

# XML-RPC

XML-RPC is a simpler RPC mechanism based on XML. It is somewhat restrictive compared to SOAP (for example, it is tightly coupled with HTTP), but it compensates for this by providing an extremely compact API for distributed applications.

XML-RPC invocations differ from SOAP's in several fundamental ways. The first is the fact that the semantics of the call are tied to the communication mechanism. The second is the simplicity of the rules for invocation and response. Let's examine these two aspects.

## Requests and Responses

An XML-RPC invocation is an HTTP request whose content is an XML document such as the one shown in Listing 14.9. The document has a `methodCall` root element containing two subelements to express the name of the function to call and its parameters, respectively. The names of the two subelements of `methodCall` are `methodName` and `param`.

As I mentioned, an XML-RPC invocation is an HTTP request, so it exhibits the headers for message size, host, and user-agent as any other.

Listing 14.9   **XML-RPC Invocation**

```
POST /RPC2 HTTP/1.0
User-Agent: Mozilla/1.0 (Win98)
Host: trinity.v-to-the-nth.com
Content-Type: text/xml
Content-length: 142

<?xml version="1.0"?>
<methodCall>
   <methodName>antonym</methodName>
   <params>
      <param>
         <value>
            <string>anathema</string>
         </value>
      </param>
   </params>
</methodCall>
```

Either a dedicated program listening on port 80 to this type of message, or a Web server capable of forwarding it to an XML-RPC engine, processes the application and transduces it to an actual C++ call. The code for a dedicated C++ implementation of XML-RPC is included on the CD.

The response from the server is a classic HTTP response with another simple document—this time with a `methodResponse` root containing a `params` element with the response value, as shown in Listing 14.10.

Listing 14.10   **XML-RPC Response**

```
HTTP/1.0 200 OK
Server: Helma XML-RPC 1.0
Connection: close
Content-Type: text/xml
Content-Length: 143

<?xml version="1.0" encoding="ISO-8859-1"?>
<methodResponse>
    <params>
        <param>
          <value>
            <string>anathema</string>
            <!--anathema, in certain cases can be a "contronym",
                i.e. a word that is its own antonym ;) -->
          </value>
        </param>
    </params>
</methodResponse>
```

As I mentioned before, the semantics of an XML response are somewhat coupled to the HTTP protocol itself. In particular, every XML response, regardless of the operation's success, must return a 200 value in the HTTP status (the first line of Listing 14.9). If a value other than that is returned, a non–XML-RPC error occurred.

## Errors

When an XML-RPC error is signaled, the response from the server is a normal 200, but the contents are different from those of a successful invocation. In particular, instead of a `param` element with the response, you have a `fault` element with a string representation of the error, as shown in Listing 14.11.

Listing 14.11   **XML-RPC Error Response**

```
HTTP/1.0 200 OK
Server: Helma XML-RPC 1.0
Connection: close
Content-Type: text/xml
```

*continues*

Listing 14.11   **Continued**

```
Content-Length: 276

<?xml version="1.0" encoding="ISO-8859-1"?>
<methodResponse>
   <fault>
     <value>
       <struct>
          <member>
            <name> No antonym found
            </name>
            <value>No antonym found at all</value>
          </member>
        <member>
        <name>
           faultCode
        </name>
      </fault>
</methodResponse>
```

# A Standalone C++ Calculator Service

Listing 14.12 shows the standalone version of a calculator service implemented in XML-RPC C++. (Compare the SOAP version in the preceding section.)

Listing 14.12   **Calculator Server in C++**

```
//Todo: add more functions

#include <stdio.h>

#include <xmlrpc.h>
#include <xmlrpc_abyss.h>

xmlrpc_value *
sample_add (xmlrpc_env *env, xmlrpc_value *param_array, void *user_data)
{
    xmlrpc_int32 x, y, z;

    /* Parse our argument array. */
    xmlrpc_parse_value(env, param_array, "(ii)", &x, &y);
    if (env->fault_occurred)
      return NULL;

    /* Add our two numbers. */
    z = x + y;

    /* Return our result. */
```

```
      return xmlrpc_build_value(env, "i", z);
}

int main (int argc, char **argv)
{
    if (argc != 2) {
      fprintf(stderr, "Usage: servertest abyss.conf\n");
      exit(1);
    }

    xmlrpc_server_abyss_init(XMLRPC_SERVER_ABYSS_NO_FLAGS, argv[1]);
    xmlrpc_server_abyss_add_method("sample.add", &sample_add, NULL);

    printf("server: switching to background.\n");
    xmlrpc_server_abyss_run();
}
```

# A Standalone C++ Client

In order to illustrate the simplicity of an application that can directly talk in XML-RPC messages, I include here a standalone client for the calculator service:

```
#define NAME "XML-RPC C Test Client"
#define VERSION "0.1"

void die_if_fault_occurred (xmlrpc_env *env)
{
    if (env->fault_occurred) {
        fprintf(stderr, "XML-RPC Fault: %s (%d)\n",
                env->fault_string, env->fault_code);
        exit(1);
    }
}

int main (int argc, char** argv)
{
    xmlrpc_env env;
    xmlrpc_value *result;
    char *state_name;

    /* Start up our XML-RPC client library. */
    xmlrpc_client_init(XMLRPC_CLIENT_NO_FLAGS, NAME, VERSION);

    /* Initialize our error-handling environment. */
    xmlrpc_env_init(&env);

    /* Call the famous server at UserLand. */
```

```
        result = xmlrpc_client_call(&env, "http://betty.userland.com/add",
                                    "add",
                                    (xmlrpc_int32) 23, (xmlrpc_int32) 42);
        die_if_fault_occurred(&env);

        /* Get our state name and print it out. */
        xmlrpc_parse_value(&env, result, "s", &state_name);
        die_if_fault_occurred(&env);
        printf("%s\n", state_name);

        /* Dispose of our result value. */
        xmlrpc_DECREF(result);

        /* Clean up our error-handling environment. */
        xmlrpc_env_clean(&env);

        /* Shutdown our XML-RPC client library. */
        xmlrpc_client_cleanup();

        return 0;
    }
```

## Summary

High-performance components in distributed applications often need to be written in C++. This chapter has shown the rationale and C++ mechanisms to implement such components using two different RPC mechanisms based on XML: SOAP and XML-RPC. Both mechanisms use HTTP to communicate XML messages across a network, and both have marshalling mechanisms to allow the passing of native data.

The complexity of both the specification and C++ implementations of XML-RPC are significantly smaller, at the cost of being less expressive and more restricted (that is, to HTTP).

The implementation of a C++ distributed calculator application (server and client) was shown for both SOAP and XML-RPC.

# 15

# XML and Databases with C++ (ODBC and DAO)

Efficient access to and manipulation of large volumes of data is one of the most common reasons to implement a component in a language such as C++. Interoperability and openness are two common reasons to choose to represent the extracted data as XML. As a result, it is not uncommon to find applications in need of C++ components for database manipulation of XML data.

This chapter discusses the general framework under which C++ XML tools for database manipulation can be understood and characterized. You'll also see relevant examples of the four main implementation options available for custom C++ classes dealing with XML and databases.

## XML's Role in Database Representation

XML documents can be used to represent the data inside a particular database table or result set, thus allowing the easy serialization and communication of database data. XML documents also let you apply the vast set of tools surrounding XML to the data on the source. (For example, when a table is represented as XML, it is not hard for an application to transform the table to XHTML using XSLT.)

XML documents representing database contents (or schema) are characterized by their data-centric nature and their usually plain structure, mimicking the flat nature of tables. By data-centric, I mean that the document has little or no mixed content, and the way it is written (entities, indentation, and so on) is not as important as the data it contains.

In short, the role of XML in database representation is that of a serialization and presentation format, based on data-centric documents. This chapter explores the implementation possibilities for C++ modules dealing with the production of these documents, using a number of strategies, platforms, and C++ XML APIs.

# C++ Implementation Options

The possibilities for implementation of C++ modules for extraction and manipulation of database data as XML documents vary according to the database paradigm (pure relational versus Data Access Objects), the API exposed by the database and native toolkits (such as the `CRecordSet` class under MFC), and the choice of XML API chosen for communication with other parts of the system (SAX versus DOM).

In the most general sense, the implementation possibilities that arise out of the combination of these factors can be classified into two main groups: dedicated middleware and adaptor APIs. By middleware, in this context, I specifically mean custom application interfaces that introduce new and often proprietary concepts (such as a map or a template) in order to bind the database to its XML representation. By adaptor APIs, I mean the custom creation of SAX or DOM interfaces on top of native APIs (such as ODBC and ADO) in order to present their results as XML data without the introduction of vendor-specific intermediate constructs.

## Middleware

Even though the most interesting and edifying work in this chapter concerns the creation of APIs later (as opposed to invoking third-party solutions), it is important for you to see the types of middleware available so that you know them as alternatives for your development.

Middleware for XML representation of database data is divided into two categories: template-based and mapping-based middleware.

### Templates

Template-based middleware allows the inclusion of result set portions in specific parts of a document by means of preprocessing an XML file such as the one shown in Listing 15.1.

Listing 15.1 **Template-Based Middleware XML**

```
<?xml version="1.0"?>
<productList>
 <name>A list of toys</name>
 <date>
    <day>23</day><month>April</month><year>2002</year>
```

```
  </date>
  <?IncludeSelect SELECT TOY_NAME,TOY_NUMBER FROM TOYS ?>
</productList>
```

The result produced by an engine designed to preprocess this document would look like Listing 15.2.

Listing 15.2  **Hypothetical Template Composition Result**

```
<?xml version="1.0"?>
<productList>
 <name>A list of toys</name>
 <date>
    <day>23</day><month>April</month><year>2002</year>
 </date>
 <row>
   <TOY_NAME>Gameboy</TOY_NAME>
   <TOY_NUMBER>0902342</TOY_NUMBER>
 </row>
 <row>
   <TOY_NAME>Playstation 2</TOY_NAME>
   <TOY_NUMBER>0902334</TOY_NUMBER>
 </row>
</productList>
```

The mere use of a particular template product (even if it is written in C++) is of little interest in this book, so all further template-driven middleware discussion is left for each product's documentation. Template-based middleware tools based on C++ can be found on the site pointed to in the "Extra C++ Database Resources" section.

## Mapping

The other common form of middleware (that is, the other common addition some middleware introduce) is the explicit mapping of table rows to element names and attributes. This is usually done via another XML document, such as the one shown in Listing 15.3.

Listing 15.3  **Hypothetical Mapping Document**

```
<?xml version="1.0"?>
<mapping>
  <element name="ToyDescription">
   <from>TOY.TOY_NAMES</from>
   <toElement>TOY_NAMES</toElement>
   <from>TOY.TOY_NUMBER</from>
   <toAttribute>TOY_NAMES</toAttribute>
  </element>
</mapping>
```

After calling a processing class with the template and a database, the result would be a composition similar to that shown in Listing 15.2, except for the representation of the toy number as an element.

Again, the mere use of a C++ middleware product that performs the process just described has no relevance for this book. So instead of further pursuing that, we will examine the development of our own C++ classes so that middleware like the preceding can be replaced and/or constructed.

# Adaptor APIs

Figure 15.1 shows the different types of adaptor APIs, organized by complexity and power.

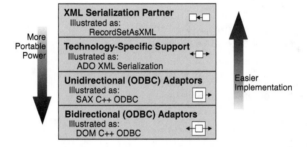

**Figure 15.1**   C++ database adaptors.

The following sections illustrate the four options for custom C++ database/XML classes, implementing reusable examples for each case. The examples are organized in ascending order of complexity, as shown in Figure 15.1.

## Class-Specific Partners

The first type of adaptor API is that coupled with only one particular class. In this case, the adaptor directly reads and writes the data from and to the XML representation in order to implement a class's XML persistence.

Even though this is a common, easy, and potentially efficient mechanism (knowing the structure of the class and making a specific SAX reader for it), it is a limited one, it is hard to reuse, and it is coupled with the particular data class.

This mechanism is helpful and congruent with classes tied to one recordset or table, such as the ones created by subclassing CRecordSet in Microsoft's MFC. The following example shows how to create a partner class to add XML persistence to a CRecordSet derivative. Because no Microsoft-specific knowledge is expected, I will devote some time to the creation and rationale of CRecordSet. If you are familiar with this process, simply skip to the "XMLSave Interface" section.

## Setting Up the Database

For the MFC recordset example, we will use a Microsoft Access database. This database contains the menu of a hypothetical restaurant, in the form of a table with three columns (Cost, Item ID, and Name).

In order to be able to use this database, you must first follow these steps in order to bind it as an ODBC source in your system:

1. Copy the restaurant.db file (see the CD) to your hard drive—say, in c:\temp.

2. Open the Control Panel and select ODBC Data Sources.

3. Add a new source, and select the MS Access driver.

4. Fill out the data source sheet as shown in Figure 15.2.

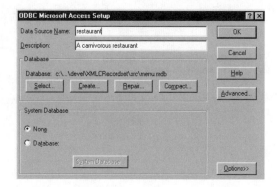

**Figure 15.2**  Creating an ODBC data source.

Now that the resource is set, you can create a subclass of `CRecordSet` and associate it with a table in it.

## Creating a *CRecordSet* Subclass

The MFC defines a simple way of binding a recordset to internal values in a program—the `CRecordSet` class. In order to bind the Menu table to variables in your program, you must encapsulate them in a subclass of `CRecordSet`, either by manually creating code, as shown in Listing 15.4, or (more conveniently) by using the Class Wizard as follows:

1. Open the Class Wizard (press Ctrl-W) and add a new class.

2. In the New Class dialog, set the name of the class and make it inherit from `CRecordSet`.

3. In the Database Options dialog, select the restaurant source that you set up in the preceding section.

These steps are shown in Figure 15.3. The result, a `CRecordSet` derivative class that watches the Menu table of the Restaurant data source, is shown in Listing 15.4.

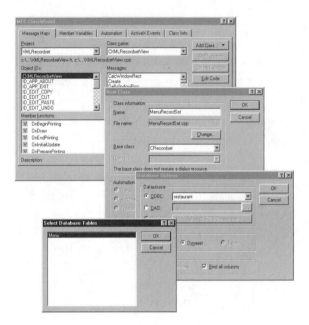

**Figure 15.3**    Creating a `CRecordSet`.

Listing 15.4    **The *MenuSet* Class (or *CMenuSet* Following MS Naming)**

```
// The following is the header file for the MenuSet class.
// Its implementation, along with a helper project to run it, is included
// on the CD-ROM


class MenuSet : public CRecordset
{
public:
    MenuSet(CDatabase* pDatabase = NULL);
    DECLARE_DYNAMIC(MenuSet)

// Field/Param Data
    //{{AFX_FIELD(MenuSet, CRecordset)
    long    m_Item;
    CString m_Name;
    long    m_Cost;
    //}}AFX_FIELD
```

```
// Overrides
    // ClassWizard generated virtual function overrides
    //{{AFX_VIRTUAL(MenuSet)
    public:
    virtual CString GetDefaultConnect();   // Default connection string
    virtual CString GetDefaultSQL();        // Default SQL for Recordset
     virtual void DoFieldExchange(CFieldExchange* pFX);  // RFX support
    //}}AFX_VIRTUAL

// Implementation
#ifdef _DEBUG
    virtual void AssertValid() const;
    virtual void Dump(CDumpContext& dc) const;
#endif
};
```

### *XMLSave* Interface

In order to add XML read and write capabilities to the MenuSet just shown, you can improve the class by either extension or inheritance. If you use extension, a helper class that watches MenuSet instances is responsible for saving them. If you use inheritance, an interface for saving and reading XML is defined, and the MenuSet class must implement it.

The following example shows the inheritance case, because the extension case with a helper class can be easily achieved by implementing a helper XMLable with the XMLable framework, as shown in Chapter 12, "Toolkit Features and Implementation Frameworks."

The general strategy for making basic XML persistence on a CRecordSet (or any other type that exhibits the same type of simple database binding) is simple: Hard-code the XML creation in a method that walks the complete table. The advantage of this is that you can fine-tune the XML output to any degree. The disadvantage is, of course, that this is a highly-coupled and nonreusable model. You are encouraged to use more-general approaches for big programs, but in case you need a quick solution such as the one depicted in Figure 15.4, Listings 15.5 and 15.6 give a sample of the code needed.

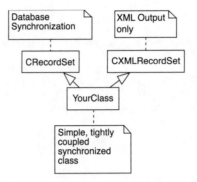

**Figure 15.4** CRecordSet and CXMLRecordSet class diagram.

Listing 15.5 **CXMLRecordSet.h**

```
#ifndef CXMLRecordSet_H
#define CXMLRecordSet_H

#include "stdafx.h"
#include <ostream>

using namespace std;
class CXMLRecordSet {
  public:

  // receive a stream in the constructor, so we can output the result
  CXMLRecordSet(ostream &a);
  void outputAsXML();

  protected:

  virtual outputRow() = 0; // every class must override this in order to
                           // output the correct info

  ostream out;
  CRecordset *m_pSet;

};

// $Log$
#endif
```

Listing 15.6  **CXMLRecordSet.cpp**

```cpp
#include "CXMLRecordSet.h"


CXMLRecordSet::CXMLRecordSet(ostream &outputStream) : out(outputStream)
{
}

void CXMLRecordSet::outputAsXML()
{
  int y = 0;
  CString str;
  if (m_pSet->IsBOF()) { // detects empty recordset
    return;
  }
  m_pSet->MoveFirst();   // fails if recordset is empty
  while (!m_pSet->IsEOF()) {
    outputRow();
    m_pSet->MoveNext();
  }
}
```

Having derived from both RecordSet and CXMLRecordSet, the process of outputting the correct XML is as simple as overloading outputRow() with code such as this:

```cpp
out << "<item id='" << m_id << "'" << ">";
...
```

The results of presenting the restaurant XML output to a window (the complete application is included on the CD) are shown in Figure 15.5.

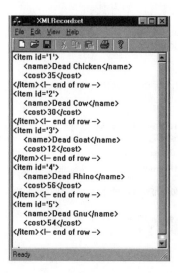

**Figure 15.5**  Presenting the XML output of a CRecordSet.

## Technology-Specific XML Support

The second category of C++-specific support for databases is that provided by particular database products and tools such as ADO and Oracle. Even though this subject is better discussed in light of the API documentation for each particular tool (see this book's Web site for that: http://www.cppxml.com), the following code can give you an idea of the look and feel of a major database API with XML support.

### ADO XML Support

Listing 15.7 is the code necessary to create XML from an ADO set. The details about ADO and other database tools are outside the scope of this book, but you are welcome to visit this book's Web site for pointers and complementary tutorials on the subject.

Listing 15.7  **ADO XML**

```
#import "msado15.dll" rename_namespace("MSXML")  rename("EOF", "ADOEOF")
#import "msxml.dll"

using namespace MSXML;

#include "stdio.h"
#include "io.h"
void dump_error(_com_error &e) ; //exception handling

void main()
{
  HRESULT r;
  CoInitialize(NULL);

  try
    {
      //open the connection, get the recordset ready
      _ConnectionPtr pConn;
      _RecordsetPtr pRs;

      r = pConn.CreateInstance(__uuidof(Connection));
      r = pRs.CreateInstance(__uuidof(Recordset));

      pConn->CursorLocation = adUseClient;
      _bstr_t strConn("Provider=sqloledb;Data Source=myDB;Initial
                    Catalog=pubs;User Id=me;Password=;");
      r = pConn->Open(strConn, "sa", "", adConnectUnspecified);
      r = pRs->Open("SELECT * from menus", pConn.GetInterfacePtr(),
                    adOpenForwardOnly, adLockReadOnly, adCmdText);

      //preparation to save RS as xml file
      struct _finddata_t xml_file;
      long hFile;
      if( (hFile = _findfirst("menus.xml", &xml_file )) != -1L)
        {
```

```
        DeleteFile("menus.xml");
        }

        r = pRs->Save("menus.xml", adPersistXML);

        _StreamPtr   pStream ; //declare one first
        pStream.CreateInstance(__uuidof(Stream));
        r = pRs->Save(pStream.GetInterfacePtr(), adPersistXML);

        IXMLDOMDocumentPtr pXMLDOMDoc;
        pXMLDOMDoc.CreateInstance(__uuidof(DOMDocument));
        r = pRs->Save(pXMLDOMDoc.GetInterfacePtr(), adPersistXML);



        r = pRs->Close();
        r = pRs->Open("menus.xml","Provider=MSPersist;",
               adOpenForwardOnly,adLockReadOnly,adCmdFile);
        r = pRs->Close();
        pStream->Position = 0;
        r = pRs->Open(pStream.GetInterfacePtr(),vtMissing,
               adOpenForwardOnly,adLockReadOnly,adCmdFile);
        r = pRs->Close();
        r = pRs->Open(pXMLDOMDoc.GetInterfacePtr(), vtMissing,
               adOpenForwardOnly, adLockReadOnly, adCmdFile);
        r = pRs->Close();
        pen call with pStream.GetInterfacePtr(), or
                  pXMLDOMDoc.GetInterfacePtr()
        r = pStream->Close();


    }
  catch(_com_error &e)
    {
      dump_error(e);
    }
}

void dump_error(_com_error &e)
{
  _bstr_t bstrSource(e.Source());
  _bstr_t bstrDescription(e.Description());

  // Print Com errors.
  printf("Error\n");
  printf("\tCode = %08lx\n", e.Error());
  printf("\tCode meaning = %s", e.ErrorMessage());
  printf("\tSource = %s\n", (LPCSTR) bstrSource);
  printf("\tDescription = %s\n", (LPCSTR) bstrDescription);

}
```

# Extra C++ Database Resources

Some topics, such as the creation of adaptors, would bring little to this chapter, because they require only the XML programming techniques seen in previous chapters. However, as reusable pieces of software, they are worth having and studying. These tools, as well as an updated list of C++ database products, resources, and extensions to this chapter's code, can be found on the database portion of this book's Web site:

    http://www.cppxml.com/db

# Summary

This chapter presented alternatives for implementing XML support for databases in C++ projects. Both SAX and DOM were used to create and manipulate C++ XML APIs for different underlying database mechanisms such as ODBC and ADO.

# V

# Appendixes

# UML

$T$HE UNIFIED MODELING LANGUAGE (UML) is a powerful tool for the graphical description and specification of a software system. It was born out of the union of the three major OO methodologies available in the mid-'90s: Booch, Jacobson's OOSE, and Rumbaugh's OMT. UML is now the de facto standard for object-oriented modeling throughout the industry and academia.

This book uses UML 1.3 (adopted in the fall of 1999) to visually describe the design of several programs. This appendix explains the three types of diagrams used in this book—class diagrams, sequence diagrams, and collaboration diagrams.

Using the types of diagrams shown here, you can express an important portion of the static and dynamic parts/views of a system. (Other mechanisms, such as the other six types of UML diagrams and prose, may also enhance the documentation.) The following sections discuss each type of diagram in detail.

## UML Resources

The complete UML 1.3 specification (a PDF bundle of over 10MB) can be downloaded from http://www.rational.com. It states the different types of diagrams (use case, sequence, collaboration, statechart, activity, class, component, object, and deployment) as well as the rationale and mechanisms of the whole language.

For a thorough and didactical exposition of the complete UML, *The Unified Modeling Language User Guide* (written by the authors of the language) is an unsurpassable source.

# Class Diagrams

Class diagrams are by far the most commonly used tool inside the UML. They are used to represent the structural view of the system, in terms of the classes that comprise it and the relationships between them.

More formally, class diagrams are sets of the following things (the term *thing* is official within the UML specification and is used to address the components of the language):

- **Classes.** Represented by rectangles with three compartments—name, attributes, and methods.
- **Interfaces.** Represented as either specially marked rectangles or small circles (if there is no need to specify their contents).
- **Relationships.** Represented as adorned lines between classes and interfaces.
- **Collaborations.** Represented as an ellipse with dashed lines. This type of element is not used in its abbreviated form in this book. It is included in this list only for the sake of completion. Collaborations define a society of classes and interactions that together achieve a higher goal. Given this definition, a class diagram itself can be viewed as the structural representation of an expanded collaboration.

## Classes

Classes are represented as rectangles with three compartments, as shown in Figure A.1. The first compartment contains the name of the class, the second its attributes, and the third its methods.

| MovieSchedule |
|---|
| - scenes : list<String><br>-$ TODAY : Date |
| + getName() : String<br>+ getNextScene(day : Date = TODAY) : scene |

**Figure A.1** UML class representation.

### Visibility

Each attribute or method of a particular class may specify its visibility using a preceding symbol:

- **+ public.** Anyone may access it.
- **- private.** Only the class itself may access it.
- **# protected.** Any descendant of the class may access it.

## Abstract Versus Concrete Classes

An abstract class is one that may not be instantiated. (It is usually included to provide a common root to a tree of related concrete classes.) In C++, an abstract class has at least one pure virtual method.

Abstract classes in UML are shown just as any other class, but with their name in italic (see Figure A.2).

**Figure A.2** Abstract versus concrete classes.

## Scope

Given a particular attribute or method, you may specify whether it is visible by every instance of the class or just by the particular instance that holds it (that is, whether it has class or instance scope).

In C++, the term *class scope* translates into *static* members. Static members in a UML diagram are marked using an underline or a preceding dollar sign, as shown in Figure A.3.

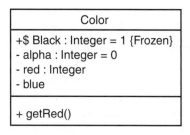

**Figure A.3** Scope.

## Attributes

Sometimes, all you need to specify is the attribute's name and its type. (Often, in the early stages of design, not even the type is necessary.) Later, however, you must enrich the design with elements such as an initial value, multiplicity indicators, and so on.

The general form of a UML attribute is

```
[visibility] name [multiplicity] [:type] [ = initial-value] [{property}]
```

Figure A.4 shows valid examples of attributes using different levels of complexity.

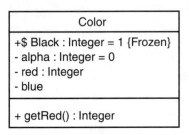

**Figure A.4**   Attributes.

The property string `{Frozen}` means the attribute may not be changed. This is mapped to a `const` attribute in C++.

### Operations

Operations have a number of extra possibilities besides just naming. The following is the general form of an operation in UML:

```
[visibility] name [{parameter-list}] [:return type] [{property-string}]
```

Figure A.5 shows increasingly well-specified versions of the same operation. (Note that you can abbreviate the class representation so that it won't show the attributes.)

**Figure A.5**   Operations.

It is important to note that the generic term *operation* can be used interchangeably with the more traditional C++ terms *member function* and *method*.

### Template Classes

One powerful and aesthetically appealing construct in the C++ language are templates. Templates in UML are represented as any other class, except for a dashed box in their upper corner, specifying the template parameters.

Figure A.6 shows the UML representation of the classic `List` template class of STL. (See Appendix B for more information on this powerful library.)

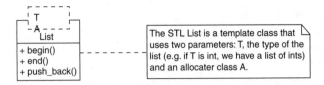

**Figure A.6** Template classes.

## Interfaces

In the most generic OO sense, an interface is the characterization of a set of operations, defining the behavior of a particular component.

In a more C++-specific way, an interface is an abstract class with only pure virtual methods.

In UML, an interface is represented by a class marked with a stereotype, or a small circle (see Figure A.8, shown later).

## Relationships

Classes do not live in isolation. Each of them is related to many others by several kinds of relationships, the most important of which are *dependency, generalization, realization,* and *association.*

UML provides the mechanisms to express all of these types of relationships. Let's discuss the details of their semantics and representation.

### Dependency

The concept of dependency is pretty much aligned with the traditional idea we all already have of the word. In formal terms, Class A depends on Class B if a change in B affects A, but not necessarily the other way around.

A dependency is shown as a dashed line with a pointed end. The arrow points to the class that is depended on, as shown in Figure A.7.

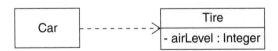

**Figure A.7** Dependency.

### Generalization

Generalization is the name given to the generic relationship between a base thing and a more specific version of it.

In terms of classes, this is simply inheritance. Inheritance is represented with a hollow arrow that goes from the derived artifact to its parent, as shown in Figure A.8.

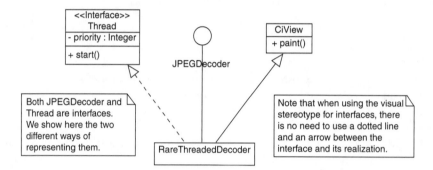

**Figure A.8**  Generalization and realization.

### Realization

A realization relationship occurs when the base artifact is an interface. It is important to note that in UML (and OO theory in general), the realization relationship can be extended to things other than interfaces and classes (such as requirements and modules), but for the sake of our current discussion, this will be enough. This is also shown in Figure A.8.

### Association

An association is a structural relationship. It is represented as a (possibly directed) line between classes. Not all the options for associations are covered in this section. However, the four most important aspects of an association (name, roles, multiplicity, and aggregation) are shown in Figure A.9.

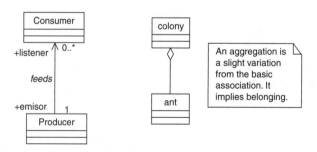

**Figure A.9**  Associations.

Using these four adornments, you can express most ideas about the associations in your design. An explicit explanation of extra adornments is included in the few diagrams that use them.

# Interaction Diagrams

So far we have explored the details of static design. Now it is time to see how to specify the behavior of the artifacts defined in class diagrams.

UML provides two semantically equivalent types of interaction diagrams: sequence and collaboration. The choice of which one to use usually is a matter of preference. This book uses both.

## Sequence Diagrams

A sequence diagram is an interaction representation focused on time and the evolution of object "conversations" through it.

The elements of a sequence diagram are objects and messages (naturally, they can also contain annotations). In a sequence diagram, the objects are aligned from left to right, and time passes from the top down, as shown in Figure A.10.

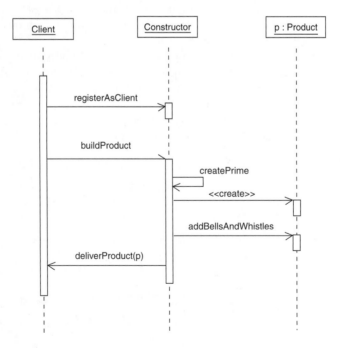

**Figure A.10** Sequence diagram.

There are several important points about this figure. Let's examine them individually:

- **Object lifeline.** The vertical dashed line denotes the object's life. It can be truncated by explicitly sending a destroy message from an object or by an external, unseen mechanism (such as garbage collection). In any case, the finish of a lifeline (not always present in the diagram) is marked by an x.

- **Focus of control.** The rectangles around the object lifeline show the object's focus of control—that is, the time during which it is active. Note that focuses of control may nest, because an object can call itself recursively.

- **Messages.** There are several kinds of messages. Some are simple, and others are stereotyped—either visually, as shown in Figure A.10, or by adding marks such as <<create>>.

Sequence diagrams are theoretically sufficient to show the different types of interaction in this book. However, sometimes you need another type of interaction representation—collaboration diagrams. This case is not very common in this book, but I wanted to mention it for the sake of completion.

## Collaboration Diagrams

Collaboration diagrams focus on the organization of the participants, as opposed to the time frame in which they talk. (Of course, there are ways within them to specify the sequence in which events occur, but that is simply not the focus.)

A collaboration diagram is basically a graph in which the nodes are objects and the arcs are the links that connect them. Through a link (which, by the way, can be marked with stereotypes if you want to do so), objects may pass messages. Messages are marked with a number that shows their time sequence. The content of the message is usually a piece of code (sometimes pseudocode) specifying the call performed. Figure A.11 shows a typical example of a collaboration diagram.

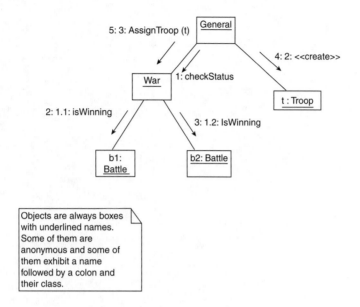

**Figure A.11**   Sequence diagram.

The organization between objects can arguably be said to be highlighted by the fact that it is shown on this type of representation.

# B

# STL

THE STANDARD TEMPLATE LIBRARY (STL) is one of the most powerful and attractive features of the C++ language. In this book, we use its most common features in order to achieve goals such as easy list maintenance and efficient associative lookups (such as between DOM nodes and Visual Tree items).

Even though the uses of STL in this book are quite intuitive and self-documenting, this appendix shows the general ideas behind every type of component in STL and gives some examples of their usage.

It is important to note that STL is a vast and deep C++ subject. This guide presents the smallest subset of ideas to make the STL parts of the book comprehensible. See the following sidebar for further reading on the topic.

### STL Resources

The most complete and easy-to-read introduction to STL is (in my opinion) the book *STL Tutorial and Reference Guide* by David R. Musser and Atul Saini (Addison-Wesley).

Other resources include the help files of your favorite C++ development environment, the STL header files themselves, and the ANSI/ISO C++ standard.

This book is quite enough for the uses of STL throughout this book.

# STL Nature and Components

The STL goal, as a library, is to provide a set of containers and algorithms for efficient, interoperable, and standard use in a wide variety of applications. It fills the gap of decades of proprietary and partial solutions in the field of data structures.

STL is rooted in the seminal ideas of Alexander Stepanov about generic programming—specifically, the notion of templates and how certain problems can be more naturally and efficiently treated by using generic algorithms outside of the classes and data types upon which they act.

The idea of encapsulating certain operations outside of the classes they treat might seem at first a little awkward, and it inevitably brings up the question, "Isn't this supposed to be OO?" among beginners. The answer can be summarized like this: Generic programming empowers OO by providing effective means to encapsulate dispersed operations.

Upon the arrival of design patterns, some ideas of generic programming have been disseminated in the form of patterns such as *iterator* and *visitor*. The fact that we have a natural syntax for their representation in C++ is the main difference between C++ and other languages' "pure OO" approaches.

Enough has been said about the idea and its quality. (You will have a chance to see for yourself the elegance that STL brings to your programs.) Let's get down to the details of the library's structure. STL has six kinds of components: *containers, iterators, generic algorithms, adaptors, function objects,* and *allocators*. The following sections introduce each by presenting an example and a summary of their role.

## Containers

A container (such as a list, a hash table, or an array) is an object that holds collections of other objects. STL provides two types of containers: *sequence containers* and *sorted associative containers*.

The first type (sequence) concentrates on linear collections:

- **Arrays.** Represented using the typical array construct of C++:

  ```
  T array[n]   // T is the type of the array, n its size
  ```

- **Vectors.** Represented with the template `vector`, provide random access to a sequence of *varying length* (which differentiates them from arrays):

  ```
  vector<T>
  ```

- **Queues.** Represented with the template `deque`, provide random access to variable-length collections. They provide a guarantee of O(1) (constant time) insertions and deletions at the beginning and end of the sequence:

  ```
  deque<T>
  ```

- **Lists.** Provide O(1) insertions at any point of the sequence, but they offer only O($n$) (sequential) access to the elements:

  ```
  list<T>
  ```

Listing B.1 shows a small application of the list container, in which we hold 10 random integers, sort them, and finally print the results to standard output.

Listing B.1 **Using an STL List to Hold Random Numbers**

```
#include "stdafx.h"
#include <stdlib.h>
#include <time.h>
#include <iostream>
#include <list>

using namespace std;
int main(int argc, char* argv[])
{
    list<int> l;
    list<int>::iterator j; // We haven't seen iterators, but their use
                           // here is obvious

    // Seed the random-number generator with current time so that
    // the numbers will be different every time we run.
     srand( (unsigned)time( NULL ) );

    for(int i=0;i<10;i++) // insert 10 random numbers
      l.push_back(rand());

    l.sort();

    for(j = l.begin();j != l.end() ; j++) // print the numbers
      cout << *j << "\n";

    return 0;
}
```

The second type of containers  (sorted associative) focus on *nonlinear* collections of arbitrary length that require random access. There are four types of sorted associative containers:

- **Sets.** Contain an arbitrarily large collection of unique elements:

  `set<T>`

- **Multisets.** Are just like sets, except that they may contain duplicates:

  `multiset<T>`

- **Maps.** Are one of the most useful types of containers. They associate keys to values, allowing for the retrieval of a value given the key. (See Listing B.2 for details.)

  `map<KeyT,ValueT>`

- **Multimaps.** Are maps that allow duplicate keys:

  `multimap<KeyT,ValueT>`

Listing B.2 **Using an STL Map**

```
void main(int argc, char *argv)
{
   map<String,Date> m;

   m[String("Mondigliani")] = Date(1920,1,24, 22,15,0);
   // Year,Month,Day,Hour, Min, Sec.

   m[String("Dali")] = Date(1984,1,23,22,15,0);

   m[String("Sicket")] = Date(1942,1,22,22,15,0);
   cout << "Enter the name you want to look up:";

   char name_b[80];
   cin >> name_b;
   String name(name_b);

   if(m.find(name) == m.end())
     cout << "\nNot found.\n";
   else
     cout << "He died on " << printDate(m[name]) << "\n";
return 0;
}
```

**Strings and Date Types**

Listing B.2 intentionally does not show the exact types used for this program, because they might change depending on the platform and clutter the example. However, if you are curious about the exact types used, the original Windows program has the following definitions:

```
#define Date COleDateTime
```

```
#define String CString
```

```
#define printDate(x) x.Format("%A %d of %B  %Y.").GetBuffer(12)
```

Here is the result of running Listing B.2:

```
Enter the name you want to look up:Mondigliani
He died on Saturday 24 of January 1920.
```

This book frequently uses maps and multimaps to deal with associations between different types of representations and objects in a standard way. The use of other associative containers is less frequent in this book.

## Iterators

Listing B.1 showed the first appearance of iterators, when j was declared a variable to be used over lists of integers:

```
list<int>::iterator j;
```

Iterators like this are the cornerstone of STL: All containers provide them, and all generic algorithms use them. In the most basic sense, iterators are the natural evolution of the pointer. They allow you to easily address a particular element of a collection while providing a set of familiar operators for their manipulation (such as ++ to advance to the next item or == to compare them with others).

Depending on the type of collection they come from, some iterators are more complex than others. Algorithms that require random access to a collection need more powerful iterators than those used by a simple algorithm that traverses the collection in only one way. Iterators are classified as shown in Figure B.1.

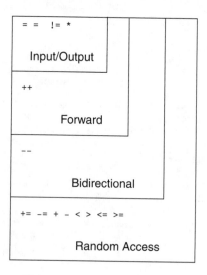

**Figure B.1**  Iterators classification.

As you can see in Figure B.1, the different classes of iterators expose different operators, thus allowing for different types of access. Getting used to which iterators are needed for each algorithm is an easy and intuitive process, but one that requires practice.

## Generic Algorithms

Generic algorithms are powerful pieces of software that allow the reuse of certain guaranteed methods, regardless of which collection they work on. STL generic algorithms are remarkable in two ways:

- They provide a natural representation for reusable methods that must be taken out of the collection of classes, without breaking the good design, efficiency, or wide applicability of the library.

- STL algorithms guarantee their performance. Unlike other libraries (perhaps in other languages), when you use a generic algorithm, you have a guarantee of complexity (in terms of Big O notation, described in Chapter 7, "Advanced C++ DOM Manipulation").

Listing B.3 shows a popular generic algorithm (and how knowing the options available to you can save a lot of coding).

Listing B.3   **Manipulating Sets with Multiples of 2 and 3**

```
#include <set>
#include <algorithm>
#include <iostream>

int main(int argc, char* argv[])
{
    set<int> a;
    set<int> b;
    // intersection1 will hold the intersection calculated the long way
    set<int> intersection1;
    // intersection2 will hold the intersection calculated the short way
    set<int> intersection2;
    set<int> intersectionMerge;

    // an iterator that we will use to traverse the sets
    set<int>::iterator r;

    for(int i=0; i < 100; i+=3) //populate with a multiple of 3
        a.insert(i);

    for(i=0; i < 100; i+=2)
        b.insert(i);
    for(r = a.begin(); r != a.end(); ++r) // Calculate the intersection
        if(b.find(*r) != b.end())
            intersection1.insert(*r);

    cout << "Numbers in [0,100) divisible both by 3 and 2: \n";
    for(r = intersection1.begin(); r != intersection1.end(); ++r)
        cout << *r << " ";

    // Now, a much easier and efficient way to do it (just 1 line, actually)
    // It uses the set_intersection function, which has two set ranges (the
    // first four parameters) and an inserter, whose role is to provide an
    // unambiguous way to populate the result.
    set_intersection(a.begin(),a.end(),b.begin(),b.end(),
                     inserter(intersection2,intersection2.end()));
    // The function inserter simply returns an output iterator for the
    // specified collection.

    // Note this nice way of outputting the result.
    ostream_iterator<int> out(cout, " ");
```

```
        copy(intersection2.begin(), intersection2.end(), out);

        cout <<"\n";

        return 0;
}
```

---

> ### What Does the Iterator Returned by *end( )* Point To?
> All the containers provide the begin() and end() methods. begin returns an iterator pointing to the first item in the collection, and end returns an "invalid" pointer to one position *beyond the last item*. This conveniently allows you to iterate through ranges that are open on one side:
>
> for(r = a.begin();  r != a.end();  ++r)  // Go from [0..n)
>
> It also allows you to signal unsuccessful searches and other invalid pointers in a safe and type-independent way:
>
> if(b.find(*r) != b.end()) { /*not found...*/ }

The output of the program is the following:

```
Numbers in [0,100) divisible both by 3 and 2:
0 6 12 18 24 30 36 42 48 54 60 66 72 78 84 90 96
Numbers in [0,100) divisible both by 3 and 2:
0 6 12 18 24 30 36 42 48 54 60 66 72 78 84 90 96
```

## Function Objects

Function objects are instances of classes that overload the function call operator (). These special objects are used by some generic algorithms in order to easily combine their implementation with complex user-defined behavior.

The following piece of code illustrates a simple use of a function object (one with no arguments for the () operator) to populate a vector with the first 15 Fibonacci numbers:

```
#include "stdafx.h"
#include <iostream>
#include <vector>
#include <algorithm>

using namespace std;

class Fibonacci
{
  public:
    Fibonacci(); // A constructor, just to initialize i and j
    int operator () ();
  private:
    int i;
```

```
        int j;
};

Fibonacci::Fibonacci()
{
  i = 0;
  j = 1;
}

int Fibonacci::operator () ()
{
  int next = i + j;
  i = j;
  j = next;
  return i;
}


int main (int argc, char* argv[])
{
  vector <int> v(15);
  Fibonacci generator;
  generate (v.begin(), v.end(), generator);
  ostream_iterator<int> out (cout, " ");
  copy (v.begin(), v.end(), out);
  cout << "\n";
  return 0;
}
```

The result is the following:

```
1 1 2 3 5 8 13 21 34 55 89 144 233 377 610
```


## A Curious Example

Yet another way to find the intersection of the two sets of numbers in Listing B.3 is to create a function object (with one argument). Given a number, this function tells you if it is divisible by both 2 and 3. Using this function, you can iterate through the union of both sets, finding qualifying numbers (using find_if). The following (certainly optional) code shows how:

```
// A function object that will tell you if a number is divisible by 2 and 3
class divisibleBy2and3
{
public:
    bool operator()(int x) const { return x%2 == 0 && x%3 == 0; }
};

void main()
{
    set<int> a;
    set<int> b;
```

```
set<int> intersectionMerge;

for(int i=0; i < 100; i+=3) // Populate with a multiple of 3
     a.insert(i);

for(i=0; i < 100; i+=2)
     b.insert(i);
// Now, let's see a convoluted (but fun) way of doing it.
// First, let's put them all together in one set, using the
// Generic Algorithm merge.
merge(a.begin(),a.end(),b.begin(),b.end(),
      inserter(intersectionMerge,intersectionMerge.end()));

// Now, let's find them
set<int>::iterator current = intersectionMerge.begin();
while(current != intersectionMerge.end())
{
    cout << *current++ << " ";
    current = find_if(current,
                      intersectionMerge.end(),
                      divisibleBy2and3());
}
     // Print as usual here.
}
```

Naturally, the number and type of arguments that the function object is expected to receive depends on the algorithm you are using. (For example, `find_if` needs a function object with one argument of the type held by the collection, and `copy` can do with a generator with no arguments at all.) Getting used to the different requirements of each function is merely a matter of practice.

## Adaptors and Allocators

Adaptors are objects used to wrap other objects and present a variation of their interface and behavior to the outside world. One common adaptor example is `reverse_iterator`, which takes a normal iterator and makes it act as if the order of the elements were reversed.

Allocators are used to change the memory models with which a particular collection works. There is usually a natural and default allocator for every operation that involves one.

Special adaptors and allocators are beyond the scope of this appendix (except for knowing what they are) and are not used in this book without in-chapter explanations.

## The STL Headers

Even though the examples in this book explicitly show the `#include` directives, it might be useful to have a description of the organization of STL. The STL components are divided among the following headers:

- Sets and multisets are on `<set>` (you include it using `#include <set>`).

- A container named X is on `<X>` (the vector is on the header `<vector>`).

- STL algorithms are all in `<algorithm>`, except for numeric algorithms in `<numeric>`.

- Predefined function objects are all in `<functional>`.

- The stack adaptor is in `<stack>`, and the queue and priority adaptors are in `<queue>`.

The preceding list is the ANSI/ISO proposed organization for STL, and it is respected in most environments. However, it is possible that a platform will show minor variations.

# C

# CD Contents and Instructions

T HIS BOOK WAS DEVELOPED UNDER THE PREMISE that every line of code in the book would be supported by a fully functional file or program on the CD. This appendix enumerates the features of the CD and offers some tips to help you get the most out of it.

## Requirements

The CD code contains source code and binaries for all the programs, so you don't need a compiler in order to see the programs working. You *will* need, naturally, a C++ compiler to develop your own programs.

## Platforms

We have strived to maximize the portability of the code, and cross-platform makefiles have been provided whenever possible. However, it is important to note that some of the examples in this book are written exclusively for either Win32 or Linux. Those cases are explicitly noted in the book and on the CD.

# Organization

The CD is organized by chapter, technology, and API type. (See Chapter 2 for a description of XML C++ in terms of these three views.)

On every view, for each example, there is an entry with the following fields:

- Name
- Snapshot (if applicable)
- Description
- Platform

# Installation Instructions

Every sample program on the CD (regardless of its platform) has the following directory structure:

```
+ bin (contains the compiled version(s) of the program)
+ src (contains all source code)
|
+ moduleA (the source code may be organized by modules)
+ moduleB
+ dsw (for windows projects, a Visual Studio project file is provided)
+ obj (temporary compilation files)
+ doc
|
+ UML (uml diagrams for the application design)
+ Requirements (TEXT/XML/PDF requirements for the application)
+ Generated API docs (HTML for the fully documented programs is generated)
+ tst (testing scripts and data)
Readme (if it exists, contains special installation/compilation instructions)
Makefile
```

To build a program that's on the CD, simply make sure you have installed the tools enumerated in the instructions for each package. (Most needed libraries are provided with each pack, so usually there is no need to do any installation.) Then type make at the command line. If you are using Visual Studio, you can issue the command nmake.

For Windows programs, you can alternatively open the project file and click the compile button on Visual C++ 6.0.

# Program Updates

The programs in this book are all fully functional and have been extensively tested and debugged. If updates or extensions are necessary, they will be published on this book's Web page at www.newriders.com.

# The Extra-Goodies Directory

The extra-goodies directory contains small (and sometimes esoteric) software and tools that are not directly related to the book's contents but that might prove of some value during XML C++ development. The programs and tools in this directory are not supported.

# Splash Screens and CSS Setup

The CD starts automatically. It assumes that you want to see the more verbose and fancier table of contents. It includes Flash splash screens, CSS configuration, and a program to copy the source code and tools. To turn off these features and browse simple HTML or pure-text versions of the contents, go to simpleIndex.html or index.txt.

# Index

## Symbols

## A

# D

## VISIT OUR WEB SITE

WWW.NEWRIDERS.COM

On our web site, you'll find information about our other books, authors, tables of contents, and book errata. You will also find information about book registration and how to purchase our books, both domestically and internationally.

## EMAIL US

Contact us at: **nrfeedback@newriders.com**

- If you have comments or questions about this book
- To report errors that you have found in this book
- If you have a book proposal to submit or are interested in writing for New Riders
- If you are an expert in a computer topic or technology and are interested in being a technical editor who reviews manuscripts for technical accuracy

Contact us at: **nreducation@newriders.com**

- If you are an instructor from an educational institution who wants to preview New Riders books for classroom use. Email should include your name, title, school, department, address, phone number, office days/hours, text in use, and enrollment, along with your request for desk/examination copies and/or additional information.

Contact us at: **nrmedia@newriders.com**

- If you are a member of the media who is interested in reviewing copies of New Riders books. Send your name, mailing address, and email address, along with the name of the publication or web site you work for.

## BULK PURCHASES/CORPORATE SALES

If you are interested in buying 10 or more copies of a title or want to set up an account for your company to purchase directly from the publisher at a substantial discount, contact us at 800-382-3419 or email your contact information to corpsales@pearsontechgroup.com. A sales representative will contact you with more information.

## WRITE TO US

New Riders Publishing
201 W. 103rd St.
Indianapolis, IN 46290-1097

## CALL/FAX US

Toll-free (800) 571-5840
If outside U.S. (317) 581-3500
Ask for New Riders
FAX: (317) 581-4663

# RELATED NEW RIDERS TITLES

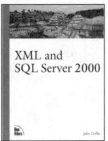

**ISBN: 0735711127**
**500 pages**
**US $44.99**

### XML and SQL Server 2000

John Griffin

*XML and SQL Server 2000* enables SQL developers to understand and work with XML, the preferred technology for integrating eBusiness systems. SQL Server 2000 has added several new features that SQL Server 7 never had, which makes working with and generating XML easier for the developer. *XML and SQL Server 2000* provides a comprehensive discussion of SQL Server 2000's XML capabilities.

**ISBN: 0735711178**
**300 pages**
**US $34.99**

### ebXML: The New Global Standard for Doing Business on the Internet

David Webber and Alan Kotok

To create an e-commerce initiative, managers need to understand that XML is the technology that will take them there. Companies understand that that in order to achieve a successful Internet presence their company needs an e-commerce methodology implemented. Many department managers (the actual people who have to design, build, and execute the plan) don't know where to begin. *ebXML* will take them there.

**ISBN: 0735710201**
**1152 pages**
**US $49.99**

### Inside XML

Steven Holzner

*Inside XML* is a foundation book that covers both the Microsoft and non-Microsoft approach to XML programming. It covers in detail the hot aspects of XML, such as DTD's vs. XML Schemas, CSS, XSL, XSLT, Xlinks, Xpointers, XHTML, RDF, CDF, parsing XML in Perl and Java, and much more.

![XML, XSLT, Java, and JSP]

**ISBN: 0735710899**
**650 pages with CD-ROM**
**US $49.99**

### XML, XSLT, Java, and JSP: A Case Study in Developing a Web Application

Westy Rockwell

A practical, hands-on experience in building web applications based on XML and Java technologies, this book is unique because it teaches the technologies by using them to build a web chat project throughout the book. The project is explained in great detail, after the reader is shown how to get and install the necessary tools to be able to customize this project and build other web applications.

![Inside XSLT]

**ISBN: 0735711364**
**600 pages**
**US $49.99**

### Inside XSLT

Steve Holzner

*Inside XSLT* is designed to be a companion guide to *Inside XML*. This example-oriented book covers XML to HTML, XML to Music, XML with Java, style sheet creation and usage, nodes and attributes, sorting data, creating Xpath expressions, using Xpath and XSLT functions, namespaces, names templates, name variables, designing style sheets and using XSLT processor API's, the 56 XSL formatting objects, the XSL DTD, and much, much more.

# Solutions from experts you know and trust.

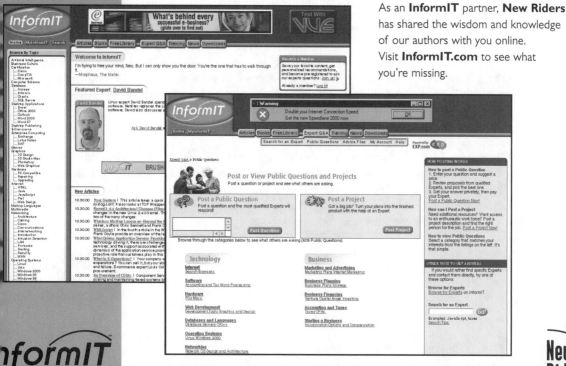

# Colophon

The image on the cover of this book is that of Neuschwanstein Castle in Bavaria, Germany. Captured by photographer Andrew Wakeford, it is the most famous of three castles built for Louis II (also known as Mad King Ludwig) of Bavaria in the nineteenth century.

Situated on a high point over the Pöllat. River gorge, this imitation of a medieval castle is said to be the model for Disney's *Sleeping Beauty* castle. Today a popular tourist attraction, the castle attracts anywhere from 10,000 visitors per day from October to April to 40,000 visitors per day during August and September.[1]

This book was written and edited in Microsoft Word, and laid out in QuarkXPress. The font used for the body text is Bembo and MCPdigital. It was printed on 50# Husky Offset Smooth paper at R.R. Donnelley & Sons in Crawfordsville, Indiana. Prepress consisted of PostScript computer-to-plate technology (filmless process). The cover was printed at Moore Langen Printing in Terre Haute, Indiana, on 12pt, coated on one side.

## License Agreement

This package contains one CD-ROM that includes software described in this book. See Appendix C for a description of these programs and instructions for their use.

By opening this package, you are bound by the following agreement:

Some of the software included with this product may be copyrighted, in which case all rights are reserved by the respective copyright holder. You are licensed to use software copyrighted by the publisher and its licensors on a single computer. You may copy and/or modify the software as needed to facilitate your use of it on a single computer. Making copies of the software for any other purpose is a violation of the United States copyright law.

This software is sold "as is" without warranty of any kind, either expressed or implied, including, but not limited to, the implied warranties of merchantability and fitness for a particular purpose. Neither the publisher nor its dealers or distributors assume any liability for any alleged or actual damages arising from the use of this program. (Some states do not allow for the exclusion of implied warranties, so the exclusion may not apply to you.)

---

1. http://www.twenj.com/bavarianeu.htm